HC
610
.E5
B63
1990

Boardman, Robert,
1945-

Global regimes and
nation-states.

$29.95

D1275754

GLOBAL REGIMES
AND
NATION-STATES
ENVIRONMENTAL ISSUES
IN AUSTRALIAN POLITICS

GLOBAL REGIMES
AND
NATION-STATES

ENVIRONMENTAL ISSUES
IN AUSTRALIAN POLITICS

Robert Boardman

Carleton University Press
Ottawa, Canada
1990

© Carleton University Press Inc. 1990

ISBN 0-88629-109-7 paperback
      0-88629-119-4 casebound

Printed and bound in Canada

Carleton Public Policy Series #4

Canadian Cataloguing in Publication Data
Boardman, Robert
Global regimes and nation-states: environmental
issues in Australian politics

(Carleton public policy series #4)
Includes bibliographical references.
ISBN 0-88629-119-4 (bound). —
ISBN 0-88629-109-7 (pbk.)

1. Environmental protection — Government policy —
Australia. I. Title. II. Series.

HC610.E5B63 1990   363.7'056'0994   C90-090142-X

Distributed by: Oxford University Press Canada
                70 Wynford Drive
                Don Mills, Ontario
                Canada. M3C 1J9
                (416) 441-2941

Cover design: Aerographics Ottawa

Acknowledgement
Carleton University Press gratefully acknowledges the support extended to its
publishing programme by the Canada Council and the Ontario Arts Council.

This book has been published with the help of a grant from the Social Science
Federation of Canada, using funds provided by the Social Sciences and Humanities
Research Council of Canada.

For Matthew

TABLE OF CONTENTS

PREFACE AND ACKNOWLEDGMENTS

International arrangements of one kind or another, on the determination of almost anything from airline routes to permitted amounts of food additives, have grown more numerous and pervasive in recent decades. What difference do they make? How do governments formulate policies to deal with the institutions and agreements that direct these activities? What impact do international arrangements have on government programmes and organization, and on the workings of domestic politics? More specifically, to turn to the subject of the present study, how effective are international arrangements for encouraging cooperation between states in the field of environmental policy?

Australia provides a sturdy vehicle for exploring these more general questions. Like Canada, it has a federal system in which responsibility for many of the domestic policy areas currently impinged on by international arrangements lies primarily, or to a significant degree, at the state or provincial level. In both Australia and Canada, environmental policy issues with important international dimensions — acid rain, protection of coastlines and offshore areas from oil pollution, living resource conservation and development, to name just a few — have climbed high on national political agendas. The politics of the preservation of the South Moresby area of British Columbia in the mid-1980s had some intriguing points in parallel with the more turbulent conflict over wilderness conservation in southwest Tasmania a few years earlier. The subject of this study is the interplay between international and domestic factors in Australian environmental policy and politics from 1965 to 1985. These two decades, from the beginnings of a national debate on environmental issues in the mid-1960s to the shifting priorities evident in the approaches of the first and second Hawke administrations in the mid-1980s, encompassed far-reaching changes in policies, programmes and government organization. The emergence of distinctively national policies, under a succession of Commonwealth governments of the 1970s, was closely tied, moreover, to the ways in which Australia began during this period to define itself as a player on the larger stage of international environmental politics.

The main body of the study is divided into two sets of chapters. In Part I, Australia is treated as an actor in the state system. The focus is on the policies and strategies adopted towards the main institutions and conventions in the environmental area. Australian policies within various international organizations are examined in Chapter 2. These centre around the organs and agencies of the United Nations system, and extend also to the environmental work of the Organization for Economic Cooperation and Development (OECD) and, at the non-governmental level, the International Union for Conservation of Nature and Natural Resources (IUCN). A group of international conventions dealing with conservation questions is discussed next (Chapter 3), including those related to the politics of the wildlife trade, questions of migratory species and their habitats, and the protection of heritage sites. Chapter 4 turns to pollution issues, with an

ix

emphasis on marine environmental questions affecting Australia that were handled in the Third United Nations Conference on the Law of the Sea (UNCLOS III) and in a number of conventions of the International Maritime Organization (IMO). The link between environmental policy and foreign policy in relation to Antarctica is investigated in Chapter 5, with particular reference to the environmental protection provisions operating in the Treaty framework and in related developments such as the 1980 convention on Antarctic Marine Living Resources.

The emphasis in Part II shifts to the policy process in Australia. Interrelations and patterns of influence among three sets of actors are analyzed: those at the federal level, particularly the various departments and agencies of the Commonwealth government; the state governments, and their interactions with the federal government in the determination of policies and programmes; and interest groups active in the environmental policy arena. Each has also had varying degrees of engagement with international organizations, both inter-governmental and non-governmental. Chapter 6 traces the evolution of a federal environmental policy role in Australia during the 1970s and 1980s, and the factors that have shaped federal-state cooperation in both the domestic and the international aspects of this policy, especially through such forums as the Australian Environment Council (AEC) and the Council of Nature Conservation Ministers (CONCOM). The formulation of approaches to international institutions, including the effects of external developments on policy, are examined in Chapter 7; and Chapter 8 assesses federal-state exchanges in relation to international conventions on conservation, pollution and Antarctica. Finally, the impact of interest groups is taken up for discussion in Chapter 9.

I carried out much of the research for the study during the course of a productive stay in 1984-85 at the Australian National University (ANU) in Canberra, as a Visiting Fellow in the Department of International Relations of the Research School of Pacific Studies. I am very much indebted to Professors J.D.B. Miller and Tom Millar for extending to me their Department's hospitality, and for allowing me to benefit, unfortunately for too short a time, from a most rewarding intellectual environment. I should also like to thank Professor R.S. Slatyer, of the Research School of Biological Sciences, for insights into the workings of Australia's international scientific programmes; Dr. Russell B. Trood for helping me to acquire some glimmering of understanding of the complex world of Australian politics, federalism and foreign policy; and, not least, my colleague Herman Bakvis, who agreed to shoulder more than an equitable share of our journal editing responsibilities during my absence. I have also benefited at Dalhousie University from the work of two graduate students, Doug Hykle and Rob Huebert, on different aspects of Canadian environmental policy. Valuable assistance was received from officials of the Australian National Parks and Wildlife Service; the Department of Home Affairs and Environment, Canberra; and Environment Canada, Ottawa. The staffs of the libraries of the Australian National University, and also of the Scott Polar Research Institute, Cambridge, were an essential resource for the research.

Earlier presentations of some of the materials in the study were made in the graduate seminar of the ANU Department of International Relations in March 1985; in the panel discussion on public policy in Canada and Australia held at the Canadian Political Science Association meetings in Hamilton in June 1987; and in a paper, "The Effectiveness of International Environmental Regimes: Lessons from the Australian Experience," presented at the American Political Science Association meetings in Chicago in September 1987. I should like to thank those who offered critical comments on these occasions, and particularly Kenneth Wiltshire, serendipitously present at Hamilton, and Marvin Soroos.

The study was completed with the aid of a Leave Fellowship from the Social Sciences and Humanities Research Council of Canada, and this support is gratefully acknowledged.

ACRONYMS

AACE	Australian Advisory Committee on the Environment
AAS	Australian Academy of Sciences
AAT	Australian Antarctic Territory
ABRS	Australian Biological Resources Study
ACAP	Advisory Committee on Antarctic Programmes
ACF	Australian Conservation Foundation
ACT	Australian Capital Territory
AEC	Australian Environment Council
AFAC	Australian Fauna Authorities Conference
AHC	Australian Heritage Commission
ALP	Australian Labor Party
AMLR	Antarctic Living Marine Resources
ANARE	Australian National Antarctic Research Expedition
ANCAR	Australian National Committee on Antarctic Research
ANPC	Australian National Parks Council
ANPWS	Australian National Parks and Wildlife Service
ANRC	Australian National Research Council
ANU	Australian National University
ANZAAS	Australia and New Zealand Association for the Advancement of Science
ARPAC	Antarctic Research Policy Advisory Committee
ASBS	Australian Systematic Botany Society
ASTEC	Australian Science and Technology Council
CAMLR	Convention on Antarctic Marine Living Resources
CCREM	Canadian Council of Resource and Environment Ministers
CITES	Convention on International Trade in Endangered Species
COMVE	Committee on Motor Vehicle Emissions
CONCOM	Council of Nature Conservation Ministers
CRSC	Chemicals Review Subcommittee
CSIRO	Commonwealth Scientific and Industrial Research Organization
CWS	Canadian Wildlife Service
DOE	Department of the Environment
EC	European Community
ECE	Economic Commission for Europe
ECOSOC	UN Economic and Social Council
EEZ	Exclusive Economic Zone
ESCAP	Economic and Social Commission for Asia and the Pacific
FAO	Food and Agriculture Organization
FOE	Friends of the Earth
GARP	Global Atmospheric Research Programme
GBRMPA	Great Barrier Reef Marine Park Authority

GEMS	Global Environment Monitoring System
GIPME	Committee on Global Investigation of Pollution in the Marine Environment
HEC	Hydroelectric Commission
IAEA	International Atomic Energy Agency
IBP	International Biological Programme
ICAO	International Civil Aviation Organization
ICOMOS	International Council of Monuments and Sites
ICSU	International Council of Scientific Unions
IDC	Inter-departmental committee
IFAW	International Fund for Animal Welfare
IGO	Inter-governmental Organization
IGY	International Geophysical Year
IIED	International Institute for Environment and Development
ILO	International Labour Organization
IMCO	Inter-governmental Maritime Consultative Organization
IMO	International Maritime Organization
IOC	Inter-governmental Oceanographic Commission
IRC	International Research Council
IRPTC	International Registry of Potentially Toxic Chemicals
IRS	International Referral System
ITU	International Telecommunications Union
IUCN	International Union for Conservation of Nature and Natural Resources
IWC	International Whaling Commission
MAB	Man and the Biosphere Programme
Marpol	Marine Pollution Convention (1973)
NACC	National Advisory Committee on Chemicals
NCSA	National Conservation Strategy for Australia
NGO	Non-governmental organization
OECD	Organization for Economic Cooperation and Development
Oilpol	Convention on Prevention of Pollution of the Sea by Oil (1954)
SCAR	Scientific Committee on Antarctic Research
SCOPE	Scientific Committee on Problems of the Environment
SCOR	Scientific Committee on Oceanographic Research
SNT	Single Negotiating Text
SPA	Specially Protected Area
TWS	Tasmanian Wilderness Society
UNCHE	United Nations Conference on the Human Environment (1972)
UNCLOS	United Nations Conference on the Law of the Sea
UNEP	United Nations Environment Programme
UNESCO	United Nations Educational, Scientific and Cultural Organization
UNICEF	United Nations Children's Fund
WHO	World Health Organization

WWF   World Wildlife Fund
WWW   World Weather Watch

In addition, the following abbreviations have been used in endnotes:

AFAR   *Australian Foreign Affairs Record*
AGD   *Australian Government Digest*
AGWD   *Australian Government Weekly Digest*
DAHE   Department of Arts, Heritage and Environment (1984-)
DEAA   Department of Environment, Aborigines and Arts (1971-72)
DEC   Department of Environment and Conservation (1972-75)
DEHCD   Department of Environment, Housing and Community
        Development (December 1975-1978)
DES   Department of Education and Science
DFA   Department of Foreign Affairs
DHAE   Department of Home Affairs and Environment (1980-84)
DOE   Department of Environment (April-December 1975)
DSE   Department of Science and Environment (1978-80)
DST   Department of Science and Technology
PP   Parliamentary Paper

CHAPTER ONE

Introduction: Global Arrangements and the Australian Polity

Arrangements for ordering the relations between states have grown more complex during the present century. The number of institutions that regulate, supervise, provide negotiating forums for, or merely dabble in, some aspect of public policy transported to the international level has expanded greatly. For many areas of policy in which governments are engaged, the world outside national borders can no longer be considered terra incognita, a blank white sheet on which ministers may hope to emblazon national insignia. Here be not dragons, but rather a more mundane universe of guidelines and rules, committees and assemblies, procedures and statutes. At any given time, however, the ways and means of organizing things internationally may also be in a state of flux. A gleam in an official's eye, or the nth resolution of a transnational organization, may eventually become a reality if the right combination of circumstances presents itself. It is this combination of order and anarchy, of rule-making by the instinctively rebellious and the instigation of change by the naturally cautious, that gives to the study of international arrangements its peculiar fascination. Such processes of governance, moreover, seep through the boundaries of states. They have in large measure ceased to be the fabric of either internationalist dreams or nationalist nightmares. How significant are they?

If the criterion is peace, the alleviation of tensions in specific inter-state conflicts, or the spread of government and law at the international level, then international organizations may with some justification be viewed as having failed to live up to earlier, and more utopian, expectations. In relation to more specific goals, such as the promotion of economic development, the record is mixed, as undoubted achievements in some areas are measured against an almost numbing sense of disorder, directionless movement, or ineffectual repetitiveness in others. Yet states continue to participate in the work of international bodies and, in varying degrees, to be influenced by what takes place within them. This momentum is a product of many factors, including the stream of recommendations that regularly flow from institutions, a desire on the part of governments to be present and to try to influence events and partake of any worthwhile outcomes, and the interplay between skeptics and enthusiasts inside national governments and in wider public debates. Within the United Nations system, outright withdrawal by states, or a refusal to join, still tends to be rare; a variety of other, less dramatic, means are available to states that wish to express degrees of satisfaction or dissatisfaction with the workings of international organizations.

1

International organizations, then, do not exist in a condition remote from the influence of the forces of international politics or the pressure of the domestic politics of states. States are located at the strategic points of decision-making in the dynamics of such bodies. Even if particular states have not been responsible for initiating specific programmes, resolutions or proposals, they are none the less important arbiters of their fate in terms of subsequent implementation. States have both shaped international arrangements in the history of institution-building from the mid-nineteenth century, and been profoundly affected by them. As power becomes a more slippery and elusive concept in international forums, and as the mosaics of international agendas change, the need to investigate processes within national governments and societies grows accordingly.

However, in part because of the different paths traditionally trod by observers of international regimes and by students of public policy in states, our knowledge of the processes that fuse the domestic and the international aspects of policy in a given area has tended to be weak. A particular area of neglect has been in the study of the attention paid by states to the implementation of decisions or regulatory instruments emanating from international institutions[1]. This neglect may reflect the inclinations of governments themselves. Problems of national follow-up tend to be less gripping than attempts to structure international rules; and not all rule-making efforts at the international level are based on the presumption that rules will, or should, be observed.

The natural environment constitutes a particularly useful policy area for the more detailed investigation of such questions. It is one that has grown in importance on the agendas of interstate relations in recent years, particularly in the decade and a half between the UN Conference on the Human Environment held at Stockholm in 1972 and the Report of the World Commission on Environment and Development in 1987. Since the early 1970s, moreover, the two sides of policy — domestic programmes and "foreign policies for the environment"[2] — have become closely interwoven in many states. It is less clear where the engine of change is located. To what extent do external pressures, such as developments in international organizations or the lessons provided by other states' experience, influence domestic programmes and policies? What kinds of factors help shape the policies and negotiating strategies of delegations in international conferences? The interconnectedness of domestic and external policies is in part a function of the issue-area: ecological processes, and the interactions of these with economies, societies and polities, cannot be contained neatly within the territorial boundaries of states. This is not to say that states lack the power to resist political influences from beyond their borders, however, or that opportunities to shift the burden of environmental adjustment on to others have ceased to be tempting.

There are also implications for government organization. Governments have had to confront the question of whether environmental agencies should be given a broad coordinating role for all of the many aspects of policies in the health, agricultural, mining, industrial and other fields that can be defined as "environmental," or whether their mandate should be more closely circumscribed. Should

2

foreign ministries, for example, or environment departments take the lead in the international arena, and by what means in practice is this dilemma resolved? In some countries, including Canada and Australia, state or provincial governments have important responsibilities in the resource and environmental fields, while external relations are traditionally and constitutionally matters for the executives of central governments. How is external environmental policy made in such cases, and what impact does the country's participation in international developments have on the practices of governments at local and regional levels?

Australia deserves special study for several reasons. In one form or another, its natural environment — the "novel and endless variety of its animal and vegetable productions," as it was described in 1821[3] — has been a focus of both domestic and external attention for several decades. While state governments have carried out various environmental and resource programmes for some time, it is only relatively recently that broader environmental movements, both national and transnational, began to exercise a significant influence over policy-making and to nudge governments towards adopting Australia-wide perspectives. The creation of a distinctive environmental policy role for the federal government during the 1970s was a related consequence. This development went hand in hand with Australia's emergence as an international actor in environmental policy areas, and this conjuncture gives us a useful opportunity to study the links between different policy strands and the factors that shape them. There is also an implicit comparative aim. Looking at Australia highlights some productive comparisons with other western countries, particularly those with federal systems. Canada, for example, also has a federal variant of the Westminster model of parliamentary and Cabinet government; as in Australia, questions of resource and environmental policy fall constitutionally within the domain of provincial or state governments; and as members of many of the same international organizations, such as the Organization for Economic Cooperation and Development (OECD) and those within the UN system, both countries have faced similar mixes of international environmental problems. There are significant differences too, and these will be discussed in a later chapter.

Before turning to the Australian record, two important perspectives on the study must be introduced: first, the character of Australia's orientation towards international organizations and law within the framework of its broader foreign policy; and, secondly, the form and content of international environmental arrangements, and the emergence of environmental questions as a policy area in Australia.

Australia in the international system

The oddity of Australia's location as an English-speaking, largely British-stocked, island of western culture situated off South-east Asia, has injected a sense of isolation from the mainstream of decision-making by western powers. T.B. Millar has concluded that most decisions on Australian foreign policy are "reactions to initiatives taken, pressures exerted, or situations developing elsewhere. Australia is too small, too satisfied, too conservative a power to have much of an impact on the outside world."[4] It took several decades for a robustly autonomous Australian foreign policy to emerge. Though staff had been stationed in London three decades earlier, Canberra opened its first full diplomatic mission abroad, in Washington, only in 1940. The events of the Second World War, particularly the southward advance of Japanese forces, brought about a reevaluation of the traditional reliance in defence and foreign policy on Britain. In later decades, the decline of British power in East Asia, that country's entry into the European Economic Community, rising nationalisms in Asia, and the momentum of closer diplomatic and security links with the United States, consolidated this trend.

It would be a mistake, however, to view Australia as a passive subject of the forces of international politics. During the 1930s, and even before, Australia was rapidly developing a distinctive voice in the leading international forums of the day. Australia played an important role, more particularly, in debates and negotiations on the organization of international economic and social cooperation in the League of Nations and the United Nations.

As the League got under way in the 1920s, it became apparent that questions were being raised that had a direct bearing on Australian interests. Indeed it has been argued by W.J. Hudson that the experience of League membership was a crucial factor in the emergence of an independent Australian foreign policy.[5] Progress was slow, however, partly for organizational reasons. Not until 1935 did the Department of External Affairs emerge from its cocoon inside the Prime Minister's Department. Australia's distance, small population, and dependence, were also factors. Officials and ministers continued to worry away at the realization that Australia's interests were not identical with those of Britain; and they were not slow to appreciate that multilateral settings could provide greater possibilities for exerting influence than was usually feasible in the more constrained dynamics of bilateral relations.

Economic and social matters held a particular attraction for Australia. The former Prime Minister, S.M. Bruce, took a keen interest in the League's work in the fields of nutrition and health. In London in 1933, at the World Monetary and Economic Conference, he warned that the western political system was in jeopardy if it could not arrange for the production and distribution of mankind's most elementary needs.[6] Australian motivations were a blend of humanitarianism, a desire for international recognition, and economic self-interest — the last a product of the calculation that any international initiative designed to alleviate the condition of the world's hungry must at some point benefit one of the world's leading agricultural producers. Bruce's thinking on these questions extended into the fundamental principles of the League system. Centralization under the League Council was the keystone of this system, with the separate existence of the International Labour Organization (ILO) as the only significant exception to the rule. By the late 1930s, critics from Australia and other western countries had become increasingly disturbed by the relative neglect of important economic and social questions by the League. In 1939, Bruce was asked by the League Council to chair a major committee on the Development of International Cooperation in Economic and Social Affairs. Its report recommended a new body be established to serve as the chief coordinating organ in these areas. By emphasizing the importance of economic and social goals, the report went a long way towards ensuring that these would have a high priority under the League's successor.[7]

Australia's reputation as an innovator was taken a step further during the wartime conferences that brought the UN into being. At San Francisco in 1945, Herbert Evatt gained recognition as a leading spokesman for the interests of smaller powers. Part of Evatt's campaigning diplomacy centred on the proposed Security Council and the provision of a veto for each of the five permanent members, and the issues surrounding the phrasing and location of Article 2(7) of the Charter, the clause protecting the domestic jurisdiction of states. More important, in practical terms, were UN structures for promoting economic and social cooperation. As a result of Australian diplomacy, and that of other small and medium powers, the Economic and Social Council (ECOSOC) became a principal organ of the UN and took on a wider range of functions than that originally envisaged for it. Evatt's delegation failed in an attempt to secure explicit guarantees of full employment, but the UN Charter did (in Article 55) include a commitment to the promotion of higher standards of living, full employment, and conditions of economic and social progress and development.[8] Too much should not be made, however, of apparent continuities between the 1930s and 1940s. For Labor's critics, and in the consensus of the 1950s and 1960s, Evatt's policies were more an aberration from the steady promotion of Australian interests through association with Britain and the US. The style of Labor's diplomacy also grated on opponents' ears. After the first flurry of excitement, how has Australia viewed the organization of which it was such an enthusiastic co-architect?

Although disenchantment with the UN began to set in in Australia, as in other western countries, in the late 1940s, Australia has remained a supportive participant. How such bodies are judged has depended in part on the circumstances of the time and the partisan hue of governments. The Charter's economic and social provisions were attractive to Labor in the 1940s and 1950s: resonant with social democratic visions of a war-free world, international cooperation to promote human welfare, and equality between nations. For conservatives, it seemed wiser to look to Australia's security needs and place faith in alignments with proven friends. Yet the swings of the electoral pendulum have not usually affected Australia's involvement in the wider UN system. Australia has remained a habitual joiner of intergovernmental bodies. It was a member of 70 by 1977 (the same number as Sweden; Canada stood at 75, the US at 78, and Britain at 91).[9] In the UN system, Australia was in the late 1970s or early 1980s a member of, among others, the UN Commission on International Trade Law, the Governing Council of the UN Development Program, the World Food Council, the UN Special Committee on Peacekeeping Operations, the UN Scientific Committee on the Effects of Atomic Radiation, the UN Committee on the Peaceful Uses of Outer

Space, the Commission on Human Rights, the Committee on Disarmament, ECOSOC, the Committee of 24, and the Council for Namibia, as well as all the Specialized Agencies.[10]

Much of this work is low-key, of little interest to Australian publics, Parliament, or the media. Indeed international economic and social questions share this fate with many Australian foreign policy questions. Building Australia in the image of shared goals has historically been a national preoccupation that has tended to exclude much interest in international affairs on the part of Australians. Translated into a society of settlers and immigrants, and a culture that valued pragmatism, individualism and egalitarianism, the deferential political attitudes of the metropole merged into a spirit of letting governments do what was necessary, so long as they did not interfere too much with the business of making a living. The distance of many Australians, both psychologically and geographically, from the federal capital has reinforced the feeling that foreign affairs could safely be ignored; elections have not been marked by much public interest in foreign policy.[11] There are exceptions, of course. Trade unions and other groups have from time to time taken strong stands on some issues, such as Indonesia's claim to West Irian in the 1960s, or French nuclear testing in the Pacific in the 1970s; and Australian debates about the Vietnam war and conscription produced an unprecedented polarization of public opinion.[12] The scope of public interest is wider, moreover, if a less restrictive definition of foreign policy issues is taken. Many Australian pressure groups have an active interest in international events related to their respective areas of interest, such as economic development in the Third World, environmental issues, women's rights, or education.

The states constitute an additional complicating layer. In their colonial form, they existed before the Commonwealth. They have maintained, through the Agents General system, their own form of quasi-diplomatic representation overseas. For many Australians, the state level is the arena of "real" politics, to be contrasted with the alleged artificialities and irrelevance of Canberra. Partisan rivalries haunt these attitudes, especially on the part of those whose own party is out of power in Canberra, or for whom the foreign policy line of the federal government has unpalatable implications. In 1982, the new Labor government in Victoria decided to ban port visits by US nuclear-armed or nuclear-powered vessels; the same year the Prime Minister of South Africa formally thanked the Premier of Queensland for his support at a time when the Fraser government was pursuing a more active anti-apartheid line.[13] The states, like Australian publics, have also been affected by the changing agendas of international relations. Appreciation of the vulnerability of the Australian economy to shifts in world economic forces has led some states to take more active steps to attract foreign investment, or to help local business-persons penetrate the Japanese market. Their international significance, however, is not great. The states lack the capabilities for full external roles; they have not tried to engage in many such activities beyond the promotion of trade, investment and tourism. The Commonwealth retains the upper hand in Australia's

6

external relations. There is no equivalent in Australia of Quebec's aspiration to a broader international cultural and economic role.[14]

The interests of the states can none the less be articulated in a variety of ways: through state and national party bodies, caucuses in the Australian Parliament, at the premiers' conferences, in public debates, through the news media, and in the structures of cooperative federalism. By these and other means, the issue of federal-state relations has been kept alive in many areas of Australia's external policies. The political parties have tended to diverge on the fundamental questions of the federal compact. Liberals have usually been more sympathetic to the general case that defence of states' rights must remain a vital component of Australian federalism; Labor, by contrast, particularly during the controversial Whitlam years of the early 1970s, has generally been more committed to forging policies within broader national frameworks. The submerged agendas of federalist principles and practice can be detected in debates in a number of areas of public policy.

Section 51(xxix) of the Constitution grants to the Parliament of Australia the power to make laws with respect to external affairs. The simplicity of the principle is deceptive. This is not the only "international" power noted in the Constitution; and the Constitution is largely silent about areas where this section potentially clashes with policy areas reserved for the states. The latter consideration has assumed progressively greater significance. As Sir Robert Menzies commented, "when the draftsmen of the Constitution wrote down the magic words 'external affairs', there did not leap into their minds any vision of the complex and novel things that were to come many years later."[15] International conventions, and international institutions, dealing with questions under the jurisdiction of the states have made the external affairs power a subject of political controversy and judicial deliberation. Whitlam, in opposition before the 1972 election, was severely critical of past federal governments that had signed international conventions, such as those of the ILO, based in part on an appreciation that state governments would be unwilling in practice to carry them through to the statute book. The issue came to a head in the Tasmanian dam crisis of 1982-83. Could the federal government, by virtue of having signed a pertinent international convention, use this (and other constitutional powers) to intervene in an area clearly within the jurisdiction of a state? The precedents were unclear. The courts concluded in a 1963 case, for example, that by ratifying a convention of the ILO the Commonwealth had not entered the relevant field of legislation; in the *Koowarta* case in 1982 a convention was held, over protests from the government of Queensland, to be a valid foundation for the federal *Racial Discrimination Act* of 1975.[16]

Australia, then, like other western countries, has experienced a steady erosion of barriers between domestic politics and policy and external relations. Domestic economic and agricultural interests, as well as longer-term foreign policy and security concerns, were reflected in Australian approaches to the League of Nations and the formation of the United Nations. In relation to issues of the natural environment, to which we now turn, Australia's geographical situation made it

7

less receptive than, say, Canada to the argument that transboundary arrangements were a prerequisite for the effective resolution of pressing domestic problems. Continuity in Australian official attention to international developments in related areas, however, combined with the rise in the 1960s of a domestic environmental policy constituency, ensured that Australian governments and interest groups would be active players in the international environmental politics of the 1970s and 1980s.

The natural environment as a policy arena

Australia's natural environment produced in its early European inhabitants a wide variety of reactions, from scientific curiosity and fascination to repulsion and horror, by way of practical, often harsh, lessons of day-to-day adaptation. In Governor Macquarie's words in 1816, this was a country "only fitt for theives and Rich men." Yet for much of their history, both before and after federation, Australians have also viewed this environment with a measure of indifference. The rise of an interest in conservation policy in the 1960s has been contrasted by one writer with a record of 150 years of neglect.[17] Neglect was compounded by urbanization, as was the later cultivation of the myth of a wilderness emblematic of the Australian identity. Environmental politics did not, however, erupt suddenly in the 1960s. If the term is defined broadly, the way was paved by developments in the nineteenth century, in the work of philosophical societies and of later field naturalists clubs and national parks associations. Inspired by the national parks movement in the United States, the Royal and Ku-ring-gai parks were established respectively in 1879 and 1891; a substantial section of the Blue Mountains was officially protected as early as 1866.[18]

It took some time for such matters to be viewed as having anything to do with "politics," and still longer for the federal government, as opposed to the states, to become an active player on the environmental stage. The reasons were partly cultural. A concern for wild nature tended to denote sentimentality: a lack of commitment to the task of building the Australian ideal, and a hankering after mannerisms more fitting in a sedate old country than in a proud and rugged new one. In part, too, there was a deep-rooted conviction that the vastness of the island continent, its resource wealth and comparatively miniscule population, together with its distance from Europe and North America, made it somehow exempt from the urban pollution and population pressures being encountered elsewhere. Australia took part in the Stockholm conference of 1972, but did not fully relinquish doubts about its relevance to Australian conditions. By the mid-1970s, environmental issues were more firmly embedded in political agendas. Looking back in 1973 to the establishment nine years earlier of the Australian Conservation Foundation, Whitlam observed that ecology in the mid-1960s had been purely of scientific interest: "Nobody really thought it was a matter that would concern the Australian Government."[19] More profound changes occurred during the subsequent decade. In 1983, a Labor government came to power following an election in which one environmental issue — the fate of wilderness areas in South-west Tasmania threatened by a proposed hydroelectric dam construction project — played a dominating, and possibly crucial, role.

Symptomatic of this transition was the enhanced ability of environmental groups during the 1970s and 1980s to generate issues and to structure the political debates on them: tourism, mining and fishing issues related to the Great Barrier Reef; the woodchips industry; instances of pollution along the coasts of Australia, particularly where oil spills were involved; the handling and regulation of toxic chemicals; the preservation of endangered species of flora and fauna; threats to temperate or tropical rainforests, or to wild rivers. Many questions became embroiled in protracted, and often bitter, partisan or federal-state disputes. The Labor government's attempt in 1972-75 to carve out an environmental policy role for the Commonwealth provoked a series of clashes with the states. The government of Victoria was not alone in 1975 in complaining about "unnecessary intrusions into areas of State responsibility."[20] Uranium mining in the 1970s sharpened the attention of groups, public opinion and political parties to a broad range of environmental issues and to their links with aboriginal rights questions.

The states, then, are the main environmental policy actors in Australia. In a sense the origins of environmental legislation in Australia date back to the protections afforded individuals by common law, as in the right of landowners to protect their property from nuisances. The years before federation produced more explicit instruments. The earliest air and water pollution regulations were promulgated in the late eighteenth century. In 1788, the first Governor of New South Wales drew up a plan for the development of Sydney which provided for main streets two hundred feet wide "so as to admit a free circulation of air."[21] The colonies took the initiative in the creation of national parks, and the label "national" was retained in the twentieth century even though these remained protected areas under state jurisdiction. It was in the period after 1945, however, and especially in the 1970s, that the main lines of environmental policies were set in place by state governments.

The legal and administrative framework that then emerged at the state level was none the less one of formidable complexity. Indeed diversity among state governments has provided the Commonwealth with some of its most persuasive arguments in favour of more genuinely national, and Canberra-led, policies. Confusion and fragmentation has also been portrayed by some environmental groups as a barrier to uniformity and progress in a policy area in which ecological principles, it is argued, ought to lead to more rational, trans-state policy-making. Bruce Davis has identified some of the factors that drive, or impede, the policy process at the state level:

> ... the overall performance is patchy, with much political expediency evident whenever private corporations seek resource exploitation rights or States are in competition to attract economic development. There is variation *between* States, seemingly influenced by the personality of their Premiers and ideology of the political party in power, but also some variation *within* States, arising from the relative strengths and influence of development-oriented agencies and interests vis-à-vis their conservation counterparts.[22]

9

Even the definitions of the subject vary. According to one South Australian statute of 1972, the "environment" includes "any matter or thing that determines or affects the conditions or influences under which any animate thing lives or exists in the State."[23] Most state laws and regulations are more specific, but the main elements of environment administration in the states still cover a vast span: general policy coordination, development and implementation; land use planning; resource management; resource development; environmental impact assessment; waste management; pollution control; conservation through reserves; wildlife protection; and the preservation of the national heritage.[24]

The weight of environmental policy authority, and experience, at the state level has seriously constrained the ability of the federal government to act as an authoritative voice domestically, and as an effective representative of the country in international forums. All states, for example, have some provisions in law for the setting aside of areas as national parks or otherwise protected areas; much of the legislation was consolidated by individual states in the period 1970-76.[25] Their constitutional preeminence in this area led some critics to question the validity of the Commonwealth's role in such matters, and to wonder aloud if the creation of the Uluru and Kakadu parks in the Northern Territory (where the federal government did have constitutional powers) was the thin end of a wedge leading to a more substantial land-use policy role for the Commonwealth. Action by Canberra on natural heritage protection matters, on which the states also introduced legislation in the 1970s, proved still more controversial. The government of Queensland, for example, passed no heritage legislation as such, did not recognize the constitutional and legal basis of the Commonwealth's advisory body in this area, and refused to nominate places in Queensland to the Register of the National Estate.[26] The federal government was in a relatively vulnerable position, with ultimately no more than a persuasive capability, backed by its constitutional powers to grant funds to the states. Listed sites could not be acquired, the Commonwealth could not legally control the use of such sites, and intervention to save a listed place from development could only come in cases where some form of Commonwealth approval was required for the project in question.[27] Protection of endangered species of flora and fauna is similarly a state responsibility. A flora protection act was passed in Queensland as early as 1930. These and related questions of wildlife conservation, however, particularly those involving trade in species or products, have since the early 1970s also become the subjects of international negotiations. This new dimension to the making of environmental policy in Australia has been central to the evolution of the federal government's role in the period since.

The constitutional authority of the states, however, is qualified both in principle and in practice. There are a number of constitutional bases for federal activity. The external affairs power, and the controversy surrounding it, was noted earlier. Other Section 51 powers include the regulation of trade and commerce with other countries and among the states; foreign corporations and trading and financial corporations formed within the limits of the Commonwealth; taxation; and power to make special laws for people of particular races — authority, that is, in relation to aboriginal populations. Under Section 96 of the Constitution the Commonwealth can grant financial assistance to states. The power to prohibit exports, for example, was used by the federal government to prevent the mineral sand mining of Fraser Island, following an environmental impact assessment made as a result of a federal statute of 1974. Environmental funding programmes for the states were established in federal acts passed in 1974 and 1977. Four statutes enacted by the Whitlam government have been described as "the cornerstones of national environmental policy": the *Environment Protection (Impact of Proposals) Act* (1974), the *Australian Heritage Commission Act* (1975), the *Australian National Parks and Wildlife Conservation Act* (1975), and the *Great Barrier Reef Marine Park Act* (1975).[28] Finally, the Commonwealth also has direct jurisdiction over the external territories, properties it owns within the states, the Northern Territory, and the Australian Capital Territory (ACT). The external territories — several islands or island groups, together with the Australian Antarctic Territory (AAT) — are relevant because of the wider significance of Antarctic policy, and also because important populations of migratory bird species have thus fallen directly under federal jurisdiction.[29]

The international component of Australian environment policy has thus grown side by side with major changes in the way these questions are handled by federal and state governments. Whether separately or in the joint mechanisms of cooperative federal structures, each level of government has had varying degrees of engagement with international developments. More formal intergovernmental arrangements for dealing with environmental issues have proliferated since the late 1960s. The transnational world of non-governmental bodies has likewise grown more complex, so that the external relations of Australian environmental groups can also be counted as a factor.

In a sense it was the latter development that occurred first. Australia's unique flora and fauna made the country a focal point of debates in the international conservation movement of the 1920s and 1930s. "The answer is unequivocal," wrote Sir James Barrett in 1925 in a book on threatened species in Australia: "Except in certain places where enlightened citizens have protected them they are all disappearing."[30] Ironically, such views were often expressed more forcibly outside the country, particularly in the United States and Britain, than in Australia itself. American conservationist pressure led to the US ban on koala imports from Australia in 1929. Indeed competition between US and British scientific groups sometimes created the impression that Australians were more subjects for study than agents managing their own affairs. A report by the American Museum of Natural History in 1921 concluded that the devastation of wildlife was more severe in Australia than elsewhere in the world. The primary causes were identified as deforestation, the fur trade and the expanding leather trade. The conditions that had led to evolution in Australia — geographical isolation combined with an early influx of primitive animals — were "now hastening that peculiar fauna towards its doom," thought the author of an article in the British scientific journal *Nature* in 1931.[31]

11

Such alarms went largely unnoticed at the time; and similar ones were still sounding in the 1980s. Changes did take place in the intervening half-century, however. Environmentalism in the later period was much more widely defined, though attention to problems of species conservation still occupied a prominent place. Groups in Australia were more numerous, and generally better organized, more alert to the political ramifications of environmental debates, better connected with their counterparts in other countries, and more visible to publics, politicians and the media. The policy environment in Australia also differed as a result of the cumulative impact of legislative changes, the initiation of environmental programmes, and the setting up of environmental bureaucracies in state and federal governments. A changing international policy milieu has been an integral part of these developments.

Four characteristics of this milieu should be noted. First, as in many other fields of international economic and social cooperation, no single, authoritative international institution dominates the environmental area. Arrangements at this level reflect basic organizing principles of the state system. Within bodies such as the Specialized Agencies of the UN system, states are either the main generators of change, or, where the initiating influence of secretariats is apparent, the actors which set policy, budgetary and other constraints on the freedom of manoeuvre and power of the organization. Secondly, institutional and other arrangements are subject to change. Fragmentation, regrouping, the formation of coalitions, and the creation of new organizations is characteristic of the web of international non-governmental environmental groups.[32] As more organs at the inter-governmental level turned their attention to environmental questions during the 1960s and 1970s, so this milieu too became more complex. Thirdly, definitions of the scope of environmental issues, and judgements about priorities and emphases, have also altered with time. Individual species, particularly endangered ones, were a preoccupation of the 1940s and 1950s in both national and international debates. This focus gave way to others — for example, the classification and conservation of ecosystem types, the integration of conservation perspectives with economic development requirements, the control of pollution and other forms of hazards, or concern for global questions such as atmospheric change — in subsequent decades. Finally, within the environmental policy arena as a whole there have emerged a number of distinct subgroupings of issues and arrangements. Organizational development has been somewhat uneven. In some areas, such as environmental conservation in Antarctica or measures for the regulation of the international wildlife trade, well-established mechanisms are in place. Even here, however, the mandates of institutions may be limited. In other areas, partial arrangements such as a single convention trying to attract signatories, may be the norm. Many of these sub-regimes, moreover, operate relatively autonomously.

Provided these caveats are kept in mind, it is useful to identify some institutions and treaties as the main components of a steadily growing international environment regime.[33] The United Nations Environment Programme (UNEP), established as a result of the landmark UN Conference on the Human Environment (UNCHE)

12

held in Stockholm in 1972, can be regarded as the flagship of world environmental cooperation. The centrality of its role, however, is qualified. It lacks broad coordinating power within the UN system, has suffered various financial and other problems, and for some countries regional organizations such as the OECD are more germane to their interests.[34] Further, several other UN institutions have programmes in the environmental area, some of which were in existence in one form or another before UNEP was created. These bodies, formally separate from the UN itself, include the World Health Organization (WHO), the United Nations Educational, Scientific and Cultural Organization (UNESCO), and the Food and Agriculture Organization (FAO). One body, the International Union for Conservation of Nature and Natural Resources (IUCN) is strictly speaking a non-governmental organization, but its mixed membership of states and government agencies as well as environmental groups gives it a far more important role in international environmental policy-making than this designation would normally imply. Although institutions such as these are autonomous, the environmental arena has also been marked by collaborative efforts. Thus the *World Conservation Strategy*, a significant 1980 document which attempted to set environmental policy guidelines for states and international organizations, was the product of joint efforts by UNEP, IUCN and the World Wildlife Fund (WWF).[35]

Much of the development of international law relating to environmental questions has been associated with such organizations. The formative stages of the Convention on International Trade in Endangered Species (CITES), for example, were closely linked with IUCN; the World Heritage convention of 1972 was constructed largely as a result of UNESCO initiatives; and the IMO has been responsible for the creation of a set of international conventions dealing with marine pollution. Several of the UN Specialized Agencies also prepare various kinds of regulatory instruments, such as the recommendations, produced by a joint committee of WHO and FAO, on additives and pesticide residue levels in foods.[36] The breadth of subject-matter of international conventions in the environmental area, though more circumscribed than the scope of issues raised in national political debates or international meetings, is impressive. Among the main treaties, in addition to the World Heritage and CITES agreements, are the Ramsar convention on the protection of wetlands (1971), the convention on conservation of migratory species (1979), and the ozone layer convention (1987); regional agreements include the African nature conservation convention of 1968, the convention on polar bear conservation signed by the Arctic nations in 1973, the 1979 convention on transboundary pollution, and the Antarctic Marine Living Resources convention (CAMLR) of 1980.[37]

Such instruments vary considerably in the obligations placed on states, and also in their effectiveness, as measured by the number of countries which undertake appropriate implementing action to strengthen them. Much depends on the interests of states and the political will of governments. Some international institutions have devices for encouraging countries to take them more seriously, for example, by compiling data on the pace of implementation of collective decisions or

13

addressing questionnaires to governments on the actions they have taken or propose to take. Yet any government's attention to international institutions and conventions in a given policy area, and particularly to the detailed work of executing agreements, is likely to be less than total. Priorities may lie elsewhere; and administrative and budgetary resources are rarely equal to the task. This applies particularly to attempts by governments to coordinate their activities across the full span of major inter-governmental organizations. As one study has concluded, "In most countries a relatively small number of bureaucrats along with a few delegates are charged with the responsibility of overseeing the work of and formulating policies for some sixty international governmental organizations. The impossibility of doing these tasks in such circumstances is obvious."[38]

Australia has brought its own interests and views to bear on regime developments in the environmental area. Among these have been wider political and foreign policy concerns. As we saw earlier, Australia has been promoting international economic and social cooperation since the early years of the League of Nations. The environmental work of organs of the UN system fits well into this tradition. Australia in the early 1970s was consequently predisposed to support new ventures such as UNEP. Similarly, a motivating factor in Australian approaches to the OECD generally, and one which is evident in the environmental arena, has been its desire to be counted as an influential participant in the deliberations of the western industrialized nations on matters of common interest. In relation to Antarctica, the evolution of Australia's environmental positions and policies has in practice been inseparable from the broader context of its historical claims to sovereignty over part of the continent. The intermeshing of these concerns is an underlying theme of the following group of four chapters.

Notes for Chapter 1

[1] Evan Luard, *International Agencies: The Emerging Framework of Interdependence* (London: Macmillan, 1977), p. 309.

[2] *Our Common Future*, Report of the World Commission on Environment and Development, (Oxford: Oxford University Press, 1987), p. 314.

[3] Philosophical Society of Australia, quoted in *The National Estate in 1981. AHC Report, June 1981* (Canberra, 1982; PP 96), p. 1.

[4] T.B. Millar, *Australia in Peace and War: External Relations, 1788-1977* (Canberra: Australian National University Press, 1978, p. 22

[5] W.J. Hudson, *Australia and the League of Nations* (Sydney: Sydney University Press for the AIIA, 1980), p. 3.

[6] *Ibid.*, pp. 176-77.

[7] *Ibid.*, pp. 178-79; and Inis L. Claude, Jr., *Swords into Plowshares: The Problems and Progress of International Organization*, 4th ed. (New York: Random House, 1971), p. 392.

[8] Alan Watt, *The Evolution of Australian Foreign Policy, 1938-1965* (Cambridge University Press, 1967), pp. 78-93.

9 Harold K. Jacobson, *Networks of Interdependence: International Organizations and the Global Political System*, 2nd ed. (New York: Knopf, 1984, p. 50.

10 Ralph Harry, "Australian Multilateral Diplomacy," in P.J. Boyce and J.R. Angel, eds., *Independence and Alliance: Australia in World Affairs, 1976-80* (Sydney: Allen and Unwin for the AIIA, 1983), pp. 87-88.

11 See for example Henry S. Albinski, *Australian External Policy under Labor: Content, Process and the National Debate* (Vancouver: University of British Columbia Press, 1977), pp. 331-32; and G. Greenwood, "Australian Foreign Policy in Action," in G. Greenwood and Norman Harper, eds., *Australia in World Affairs, 1956-1960* (Melbourne: Cheshire for the AIIA, 1963), p. 4.

12 Millar, *Australia in Peace and War*, p. 45; and Henry S. Albinski, *Politics and Foreign Policy in Australia: The Impact of Vietnam and Conscription* (Durham, N.C.: Duke University Press, 1970), pp. 3-5.

13 Brian Hocking, "Pluralism and Foreign Policy: The States and the Management of Australia's External Relations," *Yearbook of World Affairs*, 38 (1984), p. 137.

14 See for example, D.P. O'Connell and J. Crawford, "The Evolution of Australia's International Personality," in K.W. Ryan, ed., *International Law in Australia* (Sydney: Law Book Co., 1984), p. 30; and G. Sawer, "Australian Constitutional Law in Relation to International Relations and International Law," *ibid.*, p. 47.

15 Rt. Hon. Sir Robert Menzies, *Central Power in the Australian Commonwealth: An Examination of the Growth of Commonwealth Power in the Australian Federation* (London: Cassell, 1967), p. 116.

16 Attorney-General's Department, *The Australian Constitution Annotated...* (Canberra, 1980), p. 113; and F.H. Lane, *A Manual of Australian Constitutional Law* (Sydney: Law Book Co., 1984), p. 146. See also *ibid.*, for a discussion of the important 1936 case of *R. v. Burgess*.

17 H.J. Frith, *Wildlife Conservation* (Sydney: Angus and Robertson, 1979, rev. ed.), Preface.

18 See for example David Yencken, in *The Heritage of Australia* (Macmillan of Australia, 1981), p. 12; and Frank Fenner and A.L.G. Rees, eds., *The Australian Academy of Sciences: The First 25 Years* (Canberra: AAS, 1980), Ch. 1.

19 *ACF Newsl.*, 5(3), July 1973, p. 2.

20 Quoted in Alan Gilpin, *Environment Policy in Australia* (St. Lucia: University of Queensland Press, 1980), p. 29.

21 *Ibid.*, p. 6.

22 Bruce W. Davis, "Federalism and Environmental Politics: An Australian Overview," in R.L. Mathews, ed., *Federalism and the Environment* (Canberra: Centre for Research on Federal Financial Relations, 1985), p. 3.

23 G.M. Bates, *Environmental Law in Australia* (Sydney: Butterworths, 1983), p. 1.

24 *Ibid.*, p. 22. For a more compact classification, see D.E. Fisher, "An Overview of Environmental Law in Australia," *Earth Law Journal*, 3 (1977), p. 47.

25 Bates, *Environmental Law in Australia*, p. 56.

26 Kenneth Wiltshire, "Heritage," in Mathews, ed., *Federalism and the Environment*, pp. 48-49.

27 Bates, *Environmental Law in Australia*, p. 82.

28 Davis, "Federalism and Environmental Politics," p. 2.

29 Bates, *Environmental Law in Australia*, pp. 100-02.

30 Sir James Barrett, ed., *Save Australia: A Plea for the Right Use of our Fauna and Flora* (Melbourne: Macmillan, 1925), pp. 1-2.

31 "Vanishing Wildlife of Australia," *Nature*, vol. 128, no. 3228, Sept. 12, 1931, pp. 425-27; A.S. Lesouef, "Vanishing Wildlife of Australia," *Natural History* 24 (January, 1924), pp. 60-61; H.L. Raven, "Glimpses of Mammalian Life in Australia and Tasmania," *Natural History*, 24 (June 1924), pp. 16-28; and J.S. Gardner, "Harvard Museum: Expedition to Australia," *Nature*, vol. 128, no. 3228, Sept. 12, 1931, pp. 457-58.

32 See further R. Boardman, *International Organization and the Conservation of Nature* (Bloomington: Indiana University Press, 1981), Ch. 6.

15

[33] There is a substantial literature on regimes, and the conceptual and empirical problems involved in using this notion as opposed to more traditional ones. See for example Oran R. Young, "International Regimes: Toward a New Theory of Institutions," *World Politics*, XXXIX(1), October 1986; and Stephen Krasner (ed.), *International Regimes* (Ithaca: Cornell University Press, 1983).

[34] On the OECD, see Nancy K. Hetzel, *Environmental Cooperation among Industrialized Countries: The Role of Regional Organizations* (Washington, D.C.: University Press of America, 1980), esp. pp. 26-34. The regional frameworks developed by UNEP have grown in significance since the late 1970s.

[35] For overviews and analyses, see for example Jan Schneider, *World Public Order of the Environment: Towards an International Ecological Law and Organization* (University of Toronto Press, 1979), D.A. Kay and H.K. Jacobson, eds., *Environmental Protection: The International Dimension* (Totowa, N.J.: Allanheld, Osmun and Co., 1983); and L.K. Caldwell, *International Environmental Policy* (Durham, N.C.: Duke University Press, 1984).

[36] R. Boardman, *Pesticides in World Agriculture: The Politics of International Regulation* (London: Macmillan, 1986), Ch. 4.

[37] See for example S. Lyster, *International Wildlife Law* (Cambridge: Grotius Publications, 1985); and M. Trexler, "International Conservation Conventions: Are they being Implemented?" *Environmental Conservation*, Autumn 1984.

[38] Harold K. Jacobson, William M. Reisinger, and Todd Mathers, "National Entanglements in International Governmental Organization," *American Political Science Review*, 80(1), March 1986, p. 157.

I

AUSTRALIA AND INTERNATIONAL ENVIRONMENTAL ORDER

CHAPTER TWO

International Institutions: the Environment and Foreign Policy

The foreign policy dilemmas faced by Australia since the 1950s have often failed to support the thesis that functional cooperation serves tangible national interests. As in other western countries, there has been a growing irritation with the seemingly illimitable sprawl of agencies and committees in the UN system, the politicization of issues, and, in general, with the constraints affecting the capacity of the UN to enhance the security of its members. The UN's work in economic and social fields has come to be viewed by many Australians as more an extension of the industrialized world's aid and technical assistance programmes to developing countries, and less as an arena within which quantifiable gains might accrue to Australia. Yet for all its evident faults, the UN has afforded Australians an opportunity to take part directly in international events beyond the immediate confines of their own region. Participation for its own sake, or as an insurance premium, has a long history in Australia's dealings with international organizations. As one official commented on the League of Nations in 1928, it was "safer for us to be present than absent."[1] This chapter examines responses to the environmental activities of organs in the UN system, the OECD and IUCN.

Australian diplomacy in the United Nations system

Australia's approach to the environmental initiatives of the late 1960s was shaped in part by its own earlier experiences in international organizations. Several of the Specialized Agencies, included FAO, WHO, WMO and UNESCO, had already by then taken steps to expand into environmental policy areas. They handled various aspects of pollution and conservation, and, the government stated in 1970, Australia took a full interest in them where they were relevant to Australian conditions.[2] The hint of a qualification here is revealing. Australian officials and ministers tended to argue during this period that many of the environmental problems being confronted by other countries in the industrialized world did not really apply in Australia. This historical background meant that the Stockholm conference could not be viewed as a radically new departure. Any future world environment organization would have to accommodate itself to existing ones. One role for the UN, the Minister of External Affairs told the UN General Assembly in 1969, was to help to see that the relevant international agencies and other bodies actually fulfilled their opportunities and duties.[3]

The problem, then, was partly one of coordination. But it was also a problem of semantics. As the environment minister, Dr. Cass, stated in 1973, "the all-

19

embracing nature of the term 'environment programs' means that nearly all international organizations are involved in some environmental programmes and Australia has been active in many of these."[4] The starting point frequently cited by Australians in the early 1970s was the earlier Australian initiative in the field of science and technology. A proposal made in 1958 by Lord Casey, then Minister of External Affairs, led with Romanian support to the convening in 1963 in Geneva of a UN Conference on the Application of Science and Technology for the Benefit of Less Developed Areas. Australian interest in the area continued during the decade. Sir Ronald Walker, Ambassador to West Germany, was elected Chairman in 1970 of the UN Advisory Committee on the Application of Science and Technology to Development, the main body that followed up the 1963 meetings. Australian participation elsewhere in the UN system also contributed to later environmental work. In 1969, Sir William Refshange, head of the federal Department of Health, was elected Chairman of the Executive Board of WHO.[5] Australian scientists and officials took prominent roles in a number of specialized technical bodies, such as the pesticides residues monitoring activities of the Codex Alimentarius Commission, the joint food standards body established by FAO and WHO in the early 1960s.[6] Also significant in the longer term was the work of a handful of Australians in IUCN, the leading international organization handling environmental questions.

At the time of the convening of the 1968 biosphere conference, however, Australia did not have in place a national environment policy framework. In this Australia was little different from other western nations. The Commonwealth Scientific and Industrial Research Organization (CSIRO) carried out research in many environment-related areas, but it was later criticized for failing to tackle such problems systematically. In government the nearest equivalent body was the Department of Education and Science, which had itself been created only in 1966. Part of its mandate included responsibility for Australia's relations with UNESCO's scientific work. The Australian delegation to the 1968 conference was led by a member of the CSIRO executive, and included Professor J.D. Ovington of the School of Forestry at the Australian National University (ANU) in Canberra. Ovington had been active for some time in IUCN, and later became the first Director of the Australian National Parks and Wildlife Service.[7] The conference generated little publicity inside Australia, and made little impact on government policy or organization. Its significance lay more in the subsequent preparations for the resulting Man and the Biosphere (MAB) Progamme. Initial planning for the Programme was carried out in the early 1970s; Australians, particularly Professor J.O. Slatyer of the ANU School of Biology, took a leading role in both international and Australian MAB developments.[8] Australian participation in the crucial conservation aspects of the programme was confirmed in 1976 by the Standing Committee of the Council of Nature Conservation Ministers (CONCOM), the federal-state body responsible for coordinating Commonwealth and state environment policies.[9] Participation gave rise to controversy since MAB Project 8 (on "Conservation of Natural Areas and of the Genetic Material they Contain") included consideration of possible areas to be set aside as part of a world network of biosphere reserves, something which posed awkward questions for the Commonwealth's relations with the states. But essentially MAB was a scientific rather than a directly inter-governmental enterprise. Much therefore depended on the willingness of individual Australian scientists and laboratories to take an interest.

Thus Australian officials faced some difficulty in the late 1960s and early 1970s. MAB lay in the future; few knew of preparatory work for it, or appreciated the continuity from the 1968 conference to the 1972 Stockholm conference; government organization for environment policy was virtually absent at the federal level, and fragmented and weak in the states. The UN Conference on the Human Environment (UNCHE), however, was clearly more of a political venture, and more highly visible, than anything that had gone before. The prospect of a federal election in 1972 also sharpened politicians' minds to the possibility of basking in international success, and also of defusing sniping from Australian critics who were arguing that too little was being done too slowly to protect Australia's environment. Environmental issues, it appeared, would be prominent on international agendas during the 1970s; it was in Australia's interests to be as close to the forefront as possible in this new area.

The first steps on the road to Stockholm were taken by Sweden in ECOSOC in July 1968. The key UN General Assembly resolution was adopted on December 3, 1968. Australia was among the large number of co-sponsors of the Swedish resolution, and delegates took active steps to make known Australia's strong support for the move.[10] Australia failed, however, despite what one minister described as "considerable effort," to secure a seat on the preparatory body established to oversee planning for the conference. Officials registered frustration with the conventional UN geographical formulae for distributing committee placements. Australia "strongly urged that this pattern was not suitable for a committee on environmental questions if it did not ensure that important geographical areas of the world were adequately represented."[11] Objection to the "West European and Other" category was already current among Australian delegates; in a sense, the environment issue was being used as a means of settling older scores. The question became one of Australia's major concerns at Stockholm in its approach to the future world environmental organization.

Exclusion from the Preparatory Committee, though a disappointment, did not prevent Australia from taking part in preparatory work. Officials attended Committee meetings as observers. Australia also became a member of four of the Committee's Working Groups — on marine pollution, soils, conservation and monitoring — and observers were sent to the meetings of the group drafting the declaration planned as a central feature of the conference.[12] Much of this work was coordinated by the Australian mission to the UN in New York, particularly through its First Secretary, Dr. R. Merrillees. Inside Australia, preparation centred around production of the national report required from all participating countries (early in 1971), and submissions of suggestions for a case study to help focus discussion at the conference. The Australian topic selected dealt with town planning and the urban environment in Canberra and the ACT. Various submissions were made by state governments, and CSIRO prepared a formal proposal for international action on insect viruses.[13]

The Stockholm conference took place at a key juncture in Australia's own approaches to environment policy. The pressure of international events was a significant factor influencing their shape and the pace of developments. Since 1969 environment policy had been an ill-defined area of some tension between the Commonwealth and the states, especially regarding wildlife conservation. Steps were taken in 1971-72 towards creating a role for the Commonwealth, but these were far from complete at the opening of the UNCHE. Peter Howson, the federal minister responsible for the environment, finally issued the government's long-awaited statement on environment policy towards the end of May 1972, on the eve of the Stockholm meetings. The first meeting of the new Australian Environment Council (AEC) had taken place in Sydney the month before. The pace had been slow, not least because of the federal dimension. The first meeting of Commonwealth and state ministers, not a successful event, was held in September 1971; Howson's submission to the federal Cabinet on environment policy at the end of November was "the first occasion on which I've been able to get the Cabinet to think about a policy on this subject."[14]

Given this uncertainty, Australian readiness for UNCHE was no small achievement. Australia was elected to a Vice-Presidency, and to membership of the conference credentials committee. This could potentially have put Australia into the centre of the dispute over the representation of East Germany, but by the time the conference opened it was clear that the Soviet Union and its allies would be boycotting UNCHE over this issue. In the UN General Assembly in 1971 Australia had been one of the eleven countries which co-sponsored a resolution in favour of the so-called "Vienna formula," which had the effect of denying the German Democratic Republic full representation at the conference. The offer of GDR participation by way of individual experts was unacceptable to the Soviet Union. The absence of East European delegations cast a shadow over Stockholm's aspirations to universality, and was the subject of criticism in the Australian press.[15] The Australian delegation was also lobbied by representatives from South Africa and the Republic of Korea concerned about their own status at the conference.

Australia approached UNCHE with three main objectives in view: ensuring its participation in whatever form of continuing world environmental organization finally emerged; influencing the character of environmental objectives and principles set by the conference; and dealing with a number of specific issues that loomed larger than expected, notably the question of nuclear weapons testing.

The first of these was crucial. Officials lobbied informally and spoke out strongly in conference forums in favour of a larger governing council, the proposed main executive body for the future Environment Programme. Australian diplomacy led successfully to the setting up of a council of 54 (later 58) members, instead of the smaller body (of 48 members) favoured by the US. Australia's aim was

22

to press for conditions that would better guarantee it a future role. A smaller council would have reduced Australia's chances by throwing the Canberra hat in with western European contenders for geographical placings. Thus "only the higher number would provide adequate representation for all the geographic regions of the world."[16] The question brought Australia more into line with many developing countries, particularly its own regional neighbours, and away from the preferences of other western nations. The US tended to argue against a larger council on the grounds of likely efficacy. Western countries generally suspected a lack of conviction behind developing countries' views on international environmental questions, and were uneasy about the prospects of an executive still more under their control. The idea of a larger council was "strenuously resisted" by the Europeans, and Australia was the only country in the western camp to vote in favour of the Afro-Asian enlargement proposal.[17]

Active lobbying was the key to the change. It emerged from Third Committee sessions early in the conference that the size of the Council was to be set at 48. Despite this initial setback to the Australian position, the delegation decided to continue to press vigorously for an increase. Achieving a figure of 54 Howson described as "the only way in which Australia could be assured of membership."[18] The strategy was to force the issue to a head in plenary meetings, lobby developing countries, and inform the US and Britain of Australia's determination. The US delegation also tried to win support, with the aid of sympathetic Swedish and Brazilian delegates. In the final vote in plenary on the question Australia's position, expressed as an amendment to the conference report dealing with future organization, was supported by a vote of 56 to 11.[19] The momentum carried on after Stockholm, since the larger size could not in itself guarantee Australian membership in the Council. Later in 1972 Howson observed "trouble with the European group," and suggested "we may well have to go out and lobby for votes ourselves without doing the gentlemanly thing and abiding by the formula." In the event Australia was elected to membership of the Council in December.[20]

Secondly, the delegation aimed to inject what it saw as practical good sense into the conference, and check any tendency for it to degenerate into a merely exhortatory one. Australia, it was thought, was well placed to be a voice of objectivity. The main environmental threats lay in North America and Europe. As Howson stated it at Stockholm: "Australia's environmental problems are not as acute as those of some other countries. We do not have the pressures of population or resources which have contributed to environmental problems in some countries. Our geographic isolation as an island continent makes us less affected by pollution across frontiers from other countries."[21] Australia was pulled in different directions. It was firmly part of the western camp. But the Australian approach also contained echoes of Third World positions skeptical about an over-emphasis on environmental protection at the expense of economic development and international trade. In practice on most issues the delegation defined its position as that of a loyal member of the western group of nations. It was accepted as a goal that developing countries should not be allowed to water down the objectives of UNCHE. Earlier, Australia had objected to Brazilian efforts in the UN General Assembly's Second Committee on the grounds that these seemed to be aimed at preventing UNCHE from becoming an action-oriented conference. Informal lobbying, however, and a series of amendments tabled jointly with the British delegation, had failed to halt this trend.[22]

Australia's longer-term goal of participation in the future world organization remained paramount; instead of dealing with such matters, Howson commented irritably in the early stages of the conference "we're spending a lot of time on matters of detail like whales and nuclear testing."[23] Yet a number of these "details" were relevant to Australian interests.

Ocean dumping was high on the list of the Australian delegation's concerns. The meetings in Stockholm coincided with several related developments: plans for an Inter-governmental Maritime Consultative Organization (IMCO) conference on marine pollution in 1973, OECD work in this area (which Australia, as a new member, was particularly interested in following up), and discussion during 1972 of the projected negotiations in the Third UN Conference on the Law of the Sea (UNCLOS III). Australia expressed general support for the various international conventions on the environment proposed by IUCN at Stockholm. These had already been examined in the conservation group of the Preparatory Committee, of which Australia had been a member. But as the foreign minister, Nigel Bowen, told the UN General Assembly later in 1972, the main requirement in the international convention field was "most immediately in control over marine pollution."[24]

On several questions Australia tended to oppose on principle any recommendations that seemed likely to weaken the capabilities of international environmental organization. There was dissatisfaction on this score with some features of the draft Declaration on the Human Environment and the Action Plan.[25] In relation to the latter, Australia was most interested in urban pollution problems: resource management and economic development issues were seen to have been included for political reasons, for the benefit of skeptical Third World delegations. Howson specifically objected to the Plan's recommendation for compensation for exports adversely affected by environmental considerations,[26] something which likewise seemed to be a distracting ploy by developing countries. Firm support, however, was given to the "polluter pays" principle in approaches to environmental law and policy.[27] Following the relaying to Stockholm of a decision taken in Canberra during the conference, Howon was also able at a particularly opportune juncture — the lead-up to the vote on the governing council issue — to announce an Australian contribution of $2.5 million (Aus.) to the voluntary Environment Fund established by the conference.[28]

At a third level, Australian delegates were also preoccupied at Stockholm with the issue of nuclear weapons testing. This was an unrelated intrusion as far as most western countries were concerned. Australia was closely involved, however, because of the importance placed on the question by the New Zealand delegation, and also because the issue became hotly debated inside Australia. Australia's refusal to support New Zealand's campaign for a ban constituted the main news from Stockholm, as the Australian media seized on the opportunity to publicize an alleged major rift between the two countries. Duncan McIntyre, head of the New Zealand delegation, determinedly sought Australian support for anti-testing moves. The target was chiefly the French test programme, but the issue was clearly one that touched on US interests, a consideration that made for caution in the Australian approach. Australian officials discussed the matter with countries also anxious to avoid a rift with the US through escalation of the issue, notably Singapore, Malaysia, Indonesia and South Vietnam. New Zealand, rebuffing overtures, remained firmly committed to its position. The matter was finally resolved when, after a policy reversal by the Cabinet in Canberra, the Australian delegation was directed to switch sides and join New Zealand.[29]

Stockholm was important, then, for several reasons. Though the Labor administration that took office in late 1972 was to take much of the credit, or blame, for constructing Australia's federal environmental policy and organization, the foundation had already been laid before UNCHE. Australia, moreover, needed to be able to go to the conference equipped with evidence that it, too, was at least beginning to put its environmental house in order. During the conference, Howson made a point of discussing government organization with Russell Train, head of the US delegation. He found that "the Australian organization was not very different from the American, and that the American organization had not moved very much faster than ours has, although in theory it is supposed to have done."[30] The conference also had an energizing effect on environmental groups and parliamentarians in Canberra. Australia succeeded in its aim of helping to create a UNEP with an enlarged council, and later gained election to it. It also had modest success in its efforts to check trends to weaken this new organization.

However, to the extent that environmental problems at this time were defined in terms of pollution, Australia had less stake in the conference than other western countries. Stockholm was more like a vaccine. As Gordon Freeth, then foreign minister, stated in the UN General Assembly in 1969, "By taking early action now, it may be possible to prevent Australia suffering some of the more extreme afflictions that have already hit certain other countries."[31] Apart from the contribution to the voluntary fund, and subsequent annual fees, the conference did not generate any major obligations, financial or political, that future administrations in Canberra could find burdensome. International environmental developments in later years were unable to reproduce the sense of freshness and urgency that marked the Stockholm consciousness-raising exercise. After UNCHE, debates had an air of repetitiveness. The UN General Assembly's Second Committee discussions of the environment in 1973, Australian officials thought, "traversed familiar ground."[32] Criticism of UNEP's financial management, rhetoric and apparent inability to establish priorities, grew more frequent during the 1970s. Relatively more weight was attached in practice to Australia's work in the OECD. Global environmental issues became more insulated from broader political and foreign policy contexts, more technical and scientific, more development-oriented, and more low-key. Australia none the less continued to maintain a presence.

Several of the world conferences of the 1970s were "environmental" in the broad sense of the term. Australia sent delegations to the World Population Conference in Bucharest and the World Food Conference in Rome, both in 1974.[33] In common with other western countries, it tried to restrict such gatherings to their substantive focus and to prevent the encroachment of other questions. Though some spillover into commercial areas was unavoidable, for example, officials thought it would be unwise for the food conference to become involved in detailed issues of agricultural trade.[34] The Habitat conference, in Vancouver in 1976, was viewed as being in danger of suffocation by the Palestinian question and other extraneous matters. Australia's approach to Habitat was itself less well orchestrated, in part because of the unavailability of the intended leader of the delegation, Senator Greenwood.[35]

Australians held out more hope, however, for the desertification conference in 1977. The issues appeared more straightforward, and in line with environmental policy goals enunciated at Stockholm. The topic also seemed to be custom-made for Australia. It was an acknowledged world leader in the field of arid lands management, and faced regular problems of drought affecting large stretches of the country. Approximately one-third of Australia's land mass was in the arid zone. The conference was accordingly seen as "an important opportunity to highlight a serious problem that affects Australia and many other countries," and one that would "make Australia's expertise more readily available to other countries, particularly developing countries."[36] A case study of the Gascoyne area of Western Australia was submitted as a discussion document. Broader questions, however, hung over the conference. Despite what Australian officals had understood to be an informal agreement barring this, the issue of a separate fund to combat desertification arose on the final day. By forcing western delegations onto the defensive and into a common position, this served to deflect attention from policy questions explored earlier. These and other factors, in the Australian view, made a comparative failure out of what could have been a worthwhile environmental intiative. Australian observers remained highly critical later in the 1970s and early 1980s of UN inactivity in relation to world desertification problems. The component parts of the World Plan of Action that emerged from the conference were studied and shelved, but little followed.[37] Australia did continue, though, to work within a variety of bilateral and multilateral programmes in the area, for example, through consultancies by Australian experts in developing countries.

During the 1970s and 1980s UNEP provided a framework for collaboration on a number of questions of interest to Australia. Toxic chemicals were a conspicuous feature of UNCHE. Pesticides and other chemicals had acted as important spurs to Australian public concern on environmental questions since the mid-1960s. Following resolutions on chemical hazards passed at Stockholm, UNEP moved steadily during the 1970s to establish a monitoring system that could be the basis of informed international action. Progess on the International Registry of Potentially Toxic Chemicals (IRPTC) took place alongside parallel activity inside Australia. The Registry was described in 1978 as providing "an important international link for the national register of chemicals" being developed by the Australian Environment Council.[38] Talks followed between environmental officials in Canberra and IRPTC staff in Geneva on the workings of collaborative arrangements and on Australian participation in data-gathering.[39] To some extent, however, IRPTC activities were overshadowed by the greater interest Australian officials had in working through OECD on chemicals questions. The relatively slow pace of development of the Geneva network also appeared to render it less useful as a guide for policy.

More prominent a part of UNEP was the environmental information gathering and monitoring activity known as INFOTERRA. It began operations in 1975 as a consequence of plans formulated in Stockholm. The central idea, of developing information sources and channelling data in an organized fashion into a central clearing house, also pressed forward the setting up of Australia's own environmental data collection network in 1975-76. By the end of the decade, more than 500 sources had been brought into the Australian system, mostly from state governments, tertiary education institutions, and research bodies, especially the CSIRO. The Australian end of INFOTERRA answered requests for environmental information, exchanged data with INFOTERRA headquarters and other countries, and continued to evaluate the effectiveness of the system. Officials also initiated and participated in regional meetings with New Zealand and South-east Asian counterpart institutions. Training in the use and management of INFOTERRA was used as an instrument of Australian development assistance to Thailand.[40] Data gathering in the programme also stimulated other environmental statistics efforts in Australia in the 1970s and 1980s directed towards the consolidation of reliable data bases upon which policies could be built. Skeptics suggested, however, that considerably more effort went into building the INFOTERRA network than was justified by the practical consequences. Requests for information, for example, amounted to only about 30 in Canberra in 1982-83.[41]

Australia began a second three-year term as a member of the UNEP Governing Council in 1979. After several years of experience, Australians were more selective and more critical. Delegates now placed more emphasis on the regional needs of South-east Asia and the Pacific. This represented a sharpening of earlier arguments. Virtually from the inception of UNEP officials had looked on regional cooperation as a foundation for global efforts. This approach blended UNEP's thinking with that of regional institutions with which Australia was connected. Australia lent strong support to the setting up of an Environmental Coordination Unit within the Economic and Social Commission for Asia and the Pacific (ESCAP), designed to inject environmental planning considerations more soundly into its programmes. Out of this approach also came plans for a South Pacific Regional Environment Programme. Approval for this programme was given at the 18th South Pacific Conference in Noumea in 1978. It was designed as a joint venture of the South Pacific Commission and the South Pacific Bureau for Economic Cooperation.[42] These events also led to the Conference on the Human Environment in the South Pacific, held at Raratonga, Cook Islands, in 1982,[43] and to preparatory

27

work for an international convention on environmental cooperation in the South Pacific region. Australian support for such regional initiatives was autonomous. It would presumably have existed if Australia had not been a member of UNEP. The two strands — the global and the regional — were, however, mutual reinforcing, especially in light of UNEP's own fostering of a variety of regionalist enterprises in the late 1970s and 1980s. But it also strained Australian sympathy with other aspects of UNEP's work.

The second term of membership saw more criticism of UNEP than had been the case in 1973. A parliamentary committee investigating Australian participation in international environmental organizations found much evidence of public indifference. While in general the committee supported the continuation of a high level of Australian involvement, it also reported that it had received testimony indicating that UNEP was viewed variously as a brilliant failure, as badly administered, and as politically motivated.[44] Questions of administration and financial management were more central in the early 1980s. At Stockholm the government had made a commitment to the voluntary fund; it then contributed $500,000 (US) annually to the organization. From 1979 onward the delegation aimed to encourage any UNEP effort that would aid its capacity for sound financial management, the efficiency of its activity programming, and the effectiveness of its programme implementation.[45] Within government, the Treasury was becoming more agitated about the costs involved in supporting meetings of international bodies. Externally, Australia found its western friends and allies directing similar criticisms at a number of UN agencies and programmes, with UNEP, and also UNESCO, bearing much of the brunt of this scrutiny.

None of this criticism, however, acted to reduce significantly the character or level of Australian official support for UNEP. In the early 1980s the Fraser government was under renewed attack from environmental groups. In these circumstances any sizeable shift of policy would have gratuitously supplied the government's critics with valuable ammunition. Effort continued to be invested in promoting UNEP inside Australia, for example, in connection with the annual June 5 Environment Day themes.[46] Officials and NGOs also took part in the 1982 celebrations in Nairobi of UNEP's tenth anniversary. These centred around head of government and head of state meetings in a "Special Character" session. Little of practical consequence ensued. Australian official representation at the session was at a comparatively modest level,[47] perhaps out of concern lest any further involvement might add still more fuel to the already dangerously inflamed South-west Tasmanian situation.

The OECD and environmental policy

Even before 1982, UNEP appeared to many Australians to suffer from the handicaps of unwieldiness, a relentlessly Third World orientation, and lack of clearly defined programmes. More important in policy terms, though far less a target of attention and expectations by the public or environmental groups, was

28

the work of the OECD. Its Environment Committee was for Australia "the principal international forum for consultation, examination and review by industrialized countries of major environmental problems of mutual interest."[48]

Membership, in 1971, followed several years of participation by Australian officials in the work of the OECD's Development Assistance Committee (DAC). Despite the diversity of its members, the OECD was more a club of like-minded states than any of the UN bodies could be. Membership provided easier access to the more powerful countries of the world economy, and gave tacit recognition to the importance of Australia's contribution to collective decision-making. As Sir Garfield Barwick later put it, "With its membership of the OECD, Australia has considerably increased its international contacts and its sources of information on a wide range of foreign affairs, not entirely limited to the international economy or comparison of national economies. It has thus become better geared for informed participation in international discussion and planning."[49]

Australia joined the OECD within a few months of the establishment of the Environment Committee. This also coincided with Canberra's own interest in 1971 in moving more solidly into the environmental policy area. The aim of the Committee was to respond to environmental pressures within the industrialized western countries by exploring the links between economic and environmental policies, and identifying guidelines which could better ensure that ecological constraints were not economically damaging and that the environmental effects of economic or industrial programmes were minimized. As at Stockholm, the "polluter pays" principle was adopted formally in 1972 as one of its core principles, a development regarded as particularly important by Australia.[50] The OECD's work in the environmental area was seen as valuable on two counts. First, since many environmental problems were being faced by all western nations, the OECD constituted a forum in which Australia could clearly be seen to be taking part jointly with others in deliberations on important policy questions. Secondly, a number of specific aspects of OECD activity were regarded as particularly useful. In the late 1970s and early 1980s the Australian government made careful and deliberate use of OECD guidelines as the main underpinnings of its toxic chemicals management programmes. This subject will be discussed in a later chapter.

In general, Australia's participation in OECD environmental activity varied according to its own policy concerns at different times. In the early 1970s, these gravitated towards problems of air and water pollution, the themes of two key Senate committees. In 1973, the OECD's Air Management Sector Group initiated a photochemical smog survey, based on preliminary work carried out by Australia together with Japan, the Netherlands and the United States.[51] Later that year the federal environment minister announced a national approach to questions of water resources management. Here also there were productive connnections with OECD work. Australia's participation in the organization's Water Management Sector Group at the time included study of eutrophication in Australian reservoirs.[52] Other specialist groupings of the Environment Committee during the 1970s focussed on economics and the environment, chemicals, energy, waste management, transfrontier pollution, and problems of the urban environment, with environmental assessment and reporting added later.[53] This structure varied over time in response to changing circumstances. In 1976-77, for example, Australia was elected to a small high-level OECD group tasked to review Japanese environmental policies.[54]

More doubts began to be expressed, however, when it was felt that OECD agendas and priorities were being shaped more by the particular requirements of the countries of North America and Western Europe. One instance was the increasingly prominent place of transfrontier pollution issues in OECD deliberations in the late 1970s. Of great salience to some members, such as Canada and many European states, these touched Australia only marginally. Australian officials argued that a much broader range of topics needed to be tackled. To some extent the OECD was already moving in this direction. In the early 1980s the Environment Committee examined the implications of the US *Global 2000* study, the Japanese Okita Report, and the OECD's Interfutures Study.[55] More attention in the Environment Committee's second decade was devoted to global and long-term issues, including problems affecting developing countries.[56] The trend was in line with Australia's own preferred directions for the organization in the early 1980s. Many apparently exotic subjects, it was argued, could indeed affect the economic interests of western countries. These ranged from global problems of forest depletion, soils, and the build-up atmospheric carbon dioxide, to more specific questions such as the activities of western corporations in developing countries, for example Japanese forestry interests in Borneo, which had both environmental and economic ramifications. Renewed attention should also periodically be given, Australian officials maintained, to public education in western countries on environmental issues. The delegation took an initiative on this in the early 1980s which led to member-states collating, analyzing and publicizing case studies on the general educational theme "Pollution Prevention Pays."[57]

As in relation to UNEP, Australian participation in OECD was marked by a search for leadership roles. As Australia's representative, a senior official of the federal environment ministry, H.J. Higgs, served a term as Vice-Chairman of the Environment Committee and a member of the bureau in the late 1970s. Australia took over the Chairmanship for a two-year term in 1981,[58] and, in a tribute to the skilful exercise of this role by Dr. Donald McMichael, then permanent head of the department, this term was extended for a third year in 1983. The importance attached in Canberra to the organization is indicated by the practice of posting an environment counsellor to the Australian permanent mission to the OECD in Paris. Use has also been made of the mission to train or acclimatize Commonwealth officials in environmental policy areas. The OECD, then, has continued to be viewed as an organization from which Australians could gain tangible benefits, and as a result it has in some ways eclipsed UNEP as the chief focus of official environmental interest.

Non-governmental conservation networks

Australia's policies have also been affected by its association with the leading NGO in the conservation field. Formally a non-governmental body, created in 1948 as a relatively loose association of conservation groups in various countries, IUCN later developed into a hybrid institution with a mixture of state and non-state members. Australia joined in 1973.

There was some Australian interest in the earlier developments that culminated in the establishment of IUCN. Several attempts were made by US, Swiss and other conservationists in the late nineteenth and early twentieth centuries to set up a specialist international organization dealing with environmental protection. The model, an intergovernmental one, was that of the international public unions of the day. Though Australians did not participate in this planning, an Australian delegate was officially appointed to the institution that eventually emerged, the Advisory Commission for the International Protection of Nature, in 1914. A victim of policy neglect and a casualty of war, it never developed into a working intergovernmental organization.[59] Australia was more a subject than an actor in the events of the 1920s and 1930s. American and British scientists actively probed threats to Australian fauna and flora. IUCN, from the late 1940s, tended to concentrate on problems in other parts of the world. In the early and middle 1960s, African issues predominated. Yet Australia was unavoidably drawn into international debates because of widespread recognition of the uniqueness of its plant and animal life. Various Australian species were included on the international listings of endangered flora and fauna of the 1950s and 1960s. Two officers of the CSIRO Wildlife Section presented a substantial report on threatened mammals in Australia to the IUCN General Assembly meetings in Warsaw in 1960.[60]

Official Australian entry into IUCN followed participation by a number of Australian individuals and NGOs. Participation tended to be constrained by the cost and distance involved in travelling to many IUCN meetings. Preparations for UNCHE in Stockholm in 1972 were a turning point in Australian relations with IUCN. Interest in environmental questions grew, and IUCN's role in the preparatory work of the conference, particularly the sharing of its experience in running international conventions, made it a much more visible international actor. Australia's participation in the Preparatory Committee's Working Group on Conservation was an important step in forging links. Several Australians had by this time already played significant roles in IUCN. This work continued after 1972. Ovington, for example, was for many years Chairman of IUCN's Commission on Ecology, one of the key scientific advisory bodies of the organization, and was also a member of its Commission for National Parks and Protected Areas; in the 1970s McMichael served a term as a Vice-President; and from 1970-76, IUCN's Deputy Director-General was Frank Nicholls, formerly a senior research official in the Australian government.[61]

The crucial factor in the transition to membership, however, was the environmental activism of the Whitlam government. Participation in international

31

institutions and conferences, and adherence to international environmental conventions, was the external aspect of a vigorous domestic policy directed towards new legislation, government restructuring, and change in the federal-state balance. The previous Liberal coalition government had taken Australia into both the OECD and UNEP. Its absence from IUCN was an obvious gap to fill. Dr. Cass, the environment minister, announced Australia's intention to join in May 1973, following a commitment made by the Prime Minister in his capacity as Minister of Foreign Affairs (though interestingly, and erroneously, he referred to it as a "Geneva based organization" — IUCN's headquarters were in fact in the less prestigious town of Morges).[62] Australia formally became a member on June 7, and thus joined the more than thirty other countries with full state membership.[63] Membership in the IUCN was then frequently cited by the government as a rationale for important elements of Australian policies. Australia was a member of IUCN, Cass said in Parliament in 1974 in a discussion of the Specht report on plant communities, "and subscribes to the principles laid down by that Union for the conservation of wild flora and fauna."[64]

Australia's accession unfortunately coincided with a period of change and internal turmoil in IUCN. This was a product of disagreements among members about priorities and future directions, the greater expectations being directed towards the institution after Stockholm, and problems of funding and administration. A special General Assembly session in 1977 produced a new set of constitutional arrangements, including an agreement on the complex and controversial issue of the voting rights of various categories of members. Australia's delegation included both Ovington and McMichael; each also had other roles, Ovington in relation to two IUCN Commissions and McMichael as one of four Vice-Presidents (the others coming from the USSR, Iran and the US). The Australian goal was to try to encourage changes that would better assure IUCN's position as an intergovernmental, rather than a nongovernmental, actor on matters of environmental policy and law. The delegation proposed amendments to the constitutional draft dealing with membership, calling for more evidence to be presented as to applicants' qualifications for admission. Several controversial membership cases had arisen earlier, applications from East German bodies, for example, or from hunting organizations. Membership questions also had a financial aspect. One Australian group, the Tasmanian Environment Centre, was in 1977 two years in arrears in its dues, and, with 23 other offenders, had its membership rescinded. The Australian delegation also pressed for revisions to protect the interests of states (both state members and government agency members) with regard to voting powers in General Assemblies; on agreements made by the IUCN with governments and other organizations; and on international legal practice, particularly in connection with the legal capacities of the IUCN in member states.[65]

Membership of IUCN fostered connections between Australian scientists and officials and the broader international conservation network. At the time of the General Assembly in Christchurch in 1982, key positions in the organization were occupied by Ovington (still as Chairman of the Ecology Commission) and

32

McMichael (then as IUCN Treasurer and Regional Councillor). Australian experts figured prominently as members of specialist bodies such as the Commission on Ecology (which had six Australian members), the Survival Service Commission (which had five), and the Education, National Parks, and Environmental Planning Commissions (which had one Australian member each).[66] There has been some growth in NGO and agency memberships. The Tasmanian Wilderness Society, which later spearheaded the national and international campaign against the Franklin dam, joined in the mid-1970s. Shortly afterwards the Australian Heritage Commission, one of the most articulate proponents inside government of the argument that domestic obligations were inherent in the Commonwealth's international responsibilities, became a government agency member.[67] Preparation for general assemblies created a requirement for coordination. The Australian delegation to the 1984 General Assembly, in Madrid, included representatives of the Department of Home Affairs and Environment, the Australian National Parks and Wildlife Service, the Great Barrier Reef Marine Park Authority, and the Australian Heritage Commission, together with various state government agencies and NGOs.[68] The Australian Committee for IUCN, composed of various IUCN members, became an important means of coordinating outlooks in the early 1980s.

Participation in IUCN has been less demanding on budgets than UNEP. Indeed Australian officials tended to argue that the organization needed more financial support from its members. Increased fees were proposed and accepted at Kinshasa in 1975. Australian delegates declared themselves willing to accept the necessity for such revisions.[69] By the end of the decade, membership fees for Australia, as a state member, were of the order of $25,000.[70] In general, therefore, Australian activity in IUCN has been relatively immune from the charge that membership represents an unacceptably large drain on government revenues. Only occasionally has the cost of supporting Australian teams at its meetings been the subject of parliamentary or public criticism.

IUCN's mixed governmental and non-governmental character meant that Commonwealth officials took part alongside representatives from Australian environmental groups (as well as of state governments, attending either as part of the Australian government's delegation or else as agency members in their own right). This situation provoked confrontations in the organization in the 1970s. Too much power for governments, some argued, pushed the institution into the hands of faceless bureaucrats; too little, others countered, made for an irresponsible and ineffective talking shop. For the most part the possibility of serious clashes between official and non-official Australian participants has been averted, in large measure because of shared conservation goals. Having IUCN policy shaped in part by more critical NGOs could also indirectly help federal environmental officials. Faced with their own adversaries inside government in Canberra, or in state governments, federal officials could periodically cite IUCN statements and guidelines as supports for their own preferred policy options. This tactic did not always work smoothly, however. In relation to CITES, serviced for several years by a unit of the IUCN Secretariat, and giving rise to conservation issues debated in its general assemblies, Australia came under attack for its policies in several areas, and particularly with regard to some crocodile species.

Following a gestation period of several years, IUCN, together with UNEP and the World Wildlife Fund (WWF), launched its long-awaited *World Conservation Strategy* in 1980. The promptness with which the Commonwealth government took up its cause, instead of regarding it politely as innocuous shelf-fodder, is interesting, and gives a good indication of the way in which IUCN's interests have been articulated and supported in Australia both in official circles and among NGOs. Thus Prime Minister Fraser made a major statement welcoming the document in March 1980, alongside simultaneous declarations of support by other heads of government around the world. More important, work began soon afterwards on the production of a national Australian equivalent document, which would likewise blend global conservation and development concerns with adaptations to fit Australian circumstances. This process will be discussed in a later chapter. It was far more protracted than IUCN's supporters had originally hoped, and vulnerable to the injection of more compromises than many could find acceptable, but its initiation and course were evidence of the government's capacity to attach international conservation goals to national agendas.

Environmental institutions in Australian foreign policy

Australia has thus had a variety of interests in the work of international environmental organizations. As the record of Australian participation in both UNEP and the events that led to its creation indicates, these have stretched from functional and technical concerns to broader issues of foreign policy. The periodic intrusion of Middle East or Southern African questions, however, or issues such as nuclear weapons testing (at UNCHE) and the concept of common funds in North-South relations (as at the UN desertification conference), has helped to undermine the earlier presumption that environmental issues could be isolated and treated separately. Faith in the post-1945 principles of functional international cooperation also weakened. Together with growing doubts about the administrative efficacy and budgetary responsibility of UNEP, these factors tended to reinforce the view that the OECD, with a membership of like-minded western countries sharing similar mixes of economic and environmental problems, was a more hospitable and appropriate body within which Australia could pursue realistic international environmental policy goals. In both forums, ministers and officials tended to be happier when such organizations settled down to practical, even humdrum, tasks. Data-gathering through the IRPTC, for example, had its critics in Australia, particularly when specific questions of toxic chemicals regulation were being confronted by the federal and state governments in the late 1970s and early 1980s, but it was this kind of exercise that made UNEP politically defensible at home.

The crucial step was the emergence of a perception that Australia did indeed have a stake in international environmental policy developments. The first responses from Canberra were cautious. International initiatives tended to be seen at best as potentially useful ways of dealing with hypothetical problems should these materialize in the future. However, environmental issues were politically attractive domestically in 1971-72, especially with a general election looming. Added to this was the growing appreciation at three levels of government that air and water pollution — and oilspills off Australia's coasts and reefs — were not esoteric preoccupations. Much of the pace and focus of official concerns, however, can be attributed directly to the time-scale imposed by the requirement of preparing for UNCHE. This served to define much more sharply the need for effective Commonwealth, and federal-state, institutions and procedures to handle both domestic and international environmental questions. As a result, Australia was later able to inject distinctive viewpoints into international debates. In the OECD in the 1980s, for example, the character of Australia's environmental interests prompted skepticism about the emphasis other countries were placing on transboundary problems. In line with approaches to other international institutions since the establishment of the UN, a persistent theme in the environment arena was also Australia's pursuit of key positions and roles. Determined and successful diplomacy at Stockholm in 1972 prepared the ground for such strategies by bringing about an enlarged UNEP Governing Council. Compared to other international bodies, IUCN had a lower diplomatic priority. Even so, Australian membership was used by the Labor government of the early 1970s as a means of strengthening the country's capacity to influence specific international developments. The promotion of international conventions on environmental conservation, the subject of the next chapter, was among the most important of these.

Notes for Chapter 2

[1] W.J. Hudson, *Australia and the League of Nations* (Sydney: Sydney University Press for the AIIA, 1980), p. 1974.

[2] *House of Representatives*, 66, 12 March 1970, p. 448.

[3] Statement by the Hon. Gordon Freeth, in *24th Sess. of the Gen. Ass. of the UN* ... (Canberra, 1970: PP 54), Annex D, p. 104.

[4] *House of Representatives*, 85, 18 September 1973, p. 1219.

[5] *CNIA* 41(4), April 1970, p. 207; *24th Sess. of the Gen. Ass. of the UN* ... (Canberra, 1970: PP 54), para. 142, p. 75; *CNIA* 40(7), July 1969, p. 400.

[6] For example in the work of Jack Snelson, of the Department of Primary Industry. See his paper in *IUPAC Proc.* (1983), pp. 12-22. For criticism of lack of information given to Parliament on WHO, CAC and related bodies see Jenkins, *House of Representatives*, 91, 30 October 1974, pp. 3093-7.

[7] *DES, Report for Years 1967 and 1968* (Canberra, 1970; PP 172), App. IV, p. 64; "UNESCO-Biosphere Conference," *CNIA* 39(12), December 1968, pp. 523-6.

[8] *DES, Report for 1971* (Canberra, 1973; PP 116), p. 58; and *Report for 1972* (Canberra, 1974; PP 272), p. 55.

[9] ANPWS, *Report for the Period 13 March 1975 to 30 June 1976* (Canberra, 1976), p. 15.

[10] *UNCHE. Stockholm, June 1972. Summary Report of Australian Delegation* (Canberra, 1973; PP 143), para. 4, p. 3; DEA, *Annual Report 1 July 1968 - June 1969* (Canberra, 1969; PP 127), p. 54; *CNIA* 39(12), December 1968, pp. 525-6; and comments by Mr. McMahon, Minister for External Affairs, at *House of Representatives*, 66, 12 March 1970, p. 448.

[11] Bowen, *House of Representatives*, 23 November 1971, pp. 3534-5; *24th Sess. of the Gen. Ass. of the UN* ... (Canberra, 1970: PP 54), para. 37, p. 45.

[12] "Conference on the Human Environment," *CNIA* 43(3), March 1972, PP. 99-101; Bowen, *House of Representatives*, 23 November 1971, pp. 3534-5.

[13] Sen. Greenwood, *Senate*, 52, 1 June 1972, p. 2487; *UNCHE ... Summary Report of Australian Delegation*, para. 30, p. 8.

[14] Peter Howson, *The Howson Diaries: The Life of Politics*, ed. Don Aitkin (Ringwood, Victoria: The Viking Press, 1984), p. 796; *ACF Newsl.* 4(3), June 1972, p. 6.

[15] *26th Sess. of the Gen. Ass. of the UN* ... (Canberra, 1972; PP 54), para. 106, pp. 22-3; *Sydney Daily Telegraph*, 6 June 1972; DFA, *Australia and Foreign Affairs. Digest of Press Opinion*, 22/72, p. 11.

[16] *UNCHE ... Summary Report of Australian Delegation*, para. 43, p. 10.

[17] *27th Sess. of the Gen. Ass. of the UN* ... (Canberra, 1973; PP 26), para. 39, p. 7.

[18] *The Howson Diaries*, p. 879.

[19] *Ibid.*, p. 881.

[20] *Ibid.*, pp. 917, 930.

[21] *UNCHE ... Summary Report of Australian Delegation*, App. 1, pp. 13-14; *CNIA* 43(6), June 1972.

[22] *26th Sess. of the Gen. Ass. of the UN* ... (Canberra, 1972; PP 54), para. 103, p. 102. On Australian appreciation of the fears of developing countries see Mr. Bowen's remarks to the UNGA, quoted at *CNIA* 43(9), September 1972, p. 441. The press also took up this theme; see for example the editorial in the *Canberra Times*, 6 June 1972; and DFA, *Australia and Foreign Affairs. Digest of Press Opinion*, 22/72, p. 11.

[23] *The Howson Diaries*, p. 878.

[24] *CNIA* 43(9), September 1972, pp. 441-2; also Howson at UNCHE, *CNIA*, 43(6), June 1972, pp. 302-3, and *The Howson Diaries*, p. 876.

[25] *UNCHE ... Summary Report of Australian Delegation*, para. 14-16, p. 5, and App. 2.

[26] *Ibid.*, para. 19-20, pp. 6-7, and App. 3.

[27] Howson, at *CNIA* 43(6), June 1972, p. 304; and *UNCHE ... Summary Report of Australian Delegation*, App. 1, pp. 13-15.

[28] *Ibid.*, para. 48, p. 10; comments by Bowen in the UNGA, *CNIA* 43(9), September 1972, pp. 441-42; *The Howson Diaries*, p. 880.

[29] *Ibid.*, pp. 876-80, passim.

[30] *Ibid.*, p. 877.

[31] *24th Sess. of the Gen. Ass. of the UN* ... (Canberra, 1970; PP 54), Annex D, p. 102.

[32] *28th Sess. of the Gen. Ass. of the UN* ... (Canberra, 1975; PP 25), para. 126, p. 20.

[33] On the World Population Conference, see *ACF Newsl.*, 6(11), December 1974, p. 3. Senator K.S. Wriedt led a team chiefly composed of agriculture officials to the World Food Conference. See *UN. World Food Conf., Rome, 5-17 November 1974. Report of Australian Delegation* (Canberra, 1975; PP 81).

[34] *28th Sess. of the Gen. Ass. of the UN* ... (Canberra, 1975; PP 25), para. 124, p. 20.

[35] DEC, *Report for Period Dec. 1972 to June 1974* (Canberra, 1975; PP 298), p. 50; DOE, *Report for Period July 1974 to June 1975* (Canberra, 1976; PP 139), p. 20; *House of Representatives*, 102, 7 December 1976, pp. 3441-4, and 101, 21 October 1976, p. 2087.

[36] *Commonwealth Record*, 2(33), 22-8 August 1977, p. 1099.

[37] DOE, *Report for Period July 1974 to June 1975* (Canberra, 1976; PP 139), p. 20; DEHCD, *2nd Annual Report 1977* (Canberra, 1978; PP 308), p. 25; DOE, *Annual Report 1978-9* (Canberra, 1979: PP 349), p. 65; DSE, *Annual Report 1979-80* (Canberra, 1980: PP 357), p. 62; *House*

of Representatives, 108, 11 April 1978, pp. 1410-1. For later critical assessments see *ACF Newsl.*, 14(6), July 1982, p. 1, and 16(5), June 1984, p. 11.

38 *DEHCD, 3rd Annual Report. 1977-78* (Canberra, 1978; PP 433), p. 51. In general see J.W. Huismans, "The IRPTC," *Ecotoxicology and Environmental Safety*, 4, 1980, pp. 393-403.

39 DSE, *Annual Report 1978-9* (Canberra, 1979: PP 349), p. 69. On links between toxic chemicals developments internationally and the evolution of Australian policies, see also DSE, *Annual Report 1979-80* (Canberra, 1980; PP 357), pp. 66-68; DHAE, *Annual Report 1980-81* (Canberra, 1981; PP 35), p. 13.

40 *Senate*, 89, 28 April 1981, p. 1442; DSE, *Annual Report 1979-80* (Canberra, 1980; PP 357), p. 62; DHAE, *Annual Report 1980-1* (Canberra, 1981; PP 35), p. 19; *AEC Newsl.*, 3(1), March 1983, p. 3.

41 DHAE, *Annual Report 1982-3* (Canberra, 1983; PP 345), p. 13.

42 DFA, *Annual Report 1977* (Canberra, 1978; PP 159), p. 57; DSE, *Annual Report 1978-9* (Canberra, 1979; PP 349), p. 76: DHAE, *Annual Report 1980-1* (Canberra, 1982; PP 35), pp. 23-4. A significant step was the South Pacific Conference on National Parks and Reserves held in Wellington in February 1975; see DOE, *Report for Period July 1974 to June 1975* (Canberra, 1976; PP 139), p. 24.

43 For the Declaration of Principles and Action Plan see DHAE, *Annual Report 1981-82* (Canberra, 1982; PP 263), p. 19; and *AEC Newsl.*, 2(1), March 1982, p. 7.

44 Dr. Jenkins, *House of Representatives*, 130, 28 October 1982, p. 2724.

45 DHAE, *Annual Report 1980-81* (Canberra, 1982; PP 35), pp. 23-4; DFA, *Annual Report 1979* (Canberra, 1980; PP 102), p. 22.

46 For example on toxic chemicals, then an important Australian policy theme, in 1984, see *ACF Newsl.*, 16(5), June 1984, p. 11.

47 For this criticism see *ACF Newsl.*, 14(6), July 1982, p. 5. A special subcommittee of the Australian Environment Council was set up and tasked to stimulate activities nationally: *AEC Newsl.*, 2(1), March 1982, pp. 3, 5-6.

48 *Backgrounder*, 278, 8 April 1981, p. 6.

49 Rt. Hon. Sir Garfield Barwick, Foreword to K. Ryan, ed., *International Law in Australia*, 2nd ed. (Sydney: Law Book Co., 1984), p. vii. Australia was a member from 7 June 1971. See further *CNIA* 42(5), May 1971, pp. 289-90; *CNIA* 42(6), June 1971, pp. 321-3; "Australia and the OECD," *AFAR* 44(5), May 1973, pp. 312-9; and "The OECD: Aims and Achievements," *AFAR* 47(11), November 1976, pp. 572-81.

50 See the comments by Sir Ronald Walker, formerly Ambassador to the OECD, in "OECD and the Quality of Life," *Australian Financial Review*, 7 September 1973, p. 9.

51 DEC, *Report for Period December 1972 to June 1974* (Canberra, 1975; PP 298), pp. 27-8.

52 *Ibid.*, pp. 30, 41.

53 DOE, *Report for Period July 1974 to June 1975* (Canberra, 1976; PP 139), p. 21; DHAE, *Annual Report 1982-3* (Canberra, 1983; PP 345), p. 10.

54 DEHCD, *1st Annual Report 1975-76* (Canberra, 1977; PP 398), p. 15.

55 *AEC Newsl.*, 1(1), September 1981, p. 7.

56 DHAE, *Annual Report 1981-82* (Canberra, 1982; PP 263), p. 19. On the Special Session in 1981 on "The OECD and Policies for the 1980s," and the place of long-term environmental issues see also DHAE, *Annual Report 1982-83* (Canberra, 1983; PP 345), p. 10.

57 *Ibid.*, p. 11.

58 *AEC Newsl.*, 1(1), September 1981, p. 7.

59 *Report on the Conference for the International Protection of Nature. Basle, June 30 - July 7, 1946* (Swiss League for the Protection of Nature, November 1946), p. 90. Australia was one of fourteen countries that appointed delegates to the body.

60 J.H. Calaby and F.N. Ratcliffe, "Australia's Threatened Mammals," IUCN, *Proc. 7th Gen. Ass., Warsaw, 15-24 June 1960* (1960), App. II, pp. 121-6.

[61] ANPWS, *Report for Period 1 July 1976 to 30 June 1977* (Canberra, 1977), p. 20; *Report for Period 1 July 1977 to 30 June 1978* (Canberra, 1978), pp. 21-31; and *IUCN Bull.*, 7(8), August 1976, p. 43.

[62] *AGD*, 1(2), 1973, p. 583; *AFAR* 44(6), June 1973.

[63] In January 1974 there were thirty-five state members of IUCN. See DEC, *Report for Period December 1972 to June 1974* (Canberra, 1973; PP 298), p. 14. New Zealand joined in 1974; see *Australian and New Zealand Environmental Report* (1974), 16-74, p. 290. See also Prime Minister Whitlam's comments on Australia's work through the UN, OECD and IUCN for effective global environmental protection at *ACF Newsl.* 5(3), July 1973, pp. 3-4.

[64] *House of Representatives*, 91, 23 October 1974, pp. 2744-5.

[65] IUCN, *Proc. 13th (Extraordinary) Gen. Ass., Geneva, 19-21 April 1977* (1977), pp. 11, 38C, 41C, 46C, 63C, 65C; ANPWS, *Report for Period 1 July 1976 to 30 June 1977* (Canberra, 1977), p. 20.

[66] *House of Representatives*, 126, 16 February 1982, pp. 174-5.

[67] IUCN, *Proc. 13th (Extraordinary) Gen. Ass.*, p. 103; AHC, *4th Annual Report 1979-80* (Canberra, 1980; PP 330), p. 16.

[68] *AEC Newsl.*, 4(4), December 1984, p. 4. The delegation was led by Mr. C.R. Ashwin, Australian Ambassador to West Germany.

[69] IUCN, *Proc. 12th Gen. Ass., Kinshasa, 8-18 September 1975* (1976), p. 20.

[70] DSE, *Annual Report 1979-80* (Canberra, 1980; PP 357), p. 63. This was part of the environment department budget; it does not include costs of sending representatives to meetings. The Commonwealth government also supported WWF in Australia as part of its general policy of lending financial support to environmental organizations. The grant in this case was $50,000. See DSE, *Annual Report 1979-80* (Canberra, 1980; PP 357), p. 63; Senator Carrick, at *Senate*, 85, 29 April 1980, p. 1876. WWF International works in close cooperation with IUCN with secretariats housed in close vicinity to each other in Switzerland.

CHAPTER THREE

The Politics of Conservation: Wildlife, Ecosystems and Heritage

In the 1960s the term environment tended to connote pollution threats to the health of waters and air. Many Australians regarded the anxiety with which these hazards were increasingly being viewed in North America and Western Europe as on balance inappropriate to Australia's unique circumstances. It was widely felt that, though highly urbanized, Australia was not sufficiently industrialized, or its primary resource sectors so heavily dependent on high technology and agrochemicals, to warrant much concern. The politics of species and habitats, however, were central to Australian environmental debates and remained so during the later broadening of the scope of environmental questions. In this, many characteristically Australian preoccupations matched those of conservation groups in other countries, and of leading international organizations such as IUCN. Protracted controversies often surrounded particular wildlife species or groups of species. Kangaroos, for example, like polar bears in Canada in the 1950s, took such debates into areas of symbolic politics; crocodiles, like the eastern Canadian harp seal in the 1970s and 1980s, became the target of intense interest on the part of external groups. Sharply divergent viewpoints emerged. Australia's diverse bird-life formed, for the environmentalist, "thick wedges of screaming colour"[1] to be conserved as a means of enriching the quality of life and aiding the development of science; for the farmer many species were pests, the eradication or control of which was hampered by the misguided regulatory interference of city folk and politicians.

International activity helped to maintain political and administrative momentum in Australia. Following UNCHE, a number of international conventions, particularly those in which IUCN had an interest, now increased their pace of development. Those dealing with marine pollution will be discussed in the next chapter. In this chapter we look at Australian policies towards three interrelated sets of international conservation instruments. These are, first, the Convention on International Trade in Endangered Species (CITES), which has grown into one of the most organized parts of the international environmental regime; secondly, conventions dealing with migratory species and the protection of their habitats, an area in which Australia has a more immediate interest because of a 1974 bilateral agreement with Japan on the subject; and, thirdly, international heritage politics, centring on the UNESCO World Heritage convention of 1972, which later served as the external context for Australia's crisis over wilderness preservation in South-west Tasmania.

39

The international politics of the wildlife trade

The principle behind CITES, signed in Washington in 1973, dates back several decades. It is the notion that regulating the international trade in wildlife and their products is both a more effective, and a more realizable, route to conservation of endangered species of flora and fauna than more direct attempts to pressure governments into instituting domestic conservation practices. The convention itself began to take form at IUCN's General Assembly in Nairobi in 1963, and developed from subsequent work by its Survival Service Commission and Commission on Legislation in relation to an African nature conservation treaty of 1968.[2] The aim was to secure a convention obliging states to impose controls over both export and import of endangered or threatened species. As governments were drawn into the consultative process of convention-making in the late 1960s, several issues emerged. These included the listings of species (envisaged as falling into various categories in Appendices, according to relative degree of threat) and the availability of adequate data; the criteria and methodologies underlying the convention; and the international administration and national implementation of its provisions. These questions have continued since 1973 to form the main staples of debate at the meetings of the parties, which now take place every two years.

Australia would have been affected by these developments whether or not its governments had any interest in them. The uniqueness of many Australian plant and animal species, and the extent of the international trade in them and their parts and products, were each sufficient conditions for Australia to be counted as an important player. In addition, several Australian officials and scientists were among the leading participants at the international level, and they were able to encourage a more active Australian interest in CITES. From 1972 to 1975, moreover, the key period of CITES development, Australia's Labor government was keenly interested in expanding the Commonwealth's domestic and external environmental role, and hence was alert to the potential of such a convention. A related factor was controversy in the country over the wildlife trade. Much of the controversy was unrelated to CITES. It was a debate, often heated, conducted not so much in scientific terms of threats to species, but rather in more emotive terms of the fate of Australia's national emblems. For many years this meant primarily kangaroos, together with more popular bird species such as sulphur-crested cockatoos. Many such species, however, were considered pests by farmers. The fact also that many could not be considered as endangered or threatened according to the conventionally accepted scientific criteria did little to diminish conflict between conservationist and economic interests. The illegal export of Australian wild birds was the subject of a major parliamentary enquiry in the 1970s. The trade was lucrative, and difficult to detect since exporters went to considerable and ingenious lengths to hide their role in it.[3] Critics of the government's conservation measures pointed indignantly to the more bizarrely inconsistent implications. Kangaroos, one MP complained in 1975, had reached plague proportions in several parts of Australia; they could be killed legally, under controlled conditions, but could not be exported live. Galahs, similarly, could be shot as pests to crops, but could not be sold abroad, with the result, it was argued, that an illegal and cruel export trade was flourishing.[4]

The process of treaty-making that culminated in Washington in 1973 began with circulation to governments of a series of drafts by IUCN. The first was sent to ninety governments for comment in 1967; a modified draft followed in 1969.[5] This attracted little interest outside government in Australia. Senator Mulvihull, though, was quick off the mark in 1968 in questioning the "delay" in Australian signature of the convention.[6] Signature at this stage was premature. During 1968 the convention's terms were being studied by the Commonwealth and state governments prior to comments being returned to IUCN. By 1973, following IUCN's preparation of a third draft, the general principles were widely accepted. The conference took place, however, in an atmosphere of strained federal-state relations in Australia. In 1973, the Commonwealth precipitately imposed a total ban on the export of kangaroo products, a move which inflamed state anger about federal interventionism. Also during 1972-1973 Canberra successfully negotiated with US authorities the imposition of an import ban on kangaroos and kangaroo products, a move defended by the federal environment minister, Dr. Cass, as showing "a growing international awareness of the need to protect endangered species."[7] Australia as a result could not go to Washington to negotiate the final terms of CITES with the backing of a harmonized federal-state consensus on trade issues. In practice, however, this mattered less than some feared since the convention's focus on endangered species tended for the most part to divert conference attention away from many of the issues of public controversy inside Australia.

In the Washington meetings, Australian officials argued steps had already been taken in Australia to protect wildlife and to achieve effective control over trade in endangered species, but that reaching international agreement on these questions would add to the effectiveness of these steps.[8] The delegation, under McMichael, then Secretary of the Department of Environment and Conservation, pursued two sets of objectives. First, a wider role in the conference process was sought. McMichael served as a Vice-Chairman under the leadership of the veteran US diplomat Christian A. Herter, Jr. Australia was represented on the conference steering committee, the drafting committee, and the crucial first committee (which dealt with the listings of species in the Appendices). Australian officials also secured the chairmanship of the committee dealing with the listing of endangered plant species, and jointly chaired the committee on customs matters.[9] Members of the delegation also adopted an informal mediatory role in the controversial whaling issues. Both whaling and anti-whaling interests were represented at the conference, and five whale species placed under a moratorium by the International Whaling Commission (IWC) were listed in the first Appendix of CITES. This represented a compromise between opposing views over the form taken by the question at Washington: whether CITES should apply to whales and other marine species, or whether these should specifically be excluded on the grounds that the issues were distinct and were already the subject of international agreements and practices.

41

Secondly, Australia had more immediate objectives. At the heart of the politics of the conference lay the initial listings of species in the Appendices. Lists had been progressively revised since the early IUCN approaches of the 1960s. The question was not mere technical detail: it contained the important policy implication that the international community should have the right collectively to set down specific guidelines in relation to plant and animal species inside a country's territory. The debate in Washington tended on balance to be less inflammatory than in some later meetings of the parties, in part because the goal of many delegations was to secure some form of workable convention the details of which might be reviewed later, and in part because pressure of time left some questions relatively unexplored. Australia listed a total of 33 mammals, 11 birds and one reptile for inclusion in Appendix I. These included the little planigale, large desert marsupial mouse, Shark Bay mouse and New Holland mouse, the Tasmanian tiger (generally considered extinct), rusty numbat, several types of bandicoot, Gillespie's wombat, and various rat kangaroos and hare wallabies. Birds included some of the species already identified in Australian debates as targets of illicit traders: the golden-shouldered parrot, orange-bellied parrot, and paradise parrot. The West Australian swamp tortoise was the reptile species.[10] Others were proposed for addition in light of exchanges at the conference which led to revised criteria for Appendix II. Plant species were also an important Australian concern. Flora had been relatively neglected in the history of international conservation efforts. In 1973-74 a major investigation was under way in Australia on plant communities and their conservation in Australia, New Zealand and Papua New Guinea. Australia's chairmanship of the endangered plants committee connected directly with this activity. However, the conference was not able to take plant conservation far. The main reason was absence of data. Australia took the lead in pressing successfully for a resolution, not included in the Final Act, which underlined the inadequacy of world knowledge of threats to plant species.[11]

Australian signature of the convention was approved by the Cabinet at the end of June 1973. The decision, Cass said, "indicates the Government's determination to uphold the conservation principles which were a large factor in bringing Labor to power last year." It was "very important that Australia, which has so many unique forms of wildlife, should use every possible method to ensure the conservation and protection of these species. By supporting this convention, the Australian Government has served notice internationally that it is concerned to protect Australia's wildlife from exploitation and possible extinction."[12] CITES was also praised by Whitlam in marking Australia's celebration of the first World Environment Day earlier that month.[13] Ratification was a lengthier process. It was not completed until after Labor had fallen from power in the 1975 constitutional crisis. Steps were taken in 1973, however, to begin application of CITES provisions by means of a bill introduced into Parliament,[14] but ratification itself required more extensive legislative and administrative change. The machinery called for by the convention had to be put in place. This involved creation, or designation, of a national scientific authority and a management authority. Procedures had to be worked out for the issue of permits, for the regulation of the housing and transport of wildlife, and the holding of illegal imports. An important step in this process was the setting up in 1975 of the Australian National Parks and Wildlife Service (ANPWS), which became the administrative home of the convention in Australia. CITES was finally ratified in September 1976 and entered into force the following month.[15]

Because of the close connection between the convention process and internal Australian developments, CITES continued to attract attention from environmental groups. Regular meetings of the parties sustained this attention. These meetings were intended as occasions at which the international wildlife trade could be monitored, and at which governments could fine-tune the convention in the light of experience and changing circumstances. The first was held in Berne in 1976, and was followed by a special working session in 1977; since the second meeting, in Costa Rica in 1979, they have been held at two-year intervals. Australian officials have aimed both to act as good international citizens trying to make the system work well, and also to protect particular Australian interests. The two are not, of course, mutually exclusive. Proposals for significant changes in CITES have been put forward that would make the convention fit more snugly with Australian views of international wildlife trade regulation problems. Its own record has also come under fire, particularly in connection with crocodile farming.

Australian officials have gained something of a reputation at CITES meetings as conscientious and hard-working loyalists with their own, sometimes idiosyncratic, ideas about the convention's efficacy and needs. The delegation provided one of two Vice-Chairmen of the Berne meeting, Dr. R. Boden, and a Vice-Chairman of the 1983 Technical Committee. The question of establishing a steering committee, to handle issues as they arose between meetings of the parties, proved more contentious. Worry about the financial implications led the delegation to propose that the Committee's expenses should be met out of the general CITES budget. An Australian official took part as a member of the steering committee at its first meeting in Bonn in 1979.[16] As part of its general concern to improve administration of the convention Australia also discussed with Canada the idea proposed by Canadian officials in 1983 (and later withdrawn) for the CITES Secretariat to be equipped with a scientific committee to aid its work.[17] Participation in specific CITES committees has also served more tangible Australian interests. Ranching of wildlife species has been a subject of prolonged controversy. Australia's official argument has tended to be that this is not necessarily detrimental to wildlife populations, though care should be taken to ensure that products were appropriately marked. Australia chaired the committee on ranching at the 1983 meetings.[18]

Several administrative and organizational issues have propelled Australia into a more central role. These have included questions of identification of species at national borders or by national government agencies; the identification of parts, products and derivatives of species, especially by busy and inexpert customs officers; and the problems associated with sub-species. In a draft resolution submitted to the 1981 meeting Australia noted the "increasing practical problems involved in identifying the numerous species listed for varying degrees of control on the appendices of the Convention."[19] It was a member (with Denmark, Sweden, Switzerland and the US) of a working group set up to look into the possibility of developing an official CITES identification manual. The work involved extensive collaboration with other governments, with Australian officials concentrating on species that required their own expertise — the proposed sections of the manual on Marsupialiae, Brachylophus species, Australian varanids (and non-Australian varanids jointly with the Federal Republic of Germany), and lizard skins.[20] It was clear, however, that even a perfected manual could not guarantee effective import and export controls, since countries differed considerably in such matters as the training given to customs or other designated control officers.

These difficulties fed Australian suspicions that part of the problem lay with the way the appendices were constructed. Other means of organizing them, it was thought, might go a long way towards solving many of the control problems. Its proposed solution was "reverse listing." New lists would replace existing ones. These "would comprise only those species which have been proposed for commercial trade by a Party and for which there is agreement that a sufficient level of knowledge, management and control exists to ensure that the proposed trade will not threaten the species' survival."[21] The proposal did not get far. It appeared to depart too much from the spirit of Washington in 1973 and the detailed agreements reached in the 1976 and 1977 meetings. Grappling with the existing appendices was already sufficiently onerous to deter most delegations from thinking of fundamental alternatives.

A related weakness in the general workings of the convention was seen by Australia to reside in Appendix II. Article IV(3) of CITES provided for the scientific authority of a country to advise the management authority with respect to measures to be taken to regulate trade in Appendix II species. Australia was "concerned that the Convention is simply documenting the decline" of these species.[22] One problem was an apparent divergence of opinion among parties about trade controls for Appendix II species. Australian officials expressed doubts that "suitable measures . . . to limit the grant of export permits" were being taken. Such measures required detailed information on the total ecology of a group, which was lacking in most cases. Australia agreed in 1981 in New Delhi to coordinate Parties' views on this; by the time of the next meeting, however, in Gaborone in 1983, no submissions had been received.[23] The delegation continued to emphasize the severe technical and financial difficulties faced by many countries in attempting to ensure that Appendix II trade was kept within bounds, and to argue that this was not the responsibility of the range states alone. The apparent inability of CITES to curtail undesirable wildlife trade in unlisted species was also evident. The impact of the convention, Australia observed in 1979, had been that trade had apparently shifted to relatively common species not covered by it; the Australian delegation's call for a resolution on trade in unlisted species, however, ran into considerable opposition.[24]

44

Criticisms of this sort also had the self-serving purpose of highlighting Australia's conscientious efforts to administer CITES. The government's document listing proposed additions and deletions to appendices for the 1976 Berne meetings was the longest of any submitted by the parties, and was solidly backed up with extensive data summaries for each item.[25] Australia has carefully monitored trade in Appendix I and II species. In 1979, for example, Australia approved six export permits for Appendix I fauna species, and thirty-one for Appendix II species. For 1980, the figures were respectively three and 24, and for 1981 zero and seventy. For trade in Appendix I flora species, Australia approved one export permit in 1979, and fifty-four for trade in Appendix II species; the corresponding figures for 1980 and 1981 were zero and seventy, and zero and seventy-nine.[26]

Australia was engaged in a succession of debates about species at opposite ends of the threat spectrum. The Australian and British delegations formed a working group in 1979 to report on treatment of species thought to be extinct. An example was the Tasmanian tiger, proposed by Australia for Appendix I listing in 1973. The group's conclusion was that such listings should be retained; no action should be taken to remove them, but species not observed for at least fifty years despite repeated surveys should be annotated as "possibly extinct."[27] (There was a reported sighting of the Tasmanian tiger in 1982.) Exchanges have also taken place about non-threatened species. In 1981 the US and Canada expressed concern about including such species on appendices. The mass inclusion of species for monitoring or other purposes, it was argued, put the credibility of CITES at stake.[28] Confusions have indeed arisen on this point. Some countries and groups — and media reports — have interpreted the convention as a document aimed at the protection of endangered species — which it is not — instead of as one concerned with trade regulation. On balance, Australia has been sympathetic to these arguments, though officials have also seen in them a potential threat to the so-called Berne criteria. Drawn up in 1976, these, among other things, defined the biological and trade status criteria for inclusion of species in Appendices I and II. For example, species meeting the biological criteria for Appendix I should be listed "if they are or may be affected by international trade," and this included any species "that might be expected to be traded" for any purpose.[29] These provisions are clearly open to differing interpretations. Critics have continued to argue that extensive listing for educational, prestige, or monitoring purposes could potentially undermine the workings of CITES, which rests on strict trade controls and on trade data as a fundamental part of the rationale for such controls. The question remained unresolved during the 1985 and 1987 meetings.

In addition to these collective efforts, Australia has had specific interests to protect at CITES meetings. Australian plans in the late 1970s and early 1980s for crocodile farming ran into substantial international conservationist criticism in a variety of international forums. Various species had been a target of IUCN concerns for several years. Six species of crocodile and one gavial were listed in its draft of Appendix I before the 1973 meetings, and all other Crocodylia species in Appendix II. The first meeting of IUCN's Crocodile Group in 1971 concluded that "unless governments are prepared to ban totally the taking of certain of the more endangered species for an indefinite period and strictly to control the cropping of other species, it is unlikely that crocodilians will survive." There was a strong case, it maintained, for a temporary moratorium on the commercialization of all crocodilian hides until such time as governments could produce plans for cropping the resource on a sustained yield basis.[30]

Several countries, however, were interested in farming crocodiles, including Thailand and Papua New Guinea. The Australian position, in line with its general argument on ranching, was that CITES principles were compatible with the development of such programmes, provided they did not endanger the survival of the species concerned. In the late 1970s, plans were made for farming *Crocodylus porosus* in Australia, a salt-water species successfully exploited in Thailand. The plan was particularly related to measures designed to assure economic self-sufficiency for some aboriginal groups. Australia informed the 1979 CITES meeting of these plans.[31] A proposal for exemption of a Papua New Guinea population of the species listed in Appendix I was rejected at the same meeting, though by the mid-1980s that country had established a crocodile farming scheme approved by CITES. In the early 1980s, the governments of Queensland and the Northern Territory each permitted the establishment of three licensed crocodile farms. At the 1983 CITES meeting, Australia formally proposed the transfer of the Australian population of this species from Appendix I to Appendix II, having the previous year submitted a proposal to the Secretariat in which CITES' position on ranching was used as part of its defence. The question embroiled Australia in controversy. The Australian proposal was objected to in 1982-83 by the Aboriginal Northern Land Council, which among other things cited the totemic significance of the species, by environmental groups in Australia, and by both the CITES Secretariat and the main IUCN commissions. At the 1983 meeting Australia reiterated its view that the longer-term conservation of the species could be achieved "in conjunction with ranching operations and controlled farming which can be beneficial to wild populations."[32] But it decided not to proceed with the submission. The delegation insisted that this decision did not mean the population was in danger of extinction, and left open the possibility of a future proposal once consultations inside Australia and appropriate administrative arrangements had been completed. The programme had already been dealt a blow in 1982 when Applied Ecology Pty. Ltd., the management body, refused to go ahead with crocodile killings in defiance of CITES.[33]

Given the historically deleterious effects of the introduction of species, Australia was also concerned to retain control over local feral populations. Feral specimens of domesticated species should not be covered by CITES, the delegation maintained, since they could not be construed as endangered within the terms of the convention. The question arose, for example, in the case of feral cat skins. Australia defended itself from criticism by Denmark and other states by arguing that export permits were not needed and that the appropriate Australian authority exercised no control over their export.[34]

Participation in CITES, then, has been complicated by pressure from NGOs and state and territory governments. The convention has from time to time presented domestic critics of the government with extra ammunition, for example when advertisements appeared in the Australian press in 1979 for lynx fur coats.[35] Up to a point, the government could easily defend itself. The compromises built into CITES helped. This was not an instrument aimed simply against threats to endangered species: the trade criterion was crucial. Nor did appendix listings bar all trade in a species, since various exceptions — for example trade between scientific institutions — were provided for. In relation to crocodiles, the government also had a pragmatic case, arguing that population growth increasingly threatened human life in some areas, including Kakadu National Park, and therefore that regulated culls or farming were defensible ecologically, commercially and for safety reasons. However, environmental groups were not always swayed by such arguments, which seemed to smack of legalisms and red tape.

Australian participation has also been affected by budgetary, legislative and administrative considerations. In 1977, for example, the Australian delegation to the CITES special session comprised only two officials, one each from the ANPWS and Customs. This figure compared with five for Canada, eleven for the US, five for West Germany, seven for Switzerland and five for Britain.[36] During much of the 1970s the Commonwealth authorities were also involved with problems of adjusting the legislative and administrative picture to allow full implementation of the convention. The process began with signature in 1973, and continued after ratification in 1976. The most important step in this process was not finally made until 1982. Passage of a major wildlife trade act that year was aimed at strengthening "arrangements for the protection of Australia's animals and plants, and world wildlife generally, by improving the effectiveness of our import and export controls."[37] Schedules 1 and 2 of the *Wildlife Protection (Regulation of Exports and Imports) Act* were designed to protect species threatened by trade; the listings were derived mainly from CITES Appendices I and II, with additional Australian species considered to be threatened included in Schedule 1.

Finally, to turn full circle, kangaroo politics appear to be a permanent fixture of debates on the international wildlife trade. An easing of Commonwealth-state tensions in the latter half of the 1970s, and the liberalizing instincts of the Liberal-National Country coalition, combined to produce a policy shift towards resumption of trade. Farmers' and companies' criticisms of the controls were echoed in Parliament. In 1980 the government reported that the US intended to allow again imports of skins and products of three kangaroo species for a trial two-year period. After talks in Canberra, officials of the US Fish and Wildlife Service had agreed these species were "not in any risk of extermination."[38] Australian efforts were then directed towards assuring the complete removal of their listing under the terms of the US *Endangered Species Act.* This meant countering US environmentalists' criticisms of Australia being voiced in Congressional hearings. In 1983 the US body announced it had received sufficient data to warrant removal of the three species (the Red, Eastern Grey and Western Grey).[39] Ensuring that the

47

finding stood, and was implemented, required further efforts by embassy staff in Washington. The main worry on the US side related to the adequacy of Australia's capability to monitor and manage kangaroo populations. Canberra's assurances rested on two developments: progress of the 1982 wildlife trade bill, which was introduced in May of that year, and moves towards the establishment and functioning of a national kangaroo monitoring unit.[40]

In 1980 the government also lifted the ban, then in effect for about half a century, on the export of koalas, platypuses and lyrebirds. These three, ministers argued, were simply being brought into line with treatment of other species. There was "no longer any biological basis for the imposition of stricter controls on the export of these species as compared with other species."[41]

Migratory species and habitats conservation

The Australia-Japan migratory birds convention was signed in Tokyo in February 1974. From the outset the agreement had ramifications beyond its immediate subject-matter. Regular meetings between Australian and Japanese officials took place annually both before and after signature of the convention. These meetings were augmented as a consequence of the 1976 Basic Treaty of Friendship and Cooperation between the two countries.[42] The growing importance of Japan as a focus of Australian foreign policy and trade efforts during the 1970s and 1980s gave the migratory birds agreement a special significance, though it remained a relatively minor aspect of such events as the Hawke-Nakasone visits in 1984-85.

The Japan convention was a product of the Whitlam era. As Dr. Cass defended it at the time, "Migratory species cannot be protected by one country acting alone. In the case of the birds which migrate between Australia and Japan, cooperation is essential to ensure that the birds' habitats are protected in both countries. For example, it would be pointless for Japan to create sanctuaries for Japanese Snipe if Australia failed to do likewise or allowed uncontrolled hunting to take place."[43] This appeal to the functionalist logic of international cooperation did not, however, endear it to state governments. Their support was vital. State governments and the Northern Territory were invited to legislate in order to implement the convention's provisions.[44] To encourage them, the Commonwealth emphasized its permissive character. The agreement "does not oblige Australia to protect every wetland where migratory birds occur but provides a framework within which each country gives an overall commitment to the protection of migratory birds and their habitats."[45] Delay on the Australian side made for asymmetry. Japan had completed all the requirements necessary for ratification by April 1974. It took Australia until 1981 to do the same. Consensus had to be reached with the states; federal regulations were needed; sites had to be secured; data were required on migration patterns and the condition of particular wetlands.[46] Australia and Japan finally exchanged instruments of ratification in 1981. Its entry into force, the Australian foreign minister, Tony Street, said, "represented another important step forward in the broadening of our relationship with Japan" in accord with the aims of the 1976 treaty.[47]

The convention thus served a broader foreign policy end. But it was also a practical instrument of conservation policy. Its basic aim was to ensure cooperation between Australia and Japan to protect migratory birds and their habitats. A total of 66 species were identified in the convention as threatened. The 1980s marked a more active phase in the life of the agreement. The first of a series of technical meetings between Australian and Japanese experts was held in Tokyo in 1982, and was followed by one in Canberra the following year. The purpose was essentially to exchange information on the status of particular species, and to monitor actions being taken within the framework of the convention. The species particularly identified on the Australian side were Latham's Snipe, the Short-tailed Shearwater, Little Tern and various species of waders.[48] Non-governmental bodies were brought into this process as sources of expertise, among them the Royal Australian Ornithologists Union and the Bird Observers Club. Australian conservation activity examined in the talks with the Japanese included the recovery plan for the Orange-bellied parrot, monitoring of the breeding success of the Abbott's Booby, and a captive breeding programme for the Norfolk Island Parrot.

Protection of migratory species, however, required acquisition and management, or at least permitted use, of sites under the jurisdiction of state governments along migratory routes. The question was one of some delicacy in the Commonwealth's relations with the states. Conservationist groups occasionally tried to use it as a lever against state governments. In 1975 there were complaints in the Senate that the agreement was being contravened by the government of New South Wales in its efforts to create the Kooragong Island industrial site, an area of mudflats used by species protected by the convention.[49] In general, however, the Japan convention raised few problems of this kind. One reason was that, of the listed species, several required for their protection the management of areas under the jurisdiction of the Commonwealth, for example Christmas Island or Norfolk Island. Reserves to protect migratory species and endangered birds were eventually created in several states.[50] Despite its slow take-off, then, the Japan agreement was generally regarded in Canberra as a success, both in terms of the conservation of threatened species and also of its contribution to Japanese-Australian relations.

Some efforts were made to replicate the agreement. The idea of a link with China first arose in the context of a mission sent there in 1974, and the return of a Chinese mission on parks and open spaces to Australia in 1975.[51] Again, the wider political setting of the bilateral relationship was a prime motive. Pressure from the Chinese and the responsiveness of environmental officials in Canberra, grew during the early 1980s, particularly in the course of preparations for a major official visit to Australia by Chinese leaders in 1985. The federal-state relationship, however, created obstacles for Australia, and the early conclusion of an agreement was ruled out.

The impetus to pursue agreements of a more universal — rather than bilateral — kind was still weaker. Such efforts lacked the immediacy of regional concerns or the political and economic considerations that eventually helped the momentum of the Japan treaty. Thus Australia took part in the consultations on the 1979 global migratory species convention, a draft of which, prepared jointly by West Germany and IUCN in 1975, was circulated to governments. Exchanges took place between Commonwealth and state officials on the question in the late 1970s.[52] Progress of the convention was set back, however, by objections raised by a number of countries concerning its relationship to existing migratory species treaties, particularly oceans species treaties.

More importance was attached by Australia to world wetlands conservation. The Ramsar convention was drawn up at a confence in Iran in 1971. Australia signed it in May 1974. By doing so without reservation to ratification, moreover, officials claimed that Australia thus became "the first party to fully adhere to the principles of the convention."[53] Australia was also the first "new" country to sign. Previous signatories had either been closely involved in preparatory wetlands meetings leading to the convention — Iran, which signed in 1972, Finland (1973), the United Kingdom (1973), and the USSR (1974) — or else, like Switzerland in 1974, had a long history of specialized interest in international conservation issues. Contacts between Australian officials and the IUCN Secretariat and the organization's Commissions were a significant factor generating official Australian interest in the convention.

The Ramsar convention was also a potential source of federal-state friction. It could not be implemented fully without major commitments by state governments on the protection of wetlands. Under its terms, each signatory had an obligation to designate for protection a wetland of "international importance." The Australian choice was the Cobourg Peninsula. Since this was located in the Northern Territory, to the north-east of Darwin, the selection avoided a confrontation with a state government (though this was also an area complicated by aboriginal land rights questions). The government defended adherence to the convention with the argument that any such listings did "not prejudice the exclusive sovereign rights of the Contracting Party in whose territory the wetland is situated."[54] One of the hopes of the backers of this convention was that it might stimulate the collection of data upon which to base future conservation programmes. For Australia, the problems were acute. Not enough was known in the 1970s about ecosystem types and their mapping to allow informed judgements to be made about which areas ought to be protected within a worldwide network of wetlands. Some initial steps were taken in 1974 to inaugurate a national wetlands survey, an idea conceived at a 1973 meeting of the Australian Fauna Authorities Conference. Pilot projects were carried out in three areas with CSIRO advice. The enterprise ground to a halt later in the 1970s, however, over issues of cost, problems of agreement on a national approach, and differences of opinion on the extent to which survey work should concentrate on aquatic fauna or on total wetlands ecosystems.[55]

World heritage sites and the Tasmanian dam

The heritage issue surrounding conservation of wilderness areas in South-west Tasmania in the late 1970s and early 1980s had profound implications for federal-state relations, the constitutional bases of Australian federalism, and electoral politics. The World Heritage convention itself, in many ways the document at the heart of the controversy, started life innocently enough as a product of debates in UNESCO in the 1960s on preservation of the cultural and natural environment. It was strongly supported by a resolution passed at UNCHE in June 1972; IUCN endorsed it at its General Assembly in Banff in September; and the final text was adopted by the UNESCO General Conference in November.[57]

The convention provided for the listing of sites considered part of the world's natural and cultural heritage. A variety of aesthetic, scientific and conservation criteria were employed. The convention established an intergovernmental World Heritage Committee of fifteen (later twenty-one) member-states. Expert advice for the Committee came from the IUCN, on questions of natural heritage, and from the International Council of Monuments and Sites (ICOMOS), and the International Centre for the Study of the Preservation and Restoration of Cultural Property, for advice on cultural submissions. These bodies, together with UNESCO, shared secretariat functions for the convention. Provision was also made for a List of World Heritage in Danger, which would identify sites requiring urgent conservation action. The overarching concept of heritage thus embraced two quite distinct sets of concerns. In both, however, the convention, and the Committee, were essentially passive. The World Heritage List was not seen as the foundation for collective international conservation programmes. The act of listing, however, was also conceived as one that would exert a moral and political influence over governments both to protect nominated areas and to continue to search for other candidates.

Coming as it did immediately after UNCHE, the World Heritage convention fitted in well with the ambitious Labor government plans for environment and heritage policy change in Australia. The government announced in April 1974 that Australia would sign the convention. It became the fifth country to do so (after Egypt, Iraq, Bulgaria and the US). The convention "provided excellent machinery to ensure the preservation of Australia's cultural and natural heritage. By moving to adhere to the Convention the Government would acknowledge that the cultural and natural heritage constituted a world heritage, for whose protection it was the duty of the international community as a whole to cooperate."[58] Its conservation principles, particularly in Articles 4 and 5, later became an integral part of the argument by heritage supporters in Australia that the convention imposed obligations on the Commonwealth both to propose listings and to protect heritage sites.

Though closely related, environmental policy and heritage policy constituted distinct policy areas for the Australian government. Both were given a solid push forward by Labor in the period 1972-75; both also took the Commonwealth into sensitive areas of state jurisdiction. The concept of a national estate, and of the need for its preservation, had appeared in various Labor statements while the party was in opposition in 1969-72. In a policy speech in late 1972 Whitlam declared that the new Labor government would enhance and preserve the national estate. A major committee of enquiry was set up by the Prime Minister in 1973; in April 1974, he announced the government's acceptance in principle of its major recommendations.[59]

The committee's work attracted considerable public and parliamentary attention, and did much to foster a climate of questioning about the pace and character of Australian agricultural, urban and industrial development, and their costs in terms of more intangible heritage values. It also helped to consolidate the linkage between Australian heritage goals and those of the World Heritage convention. The idea of the national estate, the committee said, had been "taking shape at an increasing rate because it has been aroused by the realisation that much which is of national, and even international, value in the man-made and natural spheres is coming under very strong threats and pressures from damaging or potentially damaging human action."[60] The World Heritage convention was described as the "context against which the National Estate can be measured, as it were, for size and for relative values." Australian wildlife was described as "an asset and a resource for which we in this country and generation hold a great responsibility." More pointedly, Australia, "once it ratifies the convention, will have a strong obligation to conserve those parts of the National Estate which may be regarded as World Heritage. We regard the convention as of the highest significance for Australian National Estate policy." It seemed likely "that it will not be long before the fulfilment of the prediction that the issues which will make and break governments in the seventies will be those of conservation, pollution and the environment."[61]

The committee's report led directly to legislation in 1975 setting up the Australian Heritage Commission (AHC). Inside government, and in public, the Commission continued to articulate the same internationalist philosophy. It also took up the argument that as one of the first signatories of the convention, and as a member of the World Heritage Committee from its inception, Australia had "a special responsibility to play a part in the development of the Convention."[62] National and international events followed each other closely. The World Heritage Committee was set up at the 19th General Conference of UNESCO in 1976, and Australia was elected to a six-year term of membership.[63] The AHC confirmed its orientation to national and international questions by quickly becoming a member of the IUCN,[64] and was thus well placed to be informed about world heritage developments and to try to influence their course. Budgetary and other constraints, however, prevented Australia from being as active an international heritage actor as the Commission wanted. It was not until 1980, for example, at the World Heritage Committee's fourth meeting in Paris, that Australia was represented for the first time by an Australia-based delegate — David Yencken, head of the AHC board. At this meeting, Australia was also elected to a seat on the bureau, the Committee's executive body,[65] and the decision was taken to hold the next World Heritage meeting in Australia.

Since the convention aimed to list cultural or natural sites of world significance, only a few Australian nominations could have much chance of success. The World Heritage Committee itself encouraged governments to be highly selective in their submissions. Once the Committee had been set up, officials from various Commonwealth departments and agencies met in Canberra to consider possible nominations, and the Prime Minister formally invited the state premiers to propose sites. The procedure that emerged was for proposals to be considered by an Australian Committee for the World Heritage Convention, chaired by Yencken.[66] After the Tasmanian crisis, this procedure became the subject of tense exchanges between the Commonwealth and the states, who feared a resurgence of federal, and particularly AHC, influence over the process. In July 1984 the Council of Nature Conservation Ministers (CONCOM) was finally able to agree on a new procedure for Australian submissions of world heritage sites.[67]

In practice, relatively few obstacles arose before 1982. The first round of consultations in Australia produced agreement on the Great Barrier Reef and the Alligator Rivers region. Kakadu National Park was added in 1980. In March 1981, the environment minister, Ian Wilson, announced that Australia had lodged two additional sites for consideration, the Willandra Lakes region of western New South Wales and the Sydney Opera House.[68] Australia was not successful on all counts. The World Heritage Committee's fifth meeting, at which these nominations were considered, was held in Sydney in October 1981, and was formally opened by the Prime Minister. The Sydney Opera House proved to be a non-starter. The criteria for World Heritage listings were already strict, and had been tightened still further by the Committee at an earlier meeting in Luxor.[69] The meeting approved World Heritage status for three Australian sites: the Great Barrier Reef, Kakadu National Park, and the Willandra Lakes region. Slatyer, leader of the Australian delegation, was elected Chairman. The sites chosen, he said, "are already treasured by the Australian people and the international recognition they will now be accorded should help not only to ensure their protection for generations to come, but also will add immeasurably to the international fund of scientific and educational knowledge."[70]

In the interval between the October 1981 and December 1982 meetings of the Committee, the Tasmanian issue grew to explosive proportions in Australian politics. Other listings, such as the Great Barrier Reef, were not completely free of Commonwealth-state friction; there was a long background of disagreement between Canberra and Brisbane over the demarcation of protected areas of the Reef. The Tasmanian question, however, involved an unprecedentedly bitter confrontation between the Commonwealth and a state. The federal government tried for as long as possible to deflect, or postpone, hostilities by publicly, and repeatedly, acknowledging the constitutional rights of state governments to manage their own natural resources. South-west Tasmania, put forward in November 1981 by the Commonwealth and the then government of the state, was by far the most controversial and divisive of Australia's world heritage nominations. It covered an area called the Western Tasmania Wilderness National Parks, consisting of the South-west National Park, the Franklin-Lower Gordon Wild Rivers National Park, and Cradle Mountain-Lake St. Clair National Park, a total of 769,355 hectares. The supporting documentation itemized the natural features and aboriginal cultural values of the area, and described it as "one of the last remaining temperate wilderness areas in the world."[71]

In June 1982, the World Heritage Committee's bureau, the executive body on which Australia was also represented, approved the nomination and agreed to recommend it to the full Committee at its December meeting in Paris. The area unreservedly met the IUCN and ICOMOS interpretations of the natural and cultural criteria for listing. The submission none the less was far from clearcut. In practice, Committee members were aware of the contentious nature of the issue in Australia, and also of the structure of federalism and the limits of the Commonwealth's power. The nomination had been put forward jointly by Tasmania and the AHC, as the Commonwealth's agent. But in 1982, following a change of leadership in the state's Labor ranks, the Tasmanian government withdrew its support. At the June meeting, the Committee decided to ask the Australian authorities to provide it with a statement of intent regarding the construction of dams and other works in the nominated area, including relevant details of the area to be flooded.[72] Canberra responded by indicating that the Tasmanian government was "constructing a hydro-electric power scheme in the nominated area and that the Commonwealth has been and is discussing the scheme with the Tasmanian Government with a view to minimising the damage that the dam might cause."[73]

Australian representation at the crucial December meeting was substantial. Apart from Slatyer, serving also as the Committee's Chairman, it included McMichael, an official of the Attorney-General's Department, and Max Bourke of the AHC. The Tasmanian government was represented by Max Bingham, Deputy Premier and Attorney-General, who attended as a member of the Australian delegation.[74] The Tasmanian Wilderness Society and other groups lobbied the meeting, which took place under intense international media scrutiny. Yet in a sense the result was a foregone conclusion. The Committee's bureau had recommended support for the listing; the Australian government had provided the requested information; and IUCN and ICOMOS had registered their enthusiasm.[75] Australia, further, was chairing the Committee at the time (though Slatyer temporarily relinquished the chair when presenting the Australian case), and it would have been unusual in such circumstances for the Committee to embarrass the proposer by declining. As this was an international meeting, Tasmania was unable to mount a formal case against listing; and the Committee's own procedures, which called for the nominating country simply to respond to questions put by Committee members, also served to deflect negative arguments.

On the other hand, there was no guarantee in December 1982 that listing would protect the South-west. Tasmania had formally agreed that the Commonwealth would be consulted in the development of the management plan for the area, but the mechanism of consultation was still the subject of discussions between Canberra and Hobart.[76] Theoretically the Commonwealth had only two options: to withdraw the nomination (voluntarily, or under implicit threat of rejection by the Committee) on the grounds that enforcement action to protect the area could not be promised; or to press ahead and hope to persuade the Committee that the negotiations with Tasmania would indeed result in a workable conservation plan, and, further, that listing would add political legitimacy within Australia to Commonwealth arguments. In practice, the first option was not politically feasible at any time after November 1981. Nor would it have been the Committee's own preference. On a purist reading of its criteria, it could have maintained that the proper course was rejection, or else postponement until firmer guarantees of protection could be provided. But it was not the Committee's job to make life gratuitously difficult for an important party to the convention. In the event, the Committee chose the route of World Heritage listing as a form of moral suasion. This was combined, however, with the unusual procedural device of issuing a statement at the same time urging "the Australian authorities" to take all possible measures to protect the integrity of the property.[77]

Australia and international conservation policy

The international conventions examined in this chapter indicate the significance of federalism in the workings of international functional cooperation. (The subject is discussed in more detail later in this study.) Among the leading conservation agreements of the 1970s and 1980s, possibly only CITES allowed the federal authorities a relatively autonomous hand. Even here, however, the interests of states were clearly affected. In some states, such as New South Wales, local kangaroo and wild bird populations were regarded as pests rather than objects for preservation. Locally active conservation groups thus constituted potentially important allies of international bodies, which for the most part were restricted formally to contact with the federal government. Where agreements entailed the search for protected areas, as in the Ramsar or Japan conventions, the federal authorities were often limited in their capacity to move beyond land under the jurisdiction of the Commonwealth. The World Heritage convention raised this issue in relation to sites in Queensland, Tasmania and other states. Hence the manner in which national political debates surrounding the dam issue were increasingly structured from the late 1970s: Were there obligations inherent in the federal government's adherence to the convention and the nomination of the South-west? Was the Commonwealth government compelled, whatever the rules of federalism might suggest, to step in and halt work on the project in the name of a higher Australian interest? While the judicial and political consensus tended towards a negative answer, it was equally clear in 1981-83 that some action was needed from the federal government. In dealing with the Tasmanian issue, the various international bodies involved with the heritage convention showed

55

in practice a sensitive appreciation of Australian political realities and of the dilemma in which Canberra was caught. Listing of the South-west in 1982 by the World Heritage Committee was more a gesture of optimism and an attempt at moral suasion than a blinkered application of established procedures.

One important Australian motive in these varied cases was the more general commitment to support international law and the strengthening of world legal order. Concrete interests, however, provided a more immediate impetus than amorphous principles. Thus as we shall see in the next chapter, Australia pursued international marine pollution conventions in the 1970s and 1980s largely because of the magnitude of the threat posed by oil spills, dumping and other hazards to ecologically vulnerable reefs and coastlines. Some international agreements have also been instrumental to the achievement of wider foreign policy objectives. The convention with Japan was consistently defended on functionalist criteria: migrating species could only be protected effectively if the two governments collaborated. Yet the agreement was also seen as one element in the building of good relations with an important economic partner, a consideration which weighed more with officials of the departments of Trade and Foreign Affairs than it did with the official environmental bodies in Canberra whose task was to supervise its implementation and further growth. International conventions, moreover, have only rarely become the subjects of public controversy in Australia. The federal government has tended accordingly to move at a more leisurely pace towards signature and ratification than the comparatively few critics who took an interest in such questions usually demanded. This slowness also reflected the principle that implementing legislation at both levels of government should be in place before the final stages of adherence to conventions were completed. The fact that many conventions are not static has kept them from sliding out of view as a consequence of inertia inside government. Thus Australia has been willy-nilly an active participant in CITES developments, both in cases where Australian interests were directly affected, and also in the collective international task of regime-building.

Notes for Chapter 3

[1] Ronald McKie, *The Mango Tree* (Sydney: Collins 1974, p. 157.
[2] *IUCN Bull.*, 2(19), April-June 1971, p. 162.
[3] Enderby, *House of Representatives*, 95, 2 June 1975, p. 3099.
[4] Kelly, *House of Representatives*, 96, 2 October 1975, p. 1647.
[5] *IUCN Bull.*, 2(1), April-June 1971, p. 162; *IUCN Bull.*, 3(12), December 1972, p. 56.
[6] *Senate*, 37, 4 June 1968, p. 1359.
[7] Statement by Dr. Cass of 17 January 1973, *AGD*, 1(1), 1973, pp. 159-60. The US move added seventeen species of kangaroos and wallabies to the US Endangered Species List. On the background to the ban see Cass at *House of Representatives*, 85, 30 August 1973, p. 623.
[8] Statement by Dr. Cass of 12 February 1973, *AGD*, 1(1), 1973, p. 162. On the conference see *IUCN Bull.*, 4(3) March 1973, pp. 9-10.

[9] *Wildlife Conservation. Summary Report of the Australian Delegation to the Plenipotentiary Conf. to Conclude an International Treaty on Trade in Certain Species of Wildlife, Washington, DC, 12 February - 2 March 1973* (Canberra, 1973; PP 64), p. 5.

[10] *Ibid.*, p. 6; *AGD*, 1(2), 1973, pp. 583, 586; DEC, *Report for the Period December 1972 to June 1974* (Canberra, 1975; PP 298), p. 11.

[11] *Wildlife Conservation. Summary Report . . .*, p. 6.

[12] *AGD*, 1(2), 1973, p. 586.

[13] Statement of June 4 quoted in *AFAR*, 44(6), June 1973, p. 423.

[14] Through amendments to the Customs Act. See remarks by Mr. Daly, Minister of Services and Property, *House of Representatives*, 87, 26 November 1973, p. 3840, and Sen. Murphy at *Senate*, 58, 13 November 1973, p. 1763. The regulations required clearing up one anomaly in relation to fish.

[15] See *Wildlife Conservation, Summary Report . . .*, p. 10; *Commonwealth Record*, 1(12), 20-26 September 1976, p. 711. The implementing Customs (Endangered Species) Regulations were promulgated on 30 September 1976 (Groom, *House of Representatives* 114, 8 May 1979, p. 1973). See also DOE, *Report for Period July 1974 to June 1975* (Canberra, 1976; PP 139), pp. 11-12.

[16] Though not the second meeting, in Bonn in January 1980. See *CITES. Proc. (2nd Mtg. of Conf. of Parties, San Jose, Costa Rica. 19-30 March 1979* (Gland: IUCN, 1980), pp. 86, 107; and *CITES. Proc. 3rd Mtg. of Conf. of the Parties. New Delhi, 25 February - 8 March 1981* (Gland: IUCN, 1982), p. 256.

[17] *CITES. Proc. 4th Mtg. of Conf. of the Parties, Gaborone, 19-30 April 1983* (Gland: IUCN, 1984), p. 124.

[18] *Ibid.*, pp. 127, 129. The species are crocodiles, turtles, possibly snakes, lizards, amphibians, fish, insects. Cf. the US view, that the convention should have the flexibility to enable Parties to utilize their resources *(CITES. Proc. 2nd Mtg.*, pp. 98-9).

[19] *CITES. Proc. 3rd Mtg.*, p. 770 (Doc. 3.30.1); *CITES. Proc. 2nd Mtg.*, pp. 207-8; *ANPWS. Report for Period 1 July 1978 to 30 June 1979* (Canberra 1979), 32.

[20] *CITES. Proc. 3rd Mtg.*, pp. 169-70; *CITES. Proc. 4th Mtg.*, pp. 108-9, 387.

[21] *CITES. Proc. 3rd Mtg.*, pp. 768, 126-7 (Doc. 3.30). Australia took the lead in acting in a coordinating role for the collection of opinions on this subject.

[22] *Ibid.*, pp. 117, 127, 752, 754. Australia was in favour of an expert committee to determine guidelines to tighten the workings of IV.3; see also *CITES. Proc. 4th Mtg.*, p. 455.

[23] *Ibid.*, pp. 114-5.

[24] *CITES. Proc. 2nd Mtg.*, p. 116 (Doc. 2.30).

[25] *CITES. Proc. 1st Mtg. of Conf. of the Parties, Berne, 1-6 November 1976* (Morges: IUCN, 1977), p. 263 ff. In general on this meeting see ANPWS, *Report for Period 1 July 1976 to 30 June 1977* (Canberra, 1977), p. 20.

[26] Data from *Australia. CITES. Annual Reports for 1979, 1980, 1981* (Canberra, 1979-81).

[27] *CITES. Proc. 2nd Mtg.*, pp. 95 (Doc. 2.14), 184 (Doc. Com. 2.2).

[28] *CITES. Proc. 3rd Mtg.*, p. 115 (Doc. 3.32).

[29] "Criteria for the Addition of Species and other taxa to Appendices I and II and for the transfer of species and other taxa from Appendix II to Appendix I," in *CITES. Proc. 1st Mtg.*, pp. 31-2 (Doc. Conf. 1.1).

[30] *IUCN Bull.*, 2(19), April-June 1971, p. 163.

[31] In a document inserted after the meeting at the request of the delegation; *CITES. Proc. 2nd Mtg.*, p. 160.

[32] *CITES. Proc. 4th Mtg.*, p. 644 (Doc. 4.39.2).

[33] *Senate*, 94, 22 April 1982, p. 1449. An Applied Ecology official attended the 1981 New Delhi meetings in the Australian delegation.

[34] *CITES. Proc. 2nd Mtg.*, pp. 97, 185 (Docs. 2.3, 2.15).

[35] The issue was taken up by Friends of the Earth and other groups. See the article by M. Kennedy, *City Express*, 12 November 1980.

[36] *CITES. Proc. 1st Mtg.*, p. 167. For later meetings the delegation included also state government representatives, and some NGOs sent delegates. CITES rules permit various categories of delegates (A, B, or C) to attend meetings of the parties.

[37] *House of Representatives*, 127, 6 May 1982, pp. 2391-3.

[38] Statement by J.D. Anthony (Deputy Prime Minister and Minister of Trade and Resources) and David Thomson (Minister of Science and the Environment), *Commonwealth Record*, 5(21), 26 May - 1 June 1980, p. 763.

[39] *Federal Register*, 8 April 1983.

[40] The Unit's establishment was announced as government policy in the statement by the Govenor-General of 21 April 1983. See *Weekly Hansard* (Senate), No. 1 (1984), 28 February 1984, p. 73, remarks by Senator Ryan.

[41] *Senate*, 86, 12 September 1980, p. 898, statement by Senator Chaney. The regulations were to be amended to allow limited government-controlled export to approved zoos and scientific institutions. ("Recommended conditions for the export of koalas" and "Species of Eucalypts to be provided for koalas," *ibid.*).

[42] On the 7th annual series of bilateral meetings see *Australian Financial Review*, July 30, 1973; and for a review of later developments, *Canberra Times*, March 20, 1985.

[43] *AGD*, 2(1), 1974, p. 64.

[44] Sinclair, *House of Representatives*, 114, 7 June 1979, p. 3169.

[45] *House of Representatives*, 130, 14-15 December 1982, pp. 3522-3.

[46] *Senate*, 63, 13 February 1975, pp. 135-6; *House of Representatives*, 114, 7 June 1979, p. 3169 (Sinclair); DOE, *Report for Period July 1974 to June 1975* (Canberra, 1976; PP 139), pp. 11-2; ANPWS, *Report for Period 1 July 1977 to 30 June 1978* (Canberra, 1978), p. 19, and *Report for Period 13 March 1975 to June 1976* (Canberra, 1976), p. 17. One of the first steps was an ANPWS commissioned study on the status in Australia of migratory birds and their habitats.

[47] "Agreement for Protection of Migratory and Endangered Birds," *Backgrounder*, No. 281, 28 April 1981, p. xii; *Senate*, 97, 23 November 1982, p. 2694 (Baume); DEC, *Report for Period December 1974 to June 1975* (Canberra, 1975; PP 298), p. 11.

[48] *Commonwealth Record*, 8(49), 5-31 December 1983, p. 2171. An Australian official also took part as an observer in the US-Japan talks on nature conservation in Tokyo in May 1975; DOE, *Report for Period July 1974 to June 1975* (Canberra, 1976; PP 139), p. 24.

[49] *Senate*, 63, 13 February 1975, pp. 135-6.

[50] *Commonwealth Record*, 8(49), 5-31 December 1983, p. 2171.

[51] DOE, *Report for Period July 1974 to June 1975* (Canberra, 1976; pp 139), p. 25. The 1974 mission was under Prof. Karmel.

[52] Senator Carrick, at *Senate*, 76, 5 April 1978, p. 886; ANPWS, *Report for Period 13 March 1975 to 30 June 1976* (Canberra, 1976), p. 19, *Report for Period 1 July 1977 to 30 June 1978* (Canberra, 1978), p. 19, and *Report for Period 1 July 1978 to 30 June 1979* (Canberra, 1979), pp. 22-3.

[53] ANPWS, *Report for the Period 13 March 1975 to 30 June 1976* (Canberra, 1976), p. 16; also DEC, *Report for Period December 1972 to June 1974* (Canberra, 1975; PP 298), p. 12; Groom, *House of Representatives*, 127, 6 May 1982, p. 2392; and Sen. Mulvihull, *Senate*, 68, 25 May 1976, p. 1904.

[54] *AGD*, 2(2), 1974, p. 361.

[55] *House of Representatives*, 113, 7 June 1979, p. 3172.

[56] On the background of IUCN involvement see *IUCN. Proc. 11th Gen. Ass., Banff, 11-16 September 1972* (IUCN, 1972), p. 102.

[57] "World Heritage Convention," *IUCN Bull.*, 4(2), February 1973, p. 6.

[58] *AGD*, 2(2), 1974, pp. 360-1; DEC, *Report for Period December 1972 to June 1974* (Canberra, 1975; PP 298), pp. 12-13.

[59] Uren, *House of Representatives*, 90, 19 September 1974, pp. 1535-6; *Report of the Interim Committee on the National Estate, May 1975* (Canberra, 1976; PP 139).

[60] *National Estate. Report of the Committee of Inquiry* (Canberra, 1975; PP 195), para. 1.4, p. 20.

[61] *Ibid.*, para. 1.66, p. 30; para 3.28, pp. 49-50; para. 8.132, pp. 251-2; para. 2.6, p. 35.

62 AHC, *4th Annual Report 1979-80* (Canberra, 1980; PP 330), p. 1.
63 AHC, *1st Annual Report 1976-77* (Canberra, 1978; PP 238), p. 16.
64 *Ibid.*
65 ACH, *5th Annual Report, 1980-1* (Canberra, 1981; PP 242), p. 16.
66 ACH, *Annual Report 1977-78* (Canberra, 1978; PP 350), p. 12.
67 House of Representatives, *Weekly Hansard*, No. 13/1984, 11 October 1984, p. 2214.
68 AHC, *Annual Report 1977-78* (Canberra, 1978; PP 350), p. 122; AHC, *4th Annual Report 1979-80* (Canberra, 1980; PP 330), p. 1, and *Nomination of Kakadu National Park for Inclusion in the World Heritage List* (Canberra: ANPWS, May 1980); AHC, *5th Annual Report 1980-1* (Canberra, 1981; PP 242), p. 16, and *Commonwealth Record 1980-1* (Canberra, 1981; PP 242), p. 16, and *Commonwealth Record* 6(12), 23-9 March 1981, p. 302.
69 AHC, *4th Annual Report 1979-80* (Canberra, 1980; PP 330), p. 16.
70 "Australian Sites on World Heritage List," *Backgrounder*, 307, 28 October 1981, viii; "World Heritage Committee Meeting in Australia," *Backgrounder*, 306, 21 October 1981, iii; DFA, *Annual Report 1981* (Canberra, 1982; PP 139), p. 28.
71 *Nomination of Western Tasmania Wilderness National Parks by the Commonwealth of Australia for Inclusion in the World Heritage List* (Government of Tasmania/Australian Heritage Commission, November 1981), p. 2.
72 *Senate* 97, 23 November 1982, p. 2704.
73 Ministerial statement, McVeigh, *House of Representatives*, 130, 8 December 1982, pp. 3085-6.
74 This was "subject to the conditions which normally apply to State representatives on Australian Government delegations" (*ibid.*, p. 3086). On the background to the meeting see also Sen. Baume, at *Senate*, 97, 8 December 1982, p. 3240; and AHC, *Annual Report 1982-3* (Canberra, 1984; PP 39), p. 26.
75 Cohen, *House of Representatives*, 131, 21 April 1983, p. 53.
76 *House of Representatives*, 130, 8 December 1982, pp. 3085-6 (McVeigh).
77 *House of Representatives*, 131, 5 May 1983, p. 248.

CHAPTER FOUR

The International Regulation of Pollution

Australia tried at Stockholm in 1972 to secure more effective international action on marine pollution and ocean dumping. In many ways the government attached more importance to these concerns than to other forms of environmental hazard, for example to problems of air pollution or the regulation of pesticides and other toxic chemicals. This approach departed somewhat from the priorities being established in domestic debates in Australia. Two Senate committees had drawn widespread attention to problems of air and water pollution. For the public, and for many environmental groups, the toxic by-products of urban life and industrial activity were more pressing than more distant problems in the oceans. These problems attracted attention, however, when oil spills off the Australian coast revealed the vulnerability of the seas and the Great Barrier Reef to the mounting pace of modern shipping traffic. It was generally accepted, of course, that both terrestrial and marine pollution had to be dealt with; disagreement surfaced on the priority each should receive, and the means and the cost of tackling them.[1] This chapter discusses Australian policies in the Third Law of the Sea Conference (UNCLOS III) from 1973-82, and related responses to marine pollution conventions. As well, it discusses the control of pollution and hazards on land, particularly with regard to chemicals policy.

Australia and the UNCLOS III negotiations

In 1972 UNCHE approved a set of recommendations (86-92) on marine pollution. These called on governments, amongst other things, to support existing international marine pollution conventions, to participate fully in the work of the planned 1973 IMCO Conference on Marine Pollution and also UNCLOS III, and to support international programmes for research and monitoring in relation to marine pollution. Recommendation 92(b) urged governments "to take early action to adopt effective national measures for the control of all significant sources of marine pollution, including land-based sources, and concert and coordinate their actions regionally and where appropriate on a wider international basis...."[2] All these recommendations were in line with Australia's goals at the conference. The delegation would have preferred, however, the addition of recognition of the need for more extensive coastal state powers. But no agreement could be reached on this question in the marine pollution Working Group of which Australia was a member. The issue was shaping up into a controversial one in anticipation of UNCLOS III, and the feeling among delegations at Stockholm was that this matter could better be left for that conference to handle.

Australian emphasis on oceans questions at UNCHE reflected growing attention by Australia to these issues since the late 1960s. Early in 1970 one decisive event seemed to give convincing proof of the need for action. This was the major oil spill in the Torres Strait from the damaged tanker *Oceanic Grandeur*. The event raised an immediate public and parliamentary outcry. More than any other incident it served to alert Australians to the threats to their coasts and to the Great Barrier Reef. It prompted quick Commonwealth action. The *Navigation Act* was amended to empower the Minister for Shipping and Transport to require the owners of a ship to take appropriate measures to prevent or reduce pollution, by discharge of oil, off Australia's coast, coastal waters or reefs; or else, in default, to allow the government itself to take the necessary measures at the owners' expense. The incident renewed interest in international marine pollution controls. The traditional doctrine by which coastal states had authority only over their territorial seas was considered seriously inadequate.[3]

From 1970 Australia pursued courses of action in several international forums with the aim of bringing about and legitimizing expanded powers for coastal states to combat pollution. The Australian delegation to the FAO Technical Conference on Marine Pollution in 1970 emphasized the consequences for marine living resources of gaps in the enforcement regime.[4] More important, in London in 1971 Australia secured approval for an amendment to IMCO regulations allowing it to protect the Great Barrier Reef for up to 200 miles from the Australian coast. Australia was also active in the UN Seabed Committee from 1967. It used this position in the early 1970s to press its case for more effective coastal state powers.[5] Meanwhile, Australian official attention increasingly turned to the forthcoming Law of the Sea round, and initially to the marine pollution work of the Preparatory Committee.

Marine pollution formed only one part of the broad canvas of UNCLOS III. The issues tended to be lower in the pecking order than questions of seabed resource exploitation, the operational definition of the concept of common heritage, the scope and delineation of the exclusive economic zone, questions of rights of passage through international straits or the treatment of archipelagic states. As an island continent Australia had a wide span of interests at the conference, although maritime issues had not traditionally loomed large in the Australian consciousness. Distance from its major trading partners brought interest in problems of communication by sea. After the US and Japan, Australia in the 1970s was the world's third largest trader of dry cargo goods in ships.[6] It had important regional neighbours at the centre of the straits and archipelagic questions; in the early 1970s Australia was simultaneously engaged in bilateral negotiations with Indonesia on the delimitation of seabed boundaries. There was mounting concern about foreign fishing in Australian waters. Interest in offshore oil and gas was growing. Marine science issues also affected Australia. Indeed UNCLOS III was one of several factors — policy issues in the Southern Ocean, and wider controversy over Australia's science and technology needs prompted by OECD discussions were others — which later in the 1970s highlighted significant gaps in Australia's marine science capabilities. Australia was a co-sponsor of the UN General Assembly resolution of 1972 which defined the tasks of the Preparatory Committee. The work of UNCLOS III, the delegation said later, "promises to be enormously difficult and crucially important, not least for Australia, which has a considerable stake in every aspect of it." The leading Australian official in the negotiations, H.C. Mott, was appointed rapporteur in 1973, and Australia secured a seat on the important general (or steering) committee of the conference.[7]

Marine pollution was none the less a high priority for Australia. Mott, then adviser to the Australian delegation, told the Preparatory Committee in 1971 that experience since 1958 suggested it had "become imperative to consider the elaboration of more effective rules of international law that would inter alia give coastal states the right to exercise effective control over ships on the high seas in a broad zone contiguous to their territorial seas, so as to prevent pollution of their coastlines and damage to the marine environment." Australia wanted to see the prohibition of the disposal of noxious substances in the oceans, and the regulation of the disposal of all other materials. These matters, it claimed, should be regarded as the responsibility of the coastal state. More controversially, Australia wanted discussions of the degree to which international rules should be agreed for observance within national territories of certain minimum standards for activities such as the discharge of industrial wastes at sea. Australian officials were well aware of the fears on the part of the main maritime nations. Hence a main purpose of these rules, Mott said, "would be to promote the orderly and safe navigation of the high seas." Care would need to be taken "that the rules did not provide a basis or excuse for unduly hindering exercise of the basic rights of freedom of passage on the high seas." Australia also wanted to see rules developed that would guard against damage from seabed operations. Finally, the process of seeking international agreement on control measures "should be left wherever possible with the specialized bodies already established."[8]

Australia's objectives were thus well defined before UNCLOS III got under way. At conference sessions in 1973-74 Australia developed its case for tougher international standards and more coastal state power.[9] The latitude to be allowed coastal states was a central issue. Should their jurisdiction over pollution be limited to the enforcement of internationally agreed standards, or should they also have powers to make their own regulations and to enforce these? Australia had both to protect its interest in securing the right to make regulations of its own, while at the same time fending off criticism that such powers would be used irresponsibly by some countries. In response to US, British and other critics, Canberra's approach was to exploit the notion of reasonableness. The coastal state "should have the right, not only to enforce international standards, but to make its own regulations in certain specified circumstances and subject to certain restrictions." These regulations "would be required to be reasonable; and the primary, although not necessarily conclusive, evidence of what is reasonable would be internationally agreed standards; and in any dispute as to 'reasonableness' the matter would be subject to compulsory judicial or arbitral decision."[10]

63

The ability of Australia to influence events was limited. The second session, at Caracas in 1974, served to define opposed positions in a number of areas. In the third committee Australia's position again met with the concern of maritime states that the principle of freedom of navigation had at all costs to be protected. Agreement could not be reached on whether flag states or coastal states should carry the main enforcement responsibilities for pollution. Also unresolved was the question of the rights of coastal states to make special rules for specially defined areas, though the Australian delegation, with the Great Barrier Reef and Torres Strait area particularly in mind, detected "some recognition of the fact that States should be able to make special rules with respect to areas which were specially vulnerable in nature."[11] On these issues, the concerns of the maritime states were directed not so much at Australia as at other countries situated closer to major shipping lanes. As an active member of the coastal states group at UNCLOS III, however, Australia, particularly in the early stages of the conference, often addressed the general interests of group members. The delegation was also worried about the environmental implications of some forms of scientific research, the other focus of the third committee. Some of these activities, moreover, Senator Willessee, then foreign minister, said at Caracas, were "in essence exploration for commercial advantage."[12]

The task of persuasion, then, rested on Australia's ability to identify its own requirements with the common good. Australia was itself a trading nation — "a major user of world shipping" — and appreciated that foreign trade was a vital aspect of the economies of most coastal states. Charges of irresponsibility were thus misplaced. "The consequences of capricious or unreasonable action could be at least a rise in freight rates and even, perhaps, suspension of shipping services. No responsible State is wilfully going to run such risks ... we simply cannot proceed in this Conference on the basis that one side or another is going to be irresponsible."[13]

In this effort Australia was not alone. Australian officials found much potential for support in 1974-75 in the Canadian pursuit of a more coherent zonal approach to oceans management.[14] Increasingly, however, Australia was forced to distance itself from the position on the economic zone taken by some South American and other Group of 77 delegations. These, labelled by Australia the "extreme territorialist States," were depicted as favouring unlimited powers for coastal states. Their position, held to be quite unlike Australia's own moderate and pragmatic one, was seen to be much more related to the conception of the zone as an extension of sovereignty rather than as a means of specifying policy views on pollution control.[15] As a result, Australia occasionally found itself playing the mediator. An extreme polarization between the "coastal states rights" and the "freedom of navigation" principles would not serve its interests. Thus Australia's position on marine pollution at the fourth session, in 1976, was described as "very much a middle of the road line." This, the delegation thought, was often "influential in bringing delegations closer to agreement."[16]

The Australian position was also assisted by broader movements of opinion on major issues in the conference in the mid-1970s, notably the shift towards growing acceptance of the 200-mile exclusive economic zone (EEZ) concept as an eventual core principle of the convention. For moderate western nations such as Australia and Canada, this was no longer viewed as a radical change. Negotiations accordingly focussed more on the powers and rights of states in the zone. As a basis for discussion delegates were now using the Informal Single Negotiating Text (SNT) produced at the close of the third session. In the Third Committee, the question of pollution from ships remained the most controversial issue, and also the one that bothered Australia most. Officials took specific steps to try to ease the concerns of the maritime states. Australia argued, for example, that it was not necessary to arrest ships or persons on board in order for a coastal state to take proceedings; these could be taken in absentia, so long as there were provisions in the convention for obtaining evidence. At the minimum, though, such provisions would have to include the right to board vessels in the EEZ for investigation "when there are clear grounds for believing that a breach of applicable pollution rules has been committed."[17] Australia also moderated its position on coastal state discretionary rights in special areas. A "limited degree" of such rights should be recognized, "provided that they do not involve the right to prescribe design, construction, manning and equipment standards which are different from those agreed internationally."[18]

The consensus-making dynamics of UNCLOS III were an integral feature of this process of change. Australian delegates took part actively in the series of informal consultations on vessel-sourced pollution organized by the Third Committee chairman, Ambassador Vallarta of Mexico. The modifications, however, were insufficient to arrest what appeared to be a general conference move toward collectively defined rules and limits to the discretionary powers of coastal states. Such powers continued to be central to Australia's Third Committee objectives. Provisions of the Revised SNT at the 1977 session were regarded as still unsatisfactory. The article in question (Article 21[5]) allowed the coastal state to apply, in any Special Areas it wished to designate, only regulations of a kind that had been applied in Special Areas designated in the convention itself. The provisions, moreover, related only to standards for the discharge of pollutants, and did not cover rules such as traffic separation schemes, compulsory pilotage, or under-keel clearances. These were rules "which we might want, for example, to introduce for protection of the Great Barrier Reef." Australia, that is, wanted coastal states to have the authority to take additional measures, even though such measures might not have been incorporated into the convention.[19] The delegation proposed a number of amendments to the article, and was also receptive to criticisms from other delegations, particularly reservations expressed by several Third World countries. A near consensus was eventually reached which officials described as going a good way towards meeting the Australian position.[20] Australia also resisted, in combination with other coastal states, efforts by maritime powers to weaken the provisions of Article 28 of the Revised SNT, which dealt with port state enforcement.[21] The delegation supported the convening of a joint meeting of the Second and Third Committees to explore the scope for accommodation between coastal and maritime states on such matters as vessel-sourced pollution and innocent passage in the territorial sea, but this initiative received little support.

Following agreement in 1977 on Article 21(5), Australia became concerned to protect what had been achieved. Complicated issues still remained, particularly the respective enforcement powers of flag states, port states and coastal states. But in general by 1978 Australia favoured retaining the existing texts of the Revised SNT. This "reflected a broadly acceptable balance between the concern of maritime and other powers to facilitate freedom of navigation and the interest of coastal States in promoting the regulation and enforcement of measures to control vessel-sourced pollution in areas under their jurisdiction."[22] In most cases, the marine pollution texts were finalized at the resumed seventh session in 1978. The first two weeks were devoted to intensive informal negotiations in the small group, including Australia, meeting under Vallarta's chairmanship. Delay was caused, however, by the submission of new marine pollution amendments, and wider debate in the conference on the convention package considered as a whole and the interrelations among its component parts. The marine pollution work of the Third Committee was completed at the eighth session of UNCLOS III in March-April 1979. Marine science issues were concluded in 1980-81, and the Committee did not convene during the subsequent eleventh session.[23]

Change in the US attitude following the 1980 Presidential election left a dent in Australia's generally optimistic outlook on UNCLOS III, at least as far as its pollution elements were concerned. Concern was expressed in Parliament that resulting delays, or even the collapse of the negotiations, could jeopardize Australian interests. A series of events since the start of the negotiations had kept oceans issues alive in Australian politics. Japanese plans for dumping nuclear waste in the North Pacific received much publicity in 1981. In exchanges with Tokyo, Australia "made it clear that it is opposed to the Pacific region becoming a dumping ground" for the uncontrolled disposal of nuclear waste.[24] The convention itself was opened for signature in Jamaica in December 1982. It was "a new and promising regime for the protection of the marine environment, particularly in offshore waters, along lines sought by Australia."[25] Australia's signature of the convention, the foreign minister said, was based on a number of factors, including the achievement of its long-term objectives of freedom of navigation and access to living and non-living resources.[26] Early signature also held out the possibility of Australia's being able to bring its influence to bear on skeptics, particularly the US. At home it provided the government with evidence of its environmentalist credentials at a time when the Tasmanian issue was threatening to destroy them.

International marine pollution conventions

Despite its importance, interest in UNCLOS III tended to be restricted in Australia. A closer public and parliamentary watch was kept on the international conventions dealing with marine pollution. Indeed few things more sharply contrasted the 1960s from the 1970s as the domestic politics of this area. From the early 1950s, when the first significant international instruments were drawn up, attention was for the most part confined to shippers, traders and government agencies. From 1970, marine pollution came to be viewed as a crucial element in Australia's overall strategy for combating environmental degradation. In opposition before 1972 and after 1975, the ALP was a persistent critic of delays in the government's handling of pollution conventions. By 1980 the government had invested much effort in shaping relevant responses, particularly to problems of oil spills off Australia's coasts. The main conventions around which debate focussed were the Convention on Prevention of Pollution of the Sea by Oil, (Oilpol), in 1954, succeeded in 1973 by a new Marine Pollution convention (Marpol) which dealt with a wider range of pollutants; conventions on intervention on the high seas in cases of oil pollution casualties, and on civil liability for oil pollution damage, both of 1969; a convention on the establishment of an international fund for compensation for oil pollution damage (1971); and the Dumping Convention of 1972. Also important were a series of amendments and related agreements, for example a 1973 Protocol relating to intervention on the high seas in cases of marine pollution by substances other than oil.

Australian activity in relation to these conventions revolved around protracted federal-state exchanges. Thus, following normal practice, the Commonwealth did not take steps in the 1950s to ratify and implement the provisions of the 1954 pollution convention, as Labor critics later argued it should have done by making use of its constitutional trade and commerce and external affairs powers.[27] The practice was rather to wait for appropriate legislation to pass in the states, a process not completed until 1962, following a flurry of state Acts in 1960-61. The Commonwealth's related *Pollution of the Sea by Oil Act* of 1960, with later amendments, became the foundation for federal measures during the 1960s. Other legislative instruments contained provisions relating to marine pollution, and each of the states during the 1950s and 1960s enacted legislation covering various aspects of the subject.[28]

The pace of events accelerated gradually from the late 1960s. Environmental groups pressured the federal authorities to deal more effectively with oil pollution threats (as well as hazards posed by tourist development, mining and fishing) to the Great Barrier Reef, threats to coastal wetlands, pollution issues in the Torres and Bass Straits, ocean dumping of toxic materials, and related issues of pollution from ship- and land-based sources. Amendments to the 1954 convention approved by IMCO in 1969, while Australia was itself a Council member, were a significant step forward; but they suffered, in the Australian view, from some crucial weaknesses. The amendments limited discharge of oil to waters more than 50 miles from the nearest land, at a prescribed rate (60 litres per mile). Within 50 miles, discharge would be permitted at the same rate, but only in a very dilute mixture (100 parts or less per million). Provisions were also made for discharges to take place as far from land as possible. Debate on the 1969 amendments compelled Australia to reconsider the adequacy of the protection accorded the Great Barrier Reef. The amendments implicitly permitted the discharge of oil near the Reef, since parts are more than 50 miles from land; discharges affecting the Reef could also presumably be made in the waters separating it from the Australian mainland. In 1971, at IMCO's seventh session, Australia succeeded in securing approval for a further amendment which had the effect — for purposes of the 1954 convention only — of making the Great Barrier Reef essentially a part of the Australian coastline.[29] In the interval between the 1969 and 1971 meetings, the *Oceanic Grandeur* incident underscored the urgency of Reef protection measures, and, as we have seen, reinforced Australia's policy in the preparatory work for UNCLOS III of seeking more effective pollution control powers for coastal states. The additional powers secured by the Commonwealth through amendment of the *Navigation Act* were then used in later incidents, such as when the *Cherry Venture* ran aground.[30]

Other developments of the early 1970s kept marine pollution in the news. Arsenic dumping off Western Australia by an oil refinery in 1970-71 was raised in Parliament. The government said it had no objection to the practice, provided that the state authorities agreed, and that it took place in a recognized manner outside the limits of the continental shelf.[31] Continuing threats from oil slicks were publicized by the government's critics. Tankers using the Torres Strait, it was claimed, were missing obstructions only by inches in their attempts to reduce sailing time. Whitlam, who made the issue a central one in ALP attacks on the government in the early 1970s, noted amongst other things the dumping of waste oil in sensitive areas by a Philippines ship. Shark was being taken out of fish shops in Victoria because of mercury pollution. Despite all this, Labor maintained, state governments were still holding back from passing legislation; those that had were negligent at enforcement, as low penalties and the ease of escaping detection meant that polluters were undeterred.[32] More particularly, Whitlam argued, the government was too slow in following up the opportunities presented by international conventions in the area to strengthen its hand against such threats. By September 1970, for example, Australia had become a party to a group of 1962 amendments to the 1954 convention, but was still in the process of considering becoming a party to the 1969 amendments and also to the two 1969 oil pollution conventions.[33]

UNCHE gave further imptetus to these developments. As a member of the marine pollution working group of the Preparatory Committee, Australia paid special attention to the draft convention on ocean dumping. This, Howson said, "should be settled at the earliest practicable opportunity."[34] The new federal-state Australian Environment Council also concentrated on marine pollution issues at its post-Stockholm meeting in July 1972. The ministers "attached particular importance to the adoption of actions and procedures to check on dumping in the oceans off Australia and the implementation of adequate controls to prevent environmental damage."[35] Its Standing Committee was directed to examine urgently the final draft of the ocean dumping convention then expected to be available in November. The AEC also established a Marine Pollution Subcommittee to look at such matters as the development of the National Plan to Combat Pollution of the Sea by Oil, problems of pollution of the seas by heavy metals, investigation of pollution incidents, and the creation of a national marine pollution monitoring network.[36] Even under Labor, though, events in the 1970s continued to move relatively slowly. This was due in part to the federal dimension, and in part to the number and complexity of the international instruments themselves. The two 1969 conventions were signed by Australia in late 1970; a bill relating to the 1969 amendments to the 1954 convention was introduced into Parliament in 1972, and Australia deposited an instrument of ratification of the amendments in 1973. In preparation during the early and middle 1970s were implementing laws relating to the 1971 Great Barrier Reef amendment, and to another 1971 amendment limiting the arrangement and size of oil tanks in ships. Ratification of the 1973 convention, and the protocol of the same year, was under consideration and being discussed with state governments.[37] The 1969 convention on intervention on the high seas became internationally enforceable in 1975, and the government stated that it intended to ratify it as soon as implementing legislation was passed.

If the Labor government had survived in office beyond 1975, it is possible that this series of developments would have been brought to a speedy conclusion. In part because of some progress in federal-state discussions, but rather more because of the Whitlam government's determined efforts to elevate the Commonwealth to a position as a truly national environmental policy-maker, a major legislative package was being prepared in 1975. It was incomplete at the time of the government's dismissal, but was designed amongst other things to provide implementing legislation for all the international marine pollution conventions and their amendments, and more generally to consolidate the Commonwealth's authority as the main level of government in Australia empowered to formulate marine pollution policy.[38]

The downfall of the government brought a return to the more cautious form of cooperative federalism practised by its predecessors. This process continued to unfold in an atmosphere of public and parliamentary criticism. The Commission of Inquiry into the Maritime Industry concluded in 1976 that, in general, Australian practices and standards were well up to world standards, but it noted Australia's "slowness in acceptance" of the IMCO conventions. It conceded, in response to government officials who had prepared this line of defence, that the questions were complicated and technical. Nevertheless, it felt that "Australian acceptance of the Conventions takes too long." The Commission recommended that the scope for early acceptance of international maritime conventions should be explored and clarified. It drew attention particularly to the problems associated with the government's practice of waiting until a convention was in force internationally before it could be accepted.[39] The Marine Oil Spills Sub-Committee of the House Standing Committee on Environment and Conservation held public hearings on this and related topics in 1977. It reported that not enough emphasis was being placed on methods of preventing oil spills, and proposed further improvements to the National Plan. More especially, it called on the government to "take immediate steps" to ratify the 1969 convention on civil liability for oil pollution damage and the 1971 international fund convention. The committee acknowledged, however, that Australia could only ratify a convention when it was in a position, legally and administratively, to enforce its provisions, which usually required passage of both state and Commonwealth legislation.[40] It could also involve the furnishing of special or additional facilities. Before the 1973 marine pollution convention could be ratified, for example, Australia had to provide shore facilities for the collection of oily waste.

A major oil spill off the Queensland coast in 1978, and evidence of a continuing lax attitude on the part of some state governments, threw these problems into sharp relief in the late 1970s and early 1980s.[41] The House of Representatives oil spills committee documented persistent problems of spills from shipping, offshore drilling rigs and shore-based facilities. Deliberate discharge of tank and bilge washings by ships was the greatest threat. Though prohibited by Commonwealth and state legislation, and covered by international conventions, discharges were both "numerous and constant" and at the same time difficult to detect.[42] This question overlapped more general debate on conservation of the Great Barrier Reef, particularly in the context of the creation of a marine national park and authority for the region. Critics pointed to threats from mining and oil exploration activity, delays in implementing legislation, compromises over the extension of the coverage of protected areas of the Reef, and obstruction by the Queensland authorities.[43]

The accumulated weight of this criticism, together with the greater importance being attached to coastal zone management problems,[44] progress in Commonwealth-state exchanges (including consensus on general approaches to treaty-making procedures), and, perhaps, the vulnerability of the Fraser government to the charge of indifference to the environment, finally led to the introduction of a series of legislative measures aimed at paving the way for Australian ratification of the main international agreements. The *Environment Protection (Sea Dumping) Act* was passed in 1981. It was not proclaimed, however, until March 1984.[45] The Act was designed primarily to institute measures that would lead to accession to the dumping convention. Also in 1981, the *Protection of the Sea (Discharge of Oil from Ships) Act* was passed; this replaced the 1960 Act, and also gave effect to the 1962 and 1969 amendments of Oilpol, the 1954 convention. Towards the end of the government's tenure of power in October 1982, two bills were introduced to give effect to the 1973 marine pollution convention (Marpol). This followed another wave of public concern that arose with the grounding of the *AnroAsia* off the Queensland coast earlier in 1982: critics had renewed their attacks

70

both on the inadequacy of protection measures, and on the cost (in this case more than $280,000) of mounting pollution control and clean-up operations.[46]

It fell to the new ALP administration in 1983 to take these steps through to their conclusion. One of its earliest measures was to introduce bills essentially the same as those of 1982 designed to give effect to Marpol. This was despite the fact that administrative and operational arrangements had still not been completed. Thus the government planned initially to implement only the compulsory parts of the 1973 convention, and to defer operation of Annex II for three years in order to ensure that adequate reception facilities for the discharge of tank washings and sludge were provided at Australian ports.[47] This kind of flexibility had been built into Marpol in a 1978 Protocol which reflected unease on the part of many countries about the obligations involved in the convention itself. Notification had already been sent to governments in late 1982 that this convention would enter into force in October 1983. In November 1983, Australia lodged a total of six instruments of accession with IMCO dealing with marine pollution and other agreements.

Australian activities in international marine pollution efforts were part of a wider scientific and technical effort that mostly went unnoticed. Membership of OECD, for example, brought Australia into discussions in that organization of marine pollution problems facing member-states. The work of IMCO, later redesignated the International Maritime Organization, and of UNESCO's Intergovernmental Oceanographic Commission (IOC), has been central to international collaborative efforts to monitor and control marine pollution. Australian representatives, for example, were active in the work of the Marine Environment Protection Committee established by IMCO in 1973 to coordinate and administer activities of the organization in relation to marine pollution from ships.[48] Australian environmental officials and scientific bodies also took an early interest in the work of the Committee for Global Investigation of Pollution in the Marine Environment (GIPME), a research and monitoring programme instituted by the IOC.[49]

The western industrialized nations and toxic chemicals

An estimated 85 per cent of Australians live in coastal zones, but questions of marine pollution were for many distant concerns. Urban pollution problems were nearer to home. Their consequences could be seen, felt and heard daily. In government the Senate took an early lead in responding to environmental hazards by establishing two influential committees to investigate air and water pollution. On joining the OECD in 1971, as we saw in an earlier chapter, Australia followed up a number of questions dealing with both subjects in various technical groups surrounding the Environment Committee. For Australia, the international character of such questions was largely missing. The general area did not centre, as did problems of marine pollution, on international regulatory activity, such as the making of rules binding on the activities of foreign ships. Nor did Australia have

71

to deal with the transboundary pollution problems facing Canada and other OECD countries. Rather, dealing with pollution inside modern, industrialized societies was viewed as a common concern of all member-states of the organization. Joint approaches could help the common good; individual countries could, if they wished, apply collectively derived or comparative lessons; and cooperation might have productive consequences for economies or for other policy areas.

The problems posed by the use of toxic chemicals in modern societies had been one of the preoccupations of UNCHE in 1972. It continued as an important area for data-gathering and education under UNEP. A variety of Australian institutions, official and non-governmental, federal and state, took part in the work of the IRPTC in the late 1970s and 1980s.[50] The work was regarded as valuable to the extent that it contributed to the building of the registry being developed at the same time by the Australian Environment Council on behalf of the Commonwealth and the states. During the second half of the 1970s, however, both state and federal officials began expressing greater interest in the way the OECD was handling chemicals policy questions; other state government concerns, particularly noise abatement policies and environmental economics, also pointed them in the direction of the OECD.[51]

The organization's activities in the field of toxic chemicals dovetailed neatly with Australia's requirements. During 1978 the AEC finalized its report on environmentally hazardous chemicals, drawing on the work of the National Advisory Committee on Chemicals (NACC), a body of federal and state experts established in 1977. The committee had been tasked more specifically with the development of a national action programme on dangerous chemicals. An important aspect of this work was the development of procedures for assessing the potential environmental effects of new chemicals. This task centred on the preparation and design of an interim notification and assessment scheme for new industrial chemicals. The AEC introduced the interim scheme in 1981.

This approach drew extensively on the work of various OECD bodies in the early 1980s.[52] The background to this activity lay in the OECD's Special Programme on the Control of Toxic Chemicals, and a number of high-level ministerial meetings on hazardous chemicals in which Australia took a close interest.[53] Attention to these developments went side by side with development and implementation of the Australian scheme. In its first year of operation, a total of 58 chemicals were formally notified according to the defined procedure; only two of these, however, were considered new to Australia, and were accordingly subjected to detailed investigation by Australian officials.[54] The scheme later adopted further OECD lessons. An important part of the OECD's work in the area in the early 1980s concerned problems of the mutual acceptance by member-state governments of chemicals testing data, and the establishment of minimum pre-marketing data to be incorporated into notification schemes for new chemicals, such as that introduced in Australia. Procedures were finally agreed at two ministerial meetings in Paris in 1982. The organization's minimum pre-marketing data guidelines were then incorporated directly into Australia's Interim Notification

Scheme.[55] Australian officials also took an active part in discussions leading to OECD consensus on various other aspects of the dissemination and exchange of data on new chemicals, and compliance with good laboratory practices in chemicals testing.[56]

Pollution as an international issue

Awareness of pollution as a threat to Australian interests, then, and of the fact that the problem had a significant international dimension, emerged largely as a result of the major oil spill incident of 1970. Parliamentary, and particularly Senate, attention to problems of air and water pollution in Australia in the early 1970s was an important contributing factor. In relation to the oceans, domestic legislative and regulatory change was coupled with active diplomacy inside IMCO forums. This led to the successful passage of the 1971 amendment allowing Australia in effect to protect the Great Barrier Reef even though large sections of it lay outside territorial waters. The event marked an important turning-point not only for Australia, but also for the developments of the 1970s which culminated in broader international acceptance of the principle of expanded coastal state powers. Australia was among the countries that adopted tough stands on this general issue during the UNCLOS III negotiations. As these negotiations continued, however, some of its initial drive was deflected. Australia felt compromises were necessary, in part because it feared the consequences of being labelled a supporter of "extremist" positions. Yet the importance attached to the construction of effective international legal frameworks for managing ocean affairs did not subside; Australia's continuing concerns were evident in the sharp criticism expressed of the Reagan administration's policy reversal on UNCLOS III and of Japanese ocean dumping practices in the 1980s. Although concern for the marine environment formed only one part of Australia's interest in the oceans, several others, such as foreign fishing in Australian waters, and Australia's own stake in international shipping, had direct implications for environmental issues.

On questions of urban pollution, by contrast, Australian governments tended to follow rather than lead other western countries. At least in the early 1970s, many in Australia tended to regard these matters as for the industrialized heartlands of Western Europe and North America. Australia was none the less drawn into international discussions of pollution by virtue of its membership of the OECD Environment Committee, a factor reinforced by the high priority the federal government attached to the organization. Later in the decade and during the 1980s, more practical use was made of OECD activities in the area of toxic chemicals, particularly in connection with regulatory questions concerning the registration and assessment of potentially hazardous compounds. These issues were central to the environmental policy agendas of many western governments at the time, and Australia was quick to adapt lessons learned in OECD forums and transfer the results into domestic administrative practices. Side by side with these developments, the degree and intensity of public and group interest in pollution

73

grew substantially in the decade from the early 1970s to the early 1980s. This did not mean that Australian activities in the OECD were regularly and closely followed by an attentive public. When official participation in international meetings had to be defended within government, however, especially in an atmosphere of budgetary restraint, the existence of a domestic anti-pollution constituency was a useful asset for environmental bureaucracies.

Notes for Chapter 4

1 David Butler, *The Canberra Model: Essays on Australian Government* (London: Macmillan, 1973), p. 16.

2 *UNGA. Report of the UNCHE held at Stockholm, 5-16 June 1972* (Doc. A/CONF. 48/14, 3 July 1972), pp. 45-49.

3 "Current Developments in the Law of the Sea, " *CNIA*, 42(3), March 1971, pp. 111-2; "Law of the Sea," *CNIA*, 42(8), August 1971, p. 418.

4 *Senate*, 47, 1 April 1971, pp. 706-7.

5 See for example *3rd UNCLOS. 2nd Sess. Report of Australian Delegation* (Canberra, 1974; PP 164), Annex F, p. 44.

6 R.M. McGonigle and M.W. Zacher, *Pollution, Politics and International Law* (Vancouver: University of British Columbia Press, 1979), p. 371.

7 *UNGA. 26th Sess. of the Gen. Ass. of the UN, New York, 21 September to 22 December 1971. Report of the Australian Delegation* (Canberra, 1972; PP 54), para. 88, p. 8; see also *UNGA 28th Sess. of the UN, New York, 18 September to 18 December 1973. Report of the Australian Delegation* (Canberra, 1975; PP 25), para. 60, p. 9; *UNGA. 27th Sess. of the Gen. Ass. of the UN, New York 19 September - 19 December 1972. Report of the Australian Delegation* (Canberra, 1973, PP 26), para. 81-3, p. 16. On the importance to Australia of the work of the three subcommittees of the Preparatory Committee, and the main sections of the agenda of the 1973 conference, see "Current Developments in the Law of the Sea," *CNIA*, 42(3), March 1971, pp. 111-2.

8 Statement of 29 July 1971 to subcommittee III of the Preparatory Committee, quoted at "Law of the Sea," *CNIA*, 42(8), August 1971, pp. 417-20.

9 Statement by Senator Willessee, Minister of Foreign Affairs, at Caracas, 2 July, quoted at *AFAR*, 45(7), July 1974, pp. 481-2; see also *3rd UNCLOS. 2nd Sess. ...*, Annex A. p. 31.

10 "Preventing a Scramble for the Seas," *AFAR*, 44(10), October 1973, p. 654.

11 *3rd UNCLOS. 2nd Sess. ...*, para. 126-30, pp. 25-6. In general on this session see the reports at *AFAR*, 45(7), July 1974, pp. 464-82; "The Law of the Sea Conference in Caracas", *AFAR*, 45(10), October 1974, pp. 686-9; and DEC, *Report for Period December 1972 to June 1974* (Canberra, 1975; PP 298), p. 51.

12 *3rd UNCLOS. 2nd Sess. ...*, Annex A, p. 31.

13 Statement by Mr. J. Petherbridge, in *3rd UNCLOS. 2nd Sess....*, Annex F, p. 44. Cf. Australia's position at the 4th session: "It is important for Australia that these rights should not result in unreasonable interference with international shipping upon which Australian overseas trade depends," *3rd UNCLOS. 4th Sess. Report of Australian Delegation* (Canberra, 1976; PP 211), para. 114, p. 46.

14 Petherbridge, *3rd UNCLOS. 2nd Sess. ...*, Annex F, p. 43; also para. 131-2, p. 26.

15 *3rd UNCLOS. 5th Sess. Report of Australian Delegation* (Canberra, 1977; PP 65), p. 27. For the background of Australian statements and policy on UNCLOS III, including views of the EEZ concept in 1975-77, see the report of the parliamentary Joint Committee on Foreign Affairs and Defence, *Australia, Antarctica and the Law of the Sea. Interim Report. 1978* (Canberra, 1978; PP 198), ch. 1, 2.

16 *3rd UNCLOS. 4th Sess. ...*, para. 115, p. 47.

17 *Ibid.*, para. 111, p. 45.

18 *Ibid.*, para. 112, p. 46. See also the Minister of Foreign Affairs (Peacock) on the 200-mile zone, at *House of Representatives* 101, 19 October 1976, p. 1940.

19 *3rd UNCLOS, 5th Sess. ...*, p. 28.

20 *Ibid.*, and Annex J.

21 *Ibid.*, p. 29, and Annex H. On Australia's position in favour of the existing language of this article, see *3rd UNCLOS. 6th Sess. Report of Australian Delegation* (Canberra, 1978; PP 98), p. 60. On the 1977 meetings generally see "The UN Conference on the Law of the Sea," *AFAR*, 48(9), September 1977, pp. 448-51.

22 *3rd UNCLOS. Resumed 7th Sess., New York, 21 August - 15 September 1978. Report of the Australian Delegation* (Canberra, 1979; PP 360), p. 54. The results of the 1978 meetings were "broadly consistent with the objectives Australia had sought to achieve, but much work remains to be done." (DFA, *Annual Report 1978* [Canberra, 1979; PP 112], p. 7). See also the statement by Peacock, *House of Representatives*, 109, 9 May 1978, p. 2035; and DSE, *Annual Report 1978-9* (Canberra, 1979; PP 349), p. 10.

23 *3rd UNCLOS. Resumed 7th Sess. ...* pp. 55-7; *3rd UNCLOS. 8th Sess., Geneva, 19 March - 27 April 1979. Report of the Australian Delegation* (Canberra, 1980; PP 276), Pt. I, p. 35; Peacock, *House of Representatives*, 114, 8 May 1979, p. 1901; *UNCLOS. 9th Sess. New York, 3 March - 4 April 1980. Report of the Australian Delegation* (Canberra; 1980; PP 116), p. 22; DFA, *Annual Report 1980* (Canberra, 1981; PP 120), p. 34.

24 *House of Representatives* 123, 2 June 1981, pp. 2946-7; and in general the statement by the Minister of Foreign Affairs (Street), *House of Representatives*, 123, 26 May 1981, p. 2534 ff.

25 *3rd UNCLOS. 11th Sess. New York, 9 March to 30 April 1982. Report of the Australian Delegation* (Canberra, 1983; PP 44), vol. 1, p. 19.

26 Statement of 18 November 1982, *AFAR*, 53(11), November 1982, p. 743; see also DFA, *Annual Report 1982* (Canberra, 1983; PP 140), p. 35.

27 See remarks by Snedden, *House of Representatives*, 81, 25 October 1972, p. 3208.

28 For summaries see *Australian Maritime Legislation. Commission of Inquiry into the Maritime Industry. Report June 1976* (Canberra, 1977; PP 315), p. 214; and UNEP, *National Reports on Activities in the Priority Subject Areas Oceans and Conservation of Nature, Wildlife and Genetic Resources* (UNEP/PROG/5, 1976), report by Australia on marine pollution at pp. 8-9. In addition to the *Pollution of the Sea by Oil Act* and amendments, other relevant Commonwealth legislation was the *Beaches, Fishing Grounds and Sea Routes Protection Act* (1932 and later amendments), the *Navigation Act* (1932 and later amendments), the *Navigation Act* (1912 and later amendments), and the *Petroleum (Submerged Lands) Act* (1967).

29 Nixon, *House of Representatives*, 81, 24 October 1972, p. 3085; and 81, 25 October 1972, p. 3216.

30 *Australia and New Zealand Environmental Report* 10-75, p. 160 (statement by Mr. Jones, Minister of Transport).

31 *House of Representatives*, 72, 6-7 May 1971, p. 2858.

32 For example Everingham, *House of Representatives*, 78, 31 May 1972, p. 3402; Whitlam, *ibid.*, 80, 12 September 1972, p. 1122; Snedden, *ibid.*, 81, 25 October 1972, p. 3210.

33 *House of Representatives*, 68, 12 June 1970, pp. 3595-3612; and 69, 18 September 1970, pp. 1410-1. Several states also had their own legislation with respect to the 1962 amendments.

34 *UNCHE. Stockholm, June 1972. Summary Report of Australian Delegation* (Canberra, 1973; PP 143), App. 1, p. 15; and "UN Conference on the Human Environment," *CNIA*, 43(6), June 1972, p. 303.

35 Howson, *House of Representatives*, 79, 17 August 1972, p. 455.

36 DEC, *Report for Period December 1972 to June 1974* (Canberra, 1975; PP 198), p. 25. The AEC and the Australian Fisheries Council later formed a Joint Technical Working Group on Marine Pollution with the aim of strengthening monitoring capabilities (DEHCD, *2nd Annual Report 1977* [Canberra, 1978; PP 308], p. 24).

[37] *International Maritime Conventions. Commission of Inquiry into the Maritime Industry. Report, June 1972* (Canberra, 1977; PP 316), Part II, and pp. 25-36. On state legislation see also Peacock, *House of Representatives*, 109, 9 May 1978, p. 2093; and *Australia and New Zealand Environmental Report*, 10-75, p. 160.

[38] Henry Burmester, "Australia and the Law of the Sea — The Protection and Preservation of the Marine Environment," in K.W. Ryan, ed., *International Law in Australia*, 2nd ed. (Sydney: Law Book Co., 1984), p. 440; P. Brazil, "The Protection of the Marine Environment: Restraints on Environmental Harm" in Attorney-General's Department, *Environmental Law: The Australian Government's Role* (Canberra, 1975), pp. 40-41.

[39] *International Maritime Conventions*, para. 7-10, pp. 2-3.

[40] House of Representatives, Standing Committee on Environment and Conservation, *5th Report* (Canberra, 1978; PP 270), para. 5, p. 1; House of Representatives, Standing Committee on Environment and Conservation, *Oil Spills. Prevention and Control of Oil Pollution in the Marine Environment. September 1978* (Canberra, 1978, PP 292), pp. xi-xvii, 64, 168.

[41] *House of Representatives*, 108, 16 March 1978, pp. 803-4, and 114, 8 May 1979, p. 1960; *Commonwealth Record*, 4(18), 7-13 May 1979, p. 599.

[42] See the summary of the report introduced by Mr. Hodges, at *House of Representatives*, 111, 26 October 1978, pp. 2365-68.

[43] For example, "Coral, Politics and Oil," *National Times*, 515, December 14-20, 1980, pp. 10-14.

[44] See the summary of the report of the environment and conservation committee on the coastal zone (Hodges) at *House of Representatives* 118, 13 May 1980, pp. 2611-3.

[45] This also was designed to give effect to amendments of 1978 and 1980 to the convention, and followed state legislation. See Thomson, *House of Representatives* at 122, 14 May 1981, pp. 2442-3, and the second reading debate at 123, 2 June 1981, pp. 2943-50. On the entry into force see *AEC Newsl.*, 4(1-2), August 1984.

[46] Hunt, *House of Representatives*, 128, 18 August 1982, p. 609. Expert projections of oil spills in the early 1980s indicated a small upward trend: *Marine Oil Spill Risk in Australia*, Bureau of Transport Economics (Canberra, 1983; PP 255), pp. 32-36.

[47] *House of Representatives*, 131, 15 May 1983, pp. 939-41; and 26 May 1983, pp. 1088-91; and *Weekly Hansard*, No. 13, 1983, November 8, 1983, p. 2370.

[48] DOE, *Report for Period July 1974 to June 1975* (Canberra, 1976; PP 139), p. 23.

[49] For example, DEC, *Report for Period December 1972 to June 1974* (Canberra, 1975; PP 298), p. 26.

[50] See above Chapter 3.

[51] DHAE, *Annual Report 1981-82* (Canberra, 1982; PP 35), pp. 23-4.

[52] *AEC Newsl.*, 1(2), December 1981, pp. 1-3. On the background see DHAE, *Annual Report 1981-82* (Canberra, 1982; PP 263), p. 2.

[53] DSE, *Annual Report 1978-79* (Canberra, 1979; PP 349), p. 69; DSE, *Annual Report 1979-80* (Canberra, 1980; PP 357), p. 66; DHAE, *Annual Report 1980-81* (Canberra, 1982; PP 35), p. 13.

[54] *AEC Newsl.*, 2(4), December 1982, p. 3.

[55] *Ibid.*, pp. 3-4.

[56] *Ibid.*, and DHAE, *Annual Report 1982-83* (Canberra, 1983; PP 345), pp. 6-7.

CHAPTER FIVE

Australia, Antarctica and the Southern Ocean

Australia's participation in the environmental regime of Antarctica and its surrounding waters is both an end in itself, and also a means of attaining broader foreign policy goals. The issues themselves are intrinsically significant from both a regional and a global ecological perspective; and Australia's territorial claim to sovereignty over a large area of the continent, temporarily shelved under the terms of the 1959 Antarctica Treaty, gives the federal government a continuing and powerful vested interest in carrying out the scientific, environmental and other activities required by the treaty of all good Antarctic citizens. Never far from the surface of Antarctic policy, in other words, are fundamental national security concerns. As R.G. Casey put it in 1953, "Can we contemplate some other country getting in ahead of us on this great land mass so close to our south?"[1]

Australia has thus maintained a close interest in Antarctic developments: the treaty itself and the meetings of its parties, the Agreed Measures on environmental conservation of 1964, and the Antarctic Marine Living Resources Convention (CAMLR) of 1980. By providing headquarters facilities for the last, moreover, Australia achieved the distinction of hosting for the first time an international organization on Australian soil. Antarctic issues have been the subject of vigorous debate in Australia, particularly from the mid-1970s. The federal government has at various times come under fire from scientists and others who have argued that insufficient resources, whether financial or administrative, were being provided for research, and from some environmentalists who have taken the view that the continent should be placed under some form of permanent, collective international control, perhaps by way of the "common heritage of mankind" notions that inspired much of the drive for UNCLOS III. Behind these debates lie assessments of the economic stakes in the region. Visions of future bounty from krill in the 1970s, or of wealth from minerals exploitation in the 1980s, have focussed Australian and international attention on Antarctic and Southern Ocean resources, and also on the complex political and legal factors that govern the conduct of its affairs.

Sovereignty and policy in Antarctica

In a sense, Australia has a dual stake in Antarctica: maintenance of its claim to sovereignty over Australian Antarctic Territory (AAT), and at the same time the consolidation of its support, as a key player, for the principles and provisions

77

of the Antarctica Treaty. The two are closely related and, some critics have suggested, mutually inconsistent. The 1959 treaty is the cornerstone of Australian policies. It has been argued that the treaty supports the region's demilitarized status and thus contributes to world peace; it furthers Australia's security interests; helps to preserve the position of states which, like Australia, claim sovereignty over areas of Antarctica; encourages useful scientific research and international collaboration; supports environmental protection measures in an area which ecologically, through weather patterns and ocean currents, has a direct bearing on the Australian environment; and, finally, it constitutes a forum in which Australia can exercise international influence.[2] Peace and security have continued to rank high in official rationales for Australian support of the treaty system. Bill Hayden, Labor foreign minister in the mid-1980s, noted the "enormous importance" of the treaty as a means of preserving Antarctica from the political and military tensions that had beset the world in the past quarter-century. Further, from a strategic perspective, it was "important to remember that Antarctica dominates Australia's southern approaches."[3] The theme of sovereignty permeates all government commentary. As one account put it in 1977, Australia "has a special interest in ensuring that in the development of regimes for Antarctic resources, whether for mineral or marine living resources, nothing is done which would prejudice the exercise of our sovereignty there."[4]

The claim has a respectable pedigree. Australians were active in the early expeditions led by Sir Douglas Mawson in 1911-14 and the British, Australian and New Zealand Antarctic Expedition of 1929-31. Claims to Antarctic territory were made by the Crown in 1926; London later transferred the relevant areas to Australia (and to New Zealand), and the transfer was confirmed by the *Australian Antarctic Territory Acceptance Act* of 1933.[5] Though in the Australian view its claim was valid in international law, two other considerations have also been clear: first, that use of and continuing activity in the area would reinforce the claim should it ever be tested; and, second, that in the final analysis the claim was probably unenforceable. Organizational and administrative support for scientific activities was consolidated with the establishment in 1947 of the Antarctic Division in the Department of External Affairs (and later in the federal science department). The Division had the task of coordinating and supporting activities of the Australian National Antarctic Research Expedition (ANARE). The first Australian station (Mawson) was set up in 1954, and was later joined by others at Davis and Casey and on Macquarie Island. Yet Australians have also been conscious of their relative weakness compared to some members of the treaty framework. Sovereignty over AAT might be sound in international law, a senior Antarctic official said in 1985, "but no doubt some superpower could steamroller us."[6] The treaty itself neither helps nor hinders the claim. According to Article 4, nothing in the treaty could be interpreted as a renunciation, denial or support of any claim to sovereignty so long as the treaty was in force.

Environmental protection has been central to the work of the treaty partners since the early 1960s, as has scientific research of a kind that could ultimately lead to a strengthening of conservation measures. Both aspects are connected with Australia's claims to sovereignty. As one minister defined the connection in 1980, "As a consequence of Australian sovereignty over the Australian Antarctic Territory, we have a special responsibility to ensure that the Antarctic environment remains protected from any adverse effects of human occupation."[7] One of several Australian reports on Antarctica in the 1970s described Australian policy as being aimed at the maintenance of sovereignty over AAT, a strengthening of the treaty framework, and the maintenance of a balanced scientific programme. The last was important "as a contribution to world science and in support of Australian sovereignty and the Antarctic Treaty system." In sum, "the maintenance of Australia's sovereignty over the AAT and its standing in the Antarctic Treaty will be influenced by the extent of scientific and exploration activity in which it engages and by the scope and quality of its contribution to scientific knowledge concerning Antarctica."[8] In a sense, then, and in contrast to the policy issues posed by other international environmental institutions and agreements, Australia has not seen itself as having real choice about whether or not to participate in Antarctic and Southern Ocean regimes. It has been driven along this path by prior definitions of the importance of the region and the requirements of maintaining its territorial claims.

More areas of choice have emerged, however, as far as the degree and kind of Australia's activities are concerned. Debates have revolved around the overall Australian research effort, the amount of funding from the Commonwealth, the quality of leadership and organizational skills provided by government, the links between Antarctic science in Australia and the formulation of policy, and the organization of the networks of national and international scientific activities dealing with Antarctic matters. In 1974, in response to a rising tide of scientific controversy since the mid-1960s, the Commonwealth set up an Advisory Committee on Antarctic Programmes (ACAP) under Sir Frederick White. The Committee reported quickly, and emphasized the urgent need for greater research efforts. Antarctic policy was then the subject of a discussion paper issued by the federal Minister for Science in 1975. The paper prompted a large number of submissions and proposals, and seminars, in subsequent months. An extensive review of existing programmes was undertaken in 1978; and Prime Minister Fraser announced in 1979 the establishment of an Antarctic Research Policy Advisory Committee (ARPAC), chaired by Professor D.E. Caro of the University of Tasmania. Its report, later in 1979, stimulated a fresh round of debate on weaknesses in Australia's research efforts. Later reports of ARPAC, particularly one submitted in 1982, kept Antarctic issues to the forefront of government and public attention, and contributed to the commitments to research and reorganization made by the Labor government in the mid-1980s.[9]

Environmental conservation occupied an increasingly important place in this series of exchanges. ARPAC's terms of reference were, among other things, to advise the government on scientific and technological research related to the area's resources, "with an emphasis on increasing Australia's knowledge and expertise of both mineral and living marine resources and the possible environmental effects of resource exploitation." Its initial report stated that among the aims of Australian Antarctic policy was to "provide adequate protection for the Antarctic environment having regard both to its intrinsic values and its possible effect on our own region."[10] As examples of the importance of environmental considerations it pointed to the relation of the ice sheet to global atmospheric and oceanic circulations, the contribution of research data to understanding global weather patterns, the extensive marine living resources of the region, including whales, seals, krill, squid and fish, and to the fact that the area's freedom from pollution made it a reference point for comparison for global levels. In later reports ARPAC continued to express concern about inadequate resources, and emphasized the particular requirements for research on the Antarctic's living and mineral resources and the environmental effects of their exploitation.[11] In addition to expanding interest in minerals and krill, other activities have prompted environmentalist concern: continuing environmental problems relating to the operating procedures of expeditions, the transport to Antarctica of pollutants such as pesticides, plans for increased tourism and transportation, and the implications of depletion of the earth's ozone layer over Antarctica.

Part of Australian policy has been devoted to warding off international actions that might threaten its sovereignty claim. This has meant responding to complaints, particularly from developing countries, of the alleged exclusivity and rigidity of the treaty system.[12] In the early 1980s, Australia successfully blocked efforts by Group of 77 states in the UN, in support of a Malaysian initiative, aimed at giving the UN a greater role in Antarctic affairs on the grounds that it should be considered part of the common heritage of mankind. The ambassador, Sir Richard Woolcott, said in 1985 that the most important reason why such a notion was not applicable to Antarctica was the existence of long-standing territorial claims there. The claims were a fact, even if they were not recognized; and "to reopen this question will only provoke an unnecessary renewal of tensions which have been successfully avoided for the past twenty-five years."[13] Australian scientists were also resistant to the idea. Dr. Phillip Law, then the elder statesman of Antarctic research in Australia, commented that UN control was "so impractical because you'd have some 150 countries, most of them with not a clue about the Antarctic, and some with horrible records of lack of conservation, fighting it out."[14] Similarly, it was a concern of some critics in Parliament on Law of the Sea developments in the 1970s that a convention that institutionalized common heritage principles would lead to policies requiring a wider sharing of the resources of Antarctica with developing countries.[15]

The Australian Labor Party was divided on a number of questions of Antarctic policy in the late 1970s. Advocates of sovereignty claims and the existing treaty system on the one side, and proponents of common heritage alternatives on the other, compelled the party to adopt complicated compromise positions. It none the less entered the 1983 general election with promises of greatly increased support for Antarctic research, taking its cue from the controversial ARPAC report of 1982 which focussed criticism on the inadequacies of transportation links between Australia and its three AAT stations.[16] After the election, budgetary restraints and other priorities drove the Antarctic further out of public and government attention — as Antarctic officials and scientists tended to complain, "penguins don't vote" — and one of Australia's bases, Davis, was put on a lower level of operating activity. However, awareness of the closeness of the Antarctica treaty review due by 1991 was among the factors which led to expanded funding in 1984-86. "There has been a lull in our Antarctic research effort since the late 1970s," the minister said, "while other nations have moved to expand significantly their programmes."[17] Meanwhile, during this period environmental groups were publicizing the merits of the Antarctic becoming an internationally controlled conservation area modelled on national parks.[18] This — the New Zealand option — reinvigorated public debates later in the 1980s, with the result that traditional pro-treaty (and sovereignty) arguments were increasingly forced to compete with both resource-oriented world heritage ideas and more environmentally sensitive world park concepts.

Australian policies within the treaty framework have not for the most part been grounded in actively pursued economic interests, such as might have arisen if there had been a flourishing commercial fishery, but this has not prevented Australia from aiming for practical recognition of its role as a leading Antarctic nation. We will look first at the environmental provisions of the treaty system, and then at the management of the marine living resources of the Southern Ocean.

Environmental protection under the Antarctica Treaty

In relation to the Antarctica regime, the term environment has had a range of operational meanings. Provisions agreed on within the treaty framework have included steps for the conservation of threatened species, scientifically interesting areas, or areas of distinctive ecological diversity; and regulation of human activities, centring on the management of research stations and expeditions, and the design of regimes relating to living resource or minerals exploitation.

The Agreed Measures for the Conservation of Antarctic Fauna and Flora, finalized at the third Antarctic parties' meeting in Brussels in 1964, were for many years the centrepiece of conservation efforts. Essentially a straightforward nature conservation framework, the measures were later thought by some observers to be inadequate for coping with the environmental stresses of the late twentieth century. Article VI deals with the protection of fauna, special protection being extended to species listed in an Annex. The article prohibits the killing, wounding or capturing of any native mammal or bird. Whales were excepted on the grounds that these species were subject to the provisions of the International Whaling Convention. Governments can issue permits for scientific purposes, and criteria for the taking of animals or birds are defined for such cases. An Annex lists a number of Specially Protected Species, including various species of fur seals. Under Article VII, governments agree to take appropriate measures to minimize harmful interference with the normal living conditions of native mammals and birds, and to alleviate pollution of coastal waters; some otherwise prohibited activities are allowed where required for the maintenance of stations. Specially Protected Areas (SPAs) can be designated under Article VIII of the Agreed Measures. Such areas are defined as requiring special protection to preserve unique natural ecological systems or those of outstanding scientific interest. Human activity in such areas is strictly regulated, vehicles, for example, being forbidden. Under Article XI regulations apply also to the introduction of non-indigenous species.[19] Revisions have been made at various times since 1964. In 1972, at the seventh meeting of the parties, provisions were also made for the designation of Sites of Special Scientific Interest to be accorded a less stringent degree of protection than SPAs in order to facilitate scientific research. Meetings have also explored the implications for the Agreed Measures system of growing or potential threats to the Antarctic environment, such as those posed by tourism.[20]

Australian officials were enthusiastically present at the creation of the Agreed Measures, and have been active participants in the process of periodic revision. A number of opportunities have been taken to press particular Australian concerns. These have included problems in relation to tourist development on the continent and its neighbouring islands, the management of research stations and personnel, disposal of waste, and damage caused by feral animals, as well as the listing of sites or species according to the procedures set down in the Agreed Measures. At the eighth meeting of the Antarctic treaty states in Oslo in 1975, the Australian delegation argued vigorously, and successfully, for a ban on the disposal of nuclear waste in Antarctica.[21] This particular meeting, a landmark one in the evolution of environmental protection in the Antarctic treaty system, reached agreement on a total of fourteen recommendations. Three of these went a long way towards meeting Australian concerns in relation to expeditions, nuclear waste, and the creation of a set of general guidelines for the protection of the environment.

Although Australia in practice complied with the provisions of the Agreed Measures, it did not formally ratify them for many years. Australia's apparently lukewarm attitude cropped up increasingly during the course of the domestic debates and reviews of the 1970s. The Committee of Inquiry into the National Estate included as its only recommendation on the AAT the view that the government should incorporate the Agreed Measures into legislation as soon as possible. "The time will come when people may seek to exploit the area's resources; when that time comes any mining or other development that takes place must be done with minimum impact on the environment."[22] Australia's position was, however, more complicated than for its other international environmental agreements. Within the wider Antarctic treaty framework, Australia had not relinquished claims to sovereignty over part of this area; and particular Commonwealth measures were designed to give effect to this sovereignty — the *National Parks and Wildlife Conservation Act* of 1975, for example, extended "to every external Territory."[23] Preparation of Australian legislation took many years. Implementation of the 1964 agreements and subsequent revisions was carried out by means of administrative action taken by the federal environment department.[24] The position was finally settled in 1980 with passage of the *Antarctic Treaty (Environment Protection) Act.* This was designed to give effect to the Agreed Measures, and more generally "to provide for the protection of Antarctic wildlife and for the preservation of areas of outstanding ecological and scientific importance in the Antarctic."[25]

The Agreed Measures were a product of scientific debate in the early 1960s. Despite later revisions, they have provoked a variety of criticisms from scientific and environmental groups in Australia. They argued the magnitude of the threats to the Antarctic environment, particularly possible future mining operations, was such that this framework of environmental protection was likely to be increasingly unequal to the task. Thus in the view of the Labor opposition in the Senate, the 1980 bill did "little to provide for environment protection" in Antarctica.[26] Protection of sites and species, and rules about the management of research stations, were fine, but future economic activities on the continent had to be set in a stronger framework of environmental regulation, for example through the use of environmental impact assessments.

Periodically complaints have arisen that governments have ignored the protection mechanisms. A senior environment official of the Antarctic Division, in a 1984 submission to a Senate committee, referred to the behaviour of members of expeditions and specific problems such as waste disposal and the blowing of cement dust. There had been several "small but significant" environmental disasters. "I submit that the Commonwealth has demonstrated significant insensitivity and lack of responsibility in its regard for environmental protection in connection with its activities in Antarctica."[27] The actions of other treaty nations were also causes for unease. French plans in the mid-1980s to construct an airstrip at the Dumont d'Urville base sparked fears that this would destroy an Adelie penguin rookery in the locality and threaten a nearby Emperor penguin rookery. The Australian government expressed concern through its embassy in Paris, and indicated its view that there was evidence of a breach of the Agreed Measures. As foreign minister, however, Hayden refused to give in to environmentalists' demands that the French supply ship *Polarbjorn* be prevented from docking in Australia.[28]

The Commonwealth has remained a staunch defender of the Agreed Measures as the basis of a sound environmental management system in Antarctica. They had set up, the minister said in 1980, "a system of wildlife protection which is one of the most stringent, internationally agreed conservation measures anywhere in the world."[29] Aspects of Australia's domestic legislation, moreover, such as the *Environment Protection (Impact of Proposals) Act* and the *National Parks and Wildlife Conservation Act* of the mid-1970s, had applicability in the AAT. Thus the environment department told a joint parliamentary committee on the Antarctic and the Law of the Sea in 1978 that, as far as it was concerned, the existing treaty arrangements and the application of domestic environmental legislation provided "a satisfactory framework for protection of the Antarctic environment."[30] This show of confidence was based in part also on the incorporation of principles of environmental protection in approaches to a future minerals regime. A moratorium on minerals activity was effected by the parties from 1977. Risks to the environment were the paramount reason for the step. In the pause for reflection that this allowed, research on the environmental implications of such a regime expanded during the late 1970s and 1980s. Meeting in Wellington in 1982, the Antarctic nations reaffirmed their belief "that protection of the unique Antarctic environment and its dependent ecosystems should be a basic consideration" in any minerals regime,[31] and this was a feature of the framework eventually agreed to by the parties in 1988.

The conservation of marine living resources

In the history of Antarctic environmental conservation, attention to the oceans had tended to lag behind other developments. This is despite the fact that the area covered by the 1959 treaty, south of latitude 60° South, includes important coastal waters of Antarctica. Attention to the Southern Ocean was encouraged in the 1970s by several factors. The Law of the Sea negotiations, and particularly the spread and legitimization of 200-mile economic zones around many coastal states, clearly had implications for Antarctica in light of the territorial claims of some countries, including Australia. During the 1970s, the living marine resources of the area could no longer escape notice by governments. This meant particularly krill, in which Soviet and East European states had a rapidly growing interest, but other species, such as the crabeater seal, were thought in Australia to be likely candidates for economic exploitation in the future. The related international negotiations on whales and whaling in the 1970s also had major implications for the Antarctic treaty nations since they formed part of the spreading international regulation of Antarctica waters.

This growth of oceans interest confronted two significant gaps. First, the Antarctic treaty itself, and the Agreed Measures, were terrestrially focussed instruments. The aim of the treaty was to promote continued demilitarization of the Antarctic while encouraging international scientific cooperation, on the model of the International Geophysical year (IGY) of 1958, within a broader framework in which the consulting parties could address a variety of policy matters. Fishing, whaling and related oceanic activities, were largely outside its scope. Australian environmental critics began to seize on the significant limitations of the Agreed Measures in the 1970s. Filling some of these gaps, for example through the Antarctic seals convention of 1972, and more importantly the Antarctic marine living resources convention of 1980, occupied much Australian scientific and official attention during the 1970s. Quieter in its impact, but nevertheless important, was the 1972 decision that marine SPAs could be designated under the Agreed Measures system.

A second problem concerned marine science, particularly marine biology. The general deficiencies of several of the Antarctic states on this score were particularly felt in the case of Australia. Since such knowledge and research capabilities were viewed increasingly as crucial to Australia's future leadership role in key Antarctic issues, these weaknesses came to be a central target of scientific and government discussions. Triggered primarily by oil spill problems off Australia's coasts, complaints of lack of sustained attention to the requirements of marine science figured prominently in reports of the 1970s.[32] Australia's main Antarctic research areas at this time were meteorology, terrestrial biology, marine biology, glaciology, cosmic ray physics, upper atmosphere physics, geology and geophysics, surveying and mapping, and medical research. By the end of the 1970s, very little in practice was still being done in marine scientific studies, apart from preliminary research on krill and a number of high marine organisms. In 1977 the government approved the extension of the Antarctic Division's activities into offshore areas of Antarctica, after which it undertook significant programmes in marine biology and oceanography. Marine research generally was singled out in the work of the Caro committee in the late 1970s and early 1980s as one of the most important of the neglected Antarctic research areas.[33] Pressure to augment Australian capabilities mounted as policy issues surrounding the planned Antarctic marine living resources convention absorbed more of the time of the Antarctic parties.

The convention-making process began with the 1972 convention on seals. Australian interests were not directly affected by the convention as no commercial sealing was undertaken in Antarctica (though there was sporadic debate on crabeater seal prospects[34]). As with other international resource and environmental conventions in which Australia was interested in the early 1970s, it did not ratify the convention for some time. The convention did appear, though, as a Schedule to the *Australian National Parks and Wildlife Act* of 1975. In the early 1980s the Commonwealth authorities were preparing draft regulations that would eventually allow for ratification of the 1972 convention once their consistency with other measures, particularly the *Antarctic Treaty (Environment Protection) Act* of 1980 (designed to give effect to the Agreed Measures system), and the marine living resources convention bill, was assured.[35]

Following scientific discussion in the early 1970s, the Antarctic parties turned to a wide range of environmental policy matters at the 1975 Oslo meetings. Australian officials approached these meetings with a view to encouraging and accelerating moves towards the eventual construction of a living resources regime. Out of Oslo came an enquiry into conservation questions involved in tapping these resources.[36] Australia made clear, in 1975-77, its readiness to take a leading role in defining the proposed regime. The first important phase came with the ninth meeting of the parties in London in 1977. The Australian delegation drew particular attention to the risks presented by any future free-for-all scramble for Antarctic marine resources, including both krill and fin-fish. As Andrew Peacock, the foreign minister, said in September 1977, "The most urgent issue at the present time is the danger of uncontrolled exploitation of the Antarctic's marine living resources."[37] According to official US environmental impact assessments in 1977-78, krill was likely to be the most heavily exploited resource, which in turn meant the recovery rate for protected baleen whale species might be slowed.[38] Echoing the evolving US argument, the Australian delegation at the 1977 meetings argued that a convention would have to be based on wider ecological principles than more traditional single-species, or species groups, agreements such as those dealing with whales, seals or fish, because of the importance of krill within the broader Antarctic ecological balance. It was evident, however, that crucial disagreements on the detailed provisions of such a convention would flow from the wide range of fishing and environmental interests represented among the Antarctic parties. As a party not directly involved in economic activities, Australia increasingly took the ecological high ground. The delegation submitted its own version of a draft convention in London, and complementary and competing proposals were made by some other states, but lack of time prevented a full discussion.[39]

Time was not the only factor. Many states were just not ready to commence detailed investigations of possible texts. But the ninth meeting set the groundwork for a session devoted exclusively to this question. Australia, moreover, succeeded in London in establishing its credentials as a state acceptable to both fishing and non-fishing interests. The Second Special Antarctic Treaty Consultative Meeting on Antarctic Marine Living Resources was held in Canberra in February-March 1978. Following the proliferation of alternative conceptions of key parts of a convention in London and in subsequent exchanges, the Canberra meeting had to deal with a large number of proposals. The Australian chairman of the meeting, J.R. Rowland of the Department of Foreign Affairs, played an important role in identifying areas of potential consensus. Following informal consultations with delegates, and formal conference sessions, he drew together a new informal single draft text which reflected his assessment of the main elements in the various approaches on the table. This text was subsequently revised twice at the meeting, but still not all governments were prepared to accept it as the basis for negotiation at a final conference. The draft text which emerged from these revisions went further towards accommodating the views of the fishing states. It was, Peacock said, "a very carefully balanced package designed to bridge the gaps between the different positions and to meet some of the concerns of each country."[40] Most of Australia's "basic interests and policy objectives" were well accommodated in the text; but Canberra was concerned about the question of sovereignty, particularly since the proposed scope of the convention covered areas within its jurisdiction and also that of other claimant states. The delegation also made it known at the meetings in Canberra that Australia was interested in having the future institutional machinery of the convention established there.

Thus the strong anti-fishing line being urged on the government by environmental groups was in practice modified by the government in these continuing negotiations. Australia's effort to play a leading role reinforced the assessment that the fishery was both a fact of life, and also ecologically defensible if carefully regulated. In a major statement on Australian foreign policy in May 1978, Peacock referred specifically to "our interest in ensuring that any fishing that does take place should be carried out under conditions which will protect the integrity of the unique ecosystem of the seas surrounding Antarctica."[41]

A second session of the Special Meeting was held in Buenos Aires in July 1978. Australia renewed its pressure for phrasings and provisions that would not harm its sovereignty claims with regard to the AAT, Heard Island and MacDonald Island, and rights in the adjacent marine areas. At the close of the meeting the question remained unresolved. The preference of delegations, in line with the provisions of the Antarctica treaty, was to concentrate on substantive issues and hold over serious discussion of sovereignty questions until this momentum could make them resolvable. Growing fears of the consequences of unchecked exploitation pointed incontrovertibly, in the Australian view, to the wisdom of the ecosystem approach. Further, the convention should embrace "most of the Antarctic marine ecosystems and take note of the interrelation of all its marine living species. For this reason Australia's preference is for a convention which goes beyond the area of the Antarctic Treaty," in other words for one which took in areas north of 60° South.[42] Australian officials were now also concentrating much more on the organizational arrangements involved in implementing the convention. The politics of the convention-making process were already moving in this direction, since many key decisions on quotas, zoning and conservation practices would have to be made by the machinery established by it. There was a consensus about the need for some form of Commission of the parties signatory to the convention, and also for an advisory Scientific Committee. But delegations were divided on the crucial question of decision-making procedures. Indeed questions of the relations between these two bodies, and of procedures within each, remained largely unresolved even after conclusion of the convention itself in 1980. Australia was caught in two dilemmas. First, it wanted the convention to work. Effectiveness, however, meant recognizing the interests of fishing nations. If these had too little power in future arrangements, the convention would lack authority; if they had too much, this could amount to a veto over conservation decisions. Secondly, emphasis on the ecosystem principle behind the convention was viewed tactically by the government as a means of allowing it to steer a middle course between fishing and anti-fishing interests. The principle could, however, be interpreted to mean different things, from something akin to those governing existing international fisheries agreements on the one hand, to a rallying call against any form of resource exploitation on the other. Environmental groups in Australia tended to locate themselves nearer the latter end of this policy spectrum, so that in pursuing its goal of an effective convention the government was also potentially storing up trouble for itself at home.

Informal negotiations continued in Washington from September 1978. These eventually led to substantial agreement on the main points of a draft text. The question of sub-Antarctic islands still proved difficult to handle. As the course of the convention text progressed, other problems emerged, particularly the question of European Community (EC) representation at the final conference.[43] These issues helped delay the conference, then thought likely to be scheduled for some time in 1979. The Washington draft prepared for the conference finally emerged from negotiations there in June-July 1979, and in the course of the tenth meeting of the parties in September-October, and accommodation was reached on sub-Antarctic islands and on EC representation.[44] A sufficient basis now existed for the convening of a final conference. The Australian government supported the Washington text, pointing out that it "necessarily reflects a careful balance between the interests of states fishing in the areas and those states that place primary emphasis on the conservation aspects of the Convention." The main criterion of effectiveness was secured. The draft met "the interests of all the parties whose participation is essential to the success of the conference."[45]

The conference was held in Canberra in May 1980. By this time, most disputes had been ironed out. Australian officials averted the possibility of any last-minute doubts about an Australian headquarters by diplomatic contacts prior to the meeting and the organization of a tour for delegates of the proposed site in Hobart. A determined campaign on this point had been instituted in Parliament by Tasmanian MPs. The conference was the first to have been held in Canberra to adopt an international convention since 1947; agreement on the Tasmania headquarters also gave to Australia its first international headquarters.[46] Australia, which also acted as official depository nation for the convention, became the first country to ratify it in May 1981. It entered into force in April 1982 following ratification by New Zealand, the eighth country to take this step.[47]

A number of gaps or ambiguities in the convention, however, focussed environmentalist attention on implementation. France, for example, by means of a Note attached to the convention, was permitted to regulate fisheries zones for the islands of Kerguelen and Crozet independently of any decisions made in the Commission. This device, hammered out in Washington in 1978-79, was an important part of the final package, but it left the convention open to the criticism that its ecosystem principles had been compromised. Some Australian critics also argued that, in practice, knowledge of Antarctic marine ecology was inadequate for building a working regime based on sound conservation principles. Membership of the Commission, moreover, remained open not only to the Antarctic treaty states but also to other nations fishing in the area. The more countries that fished, the more likely was it that conservationist states would be forced into the minority position. Uncertainty about the practical implications of the provisions of the convention qualified the welcome it generally received in Australia. One Senator criticized the Washington text in 1980 as "more a charter for exploitation than a convention for conservation of Antarctic resources, especially in such sensitive areas as krill fishing and mineral exploration and exploitation."[48] The convention, one environmentalist critic argued, was "peppered with let-out clauses which are reminiscent of those which made the International Whaling Commission a paper tiger."[49]

A preparatory meeting of signatories met under Australian chairmanship in Hobart in September 1981 to discuss the establishment of the Commission, Scientific Committee and secretariat.[50] The inaugural session of the Commission

88

was held there in May-June 1982, and was attended by delegates from fifteen signatory states together with representatives of the EC and various intergovernmental and scientific organizations. Australia was elected Chairman and Japan Vice-Chairman. Decision-making rules in the Commission were the main bones of contention. The convention itself set out the principle of decision-making by consensus for important questions, for example in relation to quotas, and also allowed a period of 180 days in which parties could object formally to any decision reached by this method. At Hobart in 1982, significant differences arose over the kinds of issues to which the consensus rule should apply. There was also disagreement over the role of observers (at this meeting, the IWC, FAO, IOC, IUCN, together with the Scientific Committee for Antarctic Research [SCAR] and the Scientific Committee for Oceanographic Research [SCOR]), since some had views that conflicted with the aims of various state delegations. It was eventually agreed that observers could be excluded from specific sessions of the Commission.[51]

The Scientific Committee convened at the same time, with the Federal Republic of Germany in the chair (and the German Democratic Republic and New Zealand as Vice-Chairmen). It was unable to finalize its rules of procedure. States with significant fishing interests were not about to be outmanoeuvred by decision-making rules that would in practice favour tougher conservation decisions. After a number of attempts to break this deadlock in later months, particularly by New Zealand, the Committee was finally in a position to begin to make practical decisions at its subsequent meeting in Hobart in September 1983. This achievement came in part because the main items for discussion were only minimally contentious: the development of methods for assessing krill and fish stocks; uniform reporting formats for fisheries data; and experimental management methods.[52]

Though the convention's machinery was slowly beginning to move, Australian critics remained dubious. Environmental considerations could become secondary, some argued, in a system that encouraged various kinds of trade-offs. The ecosystem concept itself, the key to the convention, was already being "undermined ... by diplomatic manoeuvring promoted by some of the fishing states."[53] There was, however, evidence of some substantial progress. The September 1984 meetings of the Commission were described by their Australian chairman, A.D. Brown, as a "breakthrough." "We have moved past the stage of talking and are now establishing binding measures to conserve the Antarctic marine ecosystem."[54] More particularly, the Commission set restrictions on various species of fin-fish and also krill which, Australian officials argued, gave hope for the recovery of depleted fish stocks. At the same time, however, discussions in the Scientific Committee underlined the enormous difficulties of basing such decisions on reliable current data. There was evidence, for example, of significant changes in the distribution of krill, including low krill abundance in the Scotia Sea.[55] Lingering Australian doubts about the effectiveness of the regime as a constraint on fishing states were reinforced by the steady expansion of activities by Soviet and East European fleets. Though the fourth meeting of the Commission, in September 1985, adopted a third conservation regulation, dealing with a cod species, the head of the Australian delegation, John Humphreys, expressed disappointment at the direction being taken by the Commission.[56] In the Australian view, the Commission should in the future begin to consider a new strategy on conservation and management of the Antarctic's marine living resources.

Antarctic ecosystems and Australian policy

The bases of Australian engagement in the Antarctica treaty have expanded since the treaty-making process of the late 1950s. A continuing feature of Australian thinking about the region has been the security of its southern approaches and, more specifically, the maintenance of sovereign claims to part of the Antarctic land mass and its neighbouring waters. Opposition to attempts to internationalize the regime by bringing it more under UN control was both determined and successful in the 1980s. At the same time, Australia's relative weakness compared to the two super-powers present in the Antarctic system was acknowledged. Within this constraint, Australia has defined for itself a role of leadership from within the middle power ranks of the treaty partners. Negotiation of the Antarctic Living Marine Resources (AMLR) convention is a good example. Here, Australia was able to host both the conference that produced the treaty and also the scientific and administrative machinery created by the convention; Australia was in addition politically acceptable as a mediator between fishing and non-fishing states on some of the key issues in the convention-making process.

This layer of continuity in Australian policy has been gradually augmented by others. Concern for the Antarctic environment has grown. The mid-1970s can be seen in retrospect as the most significant period in this change. A decade earlier, Australia had begun the administrative implementation of the Agreed Measures, but at a relatively slow pace; full legislative recognition of these practices did not come until 1980. Attention to the fate of the krill resource in the mid-1970s, however, made environmental policy questions in Antarctica and the Southern Ocean much more salient. Anticipation of minerals exploitation towards the end of the century was another powerful incentive for action on the environmental front. Both questions highlighted regime weaknesses: the first because marine questions had traditionally been peripheral to Antarctic deliberations, and the second because existing provisions — notably the Agreed Measures of 1964 — seemed to many Australians severely inadequate as an instrument capable of setting ecologically rational checks to resource exploitation on land. The rise of these issues coincided with renewed debate inside Australia on Antarctic policy generally, and more particularly on the adequacy of the funds allocated by the government to meet policy commitments.

The Antarctic treaty arrangements, and those set up under related agreements such as the AMLR convention, were themselves subjected to criticism. The latter agreement failed to satisfy environmental critics of Australian policies. Although the underlying rationale for the convention rested on sound ecological principles, the compromises instituted by the negotiating process — on French fishing rights

90

around certain islands, for example, or the methods of determining fishing quotas — led to doubts, increasingly expressed by both environmental group representatives and government officials, about its longer-term effectiveness. Australia remained none the less a strong defender of the essentials of the treaty system. Its capacity for influencing the course of events would by comparison be minimal under the various alternative regime concepts put forward by South-east Asian and other developing countries in the UN in the 1980s. This viewpoint was not regarded as incompatible with support across a different range of issue-areas for UN environmental activities. In UNEP and related forums, environmental questions came first; in relation to Antarctica, Australia had core interests of territory and sovereignty to protect, and these dictated the desired shape of environmental policy-making structures.

This and the previous three chapters have explored the ways in which Australia came to terms with international environmental policy developments during their important formative stage from 1965-85. The chapters following focus on the policy process in Australia. Four kinds of influences are investigated: from various departments and agencies within the federal government, from state governments and in federal-state encounters, from domestic publics and pressure groups (including, for this purpose, organizations in the Australian scientific community), and from international governmental and non-governmental organizations. These are studied by looking in successive chapters at the environmental policy machinery in Australia, federal-state interactions in connection with policy in international institutions, the determination of policy responses to international conventions, and, finally, the role and influence of domestic groups.

Notes for Chapter 5

1 Cisca Spencer, "The Evolution of Antarctic Interests," in Stuart Harris, ed., *Australia's Antarctic Policy Options* (Australian National University: Centre for Resource and Environmental Studies, 1984), p. 116.

2 "The value of the Antarctic Treaty system," *Backgrounder,* 445, 14 August 1984, pp. 2-3.

3 *Australian,* January 7, 1985: *Sydney Morning Herald,* 23 January 1985.

4 "Antarctica and the question of the exploitation of its resources," *AFAR* 48(12), December 1977, p. 610.

5 For summaries see *ARPAC. Initial Report to Government. November 1979* (Canberra, 1980; PP 65), Ch. 2; Parliament, Joint Co. on Foreign Affairs and Defence, *Australia, Antarctica and the Law of the Sea. Interim Report 1978* (Canberra, 1978; PP 168), Ch. VII.

6 Dr. John Boyd, Antarctic Division deputy director, *Sydney Morning Herald,* January 23, 1985.

7 Thomson, *House of Representatives,* 118, 23 April 1980, pp. 2185-6.

8 *ARPAC. Initial Report,* pp. 1-5.

9 *Towards New Perspectives for Australian Scientific Research in Antarctica. Discussion Paper presented by the Hon. W.L. Morrison, MP, Minister for Science, March 1975* (Canberra, 1975; PP 34); *AFAR* 46(3), March 1975, p. 140; DOS, *Annual Report 1975-76* (Canberra, 1977; PP 374), p. 4-5; *ARPAC. Initial Report; Commonwealth Record* 4(49), 10-31 Dec. 1979, p. 1915, and 5(11), 17-23 March 1980, p. 368.

Global Regimes and Nation-States

10 *ARPAC. Initial Report,* p. 1.

11 *ARPAC. Report for Period 1 December 1979 to November 1981* (Canberra, 1982), p. vi; and Thomson earlier, on the government's commitment to research and the appointment of a Planning Committee of scientists, *House of Representatives,* 117, 20 March 1980, pp. 1070-1.

12 See for example Peacock's comments on common heritage and in defence of Australian sovereignty, *House of Representatives,* 106, 15 September 1977, pp. 1164-5.

13 Remarks at the Beardmoor Glacier seminar, *Sydney Morning Herald* and *Age,* 14 January 1985. On Australia and Third World demands see Bryan Boswell, "The Antarctic cake — everybody wants a slice," *Australian,* 29 December 1983. The resolution on Antarctica passed by the 1984 Nonaligned Summit also produced parliamentary questions.

14 *Australian,* 7 January 1985. Cf. "There is no certainty that internationalization of the Antarctic would enhance protection of the Antarctic environment. It is possible that it would lead to a 'free for all' grab for resources (so far avoided in the Treaty arrangement) which could have harmful consequences" (Joint Committee on Foreign Affairs and Defence, *Australia, Antarctica and the Law of the Sea,* p. 59).

15 E.g. Sen. Button on the second reading debate on the AMLRs bill, *Senate* 89, 7 April 1981, p. 1155.

16 Jane Ford, "Research in Antarctica comes in from the cold," *Australian,* February 18, 1983. The report was apparently withheld for several months because of its criticisms (*Weekend Australian,* 25 September 1982). In an earlier ALP view a future Labor government, while maintaining sovereign claims, "would be prepared to enter into discussion with other interested nations to investigate the desirability and practicability of international control of Antarctica" (quoted at *House of Representatives,* 117, 30 March 1980, p. 1072).

17 Jones, quoted in *Telegraph* (Sydney), 9 October 1985. The budget was to be $33.9 million for the forthcoming financial year, an increase of 9.8 per cent. On the Davis base see his statement in *Age,* 19 August 1983; there were various media reports earlier that the station would be closed. On Antarctic policy and the budgetary problems see also *Sydney Morning Herald,* 23 January 1985.

18 Geoff Mosley, "The natural option: the case for an Antarctic world park," in Stuart Harris, ed., *Australia's Antarctic Policy Options* (Australian National University: Centre for Resource and Environmental Studies, CRES Monograph 11, 1984), pp. 307-27.

19 For summaries see B. Sage, "Conservation and Exploitation," in W.N. Bonner and D.W.H. Walton, eds., *Key Environments: Antarctica* (Oxford: Pergamon Press for IUCN, 1985), pp. 362-4; and W.N. Bonner, "Conservation and the Antarctic," in R.M. Laws, ed., *Antarctic Ecology,* vol. 2 (London: Academic Press, 1984), pp. 840-3.

20 *Ibid.*

21 "Antarctic Treaty Meeting: A turning point," *AFAR* 46(8), August 1975, pp. 432-4.

22 *National Estate. Report of the Committee of Inquiry* (Canberra, 1975; PP 195), pp. 244-5, para. 8.101.

23 ANPWS, *Report for the Period 1 July 1976 - 30 June 1977* (Canberra 1977), pp. 15-16.

24 ANPWS, *Report for the Period 1 July 1978 - 30 June 1979* (Canberra, 1979), p. 19.

25 Thomson, *House of Representatives,* 118, 23 April 1980, pp. 2185-6; and *Senate* 85, 23 May 1980, pp. 2790-1. Covered were the activities of Australians anywhere on the continent, and of any national within AAT; the bill gives the minister power to regulate organizations and individuals with regard to wildlife and their habitat; and provides for the making of regulations on pollution, the use of motor vehicles and other matters.

26 The bill was not opposed. See Sibraa, *Senate,* 85, 23 May 1980, p. 2797. Cf. N. Klugman, *House of Representatives,* 118, 22 May 1980, pp. 3110-1, who complained that the bill did not go far enough.

27 Dr. Gavin Johnstone, in a private submission to the Senate Standing Committee on Natural Resources, quoted in the *Canberra Times,* 10 February 1984. See also Peter Roberts, "Rubbish, bane of Antarctica," *Age,* 3 March 1983.

28 *Canberra Times,* 4 December 1984.

92

29 Thomson, *House of Representatives,* 118, 23 April 1980, pp. 2185-6. "Antarctic nature conservation and environment protection rank high in priority in both the Antarctic Treaty and Australian Government policy."

30 Joint Committee on Foreign Affairs and Defence, *Australia, Antarctica and the Law of the Sea,* p. 59.

31 Australia would "continue to stress the importance of environmental aspects": DFA, *Annual Report 1982* (Canberra, 1983; PP 140), p. 35. On the 11th Consultative Meeting in Buenos Aires see DFA, *Annual Report 1981* (Canberra, 1982; PP 139), p. 36; *Backgrounder* 292, 15 July 1981, pp. 1-2; and Street, *House of Representatives,* 123, 28 May 1981, p. 2747. On the later Wellington meetings on the environment, see *Financial Review* (Sydney), 19 January 1983.

32 *Science and Technology in Australia. 1977-8. A Report to the Prime Minister by the ASTEC* (Canberra, 1978; PP 240), Ch. 7, esp. para. 7.2.12, p. 131; and more generally, ASTEC, *Towards a Marine Sciences and Technologies Programme for the 1980s* (Canberra, 1981; PP 168).

33 *ARPAC. Initial Report,* pp. 7 ff., App. 4. Earlier work was carried out at Mawson on marine biology, and studies of seabird populations on Macquarie Island: DOS, *Antarctic Division, Report for Year 1972-3* (Canberra, 1974; PP 251), pp. 3, 14-17.

34 *Towards New Perspectives for Australian Scientific Research in Antarctica,* p. 13.

35 Barrie, *Senate,* 89, 7 April 1981, p. 1166. On the background see DEC, *Report for Period December 1972 - June 1974* (Canberra, 1975; PP 298), p. 15; ANPWS, *Report for Period 1 July 1976 to 30 June 1977* (Canberra, 1977), p. 15.

36 DFA, *Annual Report 1975* (Canberra, 1976; PP 142), p. 14. In general see "Antarctic Treaty Meeting: A turning point," *AFAR* 46(8), August 1975, pp. 432-4.

37 *House of Representatives* 106, 15 September 1977, pp. 1164-5.

38 Department of State, *Final Environmental Impact Statement on the Negotiations of a Regime for Conservation of Antarctic Marine Living Resources* (Washington, D.C.: June 1978).

39 On the 9th meeting see "Antarctica and the question of the exploitation of its resources," *AFAR* 48(12), December 1977, pp. 604-11; and Peacock, *House of Representatives,* 107, 8 November 1977, pp. 3124-5 and 107, 11 October 1977, p. 1815.

40 On the Canberra meetings see DFA, *Annual Report 1978* (Canberra, 1979; PP 112), pp. 8-9; "Antarctic Meeting in Canberra," *AFAR,* 49(3), March 1978, pp. 123-6; and Peacock, *House of Representatives* 108, 10 April 1978, p. 1267.

41 *House of Representatives* 109, 9 May 1978, p. 2035.

42 Peacock, *AFAR,* 49(7), July 1978, p. 369.

43 DFA, *Annual Report 1978* (Canberra, 1979; PP 112), pp. 8-9.

44 *AFAR* 50(7) July 1979, p. 404; DFA, *Annual Report 1979* (Canberra, 1980; PP 102), p. 24.

45 See Sens. Puplick and Carrick, *Senate* 85, 28 April 1980, pp. 1808-9. Environmental concerns are discussed at "Antarctica — a continent of international harmony?" *AFAR* 51(2), February 1980, pp. 4-12.

46 McVeigh, Acting Minister of Science and Technology, *House of Representatives,* 122, 26 March 1981, p. 1007. Pressure for a Hobart base was maintained particularly by Mr. Hodgman; see his comments at *House of Representatives,* 118, 22 April 1980, p. 2071, and 119, 10 September 1980, p. 1139. See also Peacock's remarks on the conference at *House of Representatives,* 118, 20 May 1980, p. 2886; and "Antarctic marine living resources conference," *AFAR,* 51(5), May 1980, pp. 144-7.

47 Statement by Peacock and Thomson, *AFAR,* 51(9), September 1980, p. 35; "Antarctica in the 80s," *AFAR* 52(1), January 1981, pp. 4-14; statement by Street and Thomson, *AFAR* 52(5), May 1981; *Backgrounder* 283, 13 May 1981, III; statement by Street, *AFAR,* 53(3), March 1982, p. 112.

48 Puplick, *Senate,* 85, 28 April 1980, pp. 1808-9.

49 Peter Roberts, "Testing the waters for krill," *Age,* 16 March 1983.

50 Statement by Thomson and Street, *AFAR* 52(9), September 1981, pp. 464-5; DFA, *Annual Report 1981* (Canberra, 1982; PP 139), p. 25; "Antarctic marine living resources: Hobart meeting," *Backgrounder* 305, 14 October 1981, p. 1. Delegations of fourteen of the fifteen signatories (Poland was absent) attended, with observers from the EEC and intergovernmental organizations.

93

[51] *AFAR,* 53(5) May 1982, pp. 325-6; *Backgrounder* 334, 26 May 1982, p. 3; "Antarctic marine living resources," *Backgrounder* 337, 16 June 1982, pp. 6-8; DFA, *Annual Report 1982* (Canberra, 1983; PP 140) p. 37.

[52] DST, *Antarctic Division, Annual Review 1983-4* (Canberra, 1984), p. 2; and reports at J.C. Hamilton, "Important conservation role for Hobart," *Bulletin,* 13 September 1983; and *Mercury,* 29 August 1983.

[53] See articles by Roger Wilson in *Canberra Times,* 28 August 1983, and *Sydney Morning Herald,* 12 July 1983.

[54] "Antarctic marine living resources." *Backgrounder* 449, 26 September 1984.

[55] Scientific Committee for the Conservation of Antarctic Marine Living Resources, *Report of the 3rd Meeting of the Scientific Committee, Hobart, 3-13 September 1984* (SC-CAMLR-III), para. 8.6, p. 24.

[56] *West Australian,* 16 September 1985.

II

CHARTING THE POLICY PROCESS

CHAPTER SIX

Institution-building and Cooperative Federalism

The 1970s saw the federal government emerge as an actor in Australian environmental policy. This emergence was partly in response to international developments, especially the experience of preparing for and taking part in UNCHE. Canberra initiated a variety of steps before this event to bring about a greater degree of coordination on environmental matters among Australia's governments. The obstacles were considerable. As the minister, Peter Howson, noted in 1971, some states at that time had no environment departments; "In fact, it's obvious at the moment that we are trying to move too quickly in this field."[1] Following the election of late 1972, other factors entered the picture. Environmental policy in the period 1972-75 was in part a function of the determination of Labor to tilt the federal-state balance in the direction of the Commonwealth. Domestic and international considerations were connected. Whitlam was interested in exploring the possibility of using international developments such as conventions and conferences as a means of legitimizing the expansion of Canberra's role in the formulation of domestic Australian environmental policy. These areas, as we saw in Chapter 1, fall primarily under the jurisdiction of the states in the Australian constitution. The period since the end of the 1960s has been marked by a protracted struggle to establish mutually agreed institutional and policy-making mechanisms that would recognize the respective spheres of each level of government and also the value of cooperative efforts between the two. These developments laid the foundation for joint approaches to international environment policy, and served as the crucial connecting points linking the domestic and external aspects of Australian policies.

The Australian states as environmental actors

As the inheritors of the constitutional mantle, as practitioners for decades in the arts of land use and resource management, and, in many ways, as the primary arenas of politics in the Australian political system, the states were quick to defend both their record and their jurisdictional rights when environmental issues began to take on greater political significance in the middle and late 1960s. Environmental law and policy were matters indisputably under the authority of the states. This argument related not so much to broader environmental policy as to the individual pieces of the jig-saw puzzle, many of which were in any case missing. States were proud of their record at the forefront of the history and growth of Australia's national parks, even though the term "national" in this context was something

97

of a misnomer. As one speaker in the New South Wales legislature said in 1979, moreover, these parks were "— so far as possible — the major repository of untouched flora and fauna in the Australian landscape."[2] For the Commonwealth to attempt to move into such areas, and other aspects of environment policy, smacked of meddlesome interference. Some detected more sinister motives. The Labor government of 1972-75 funded environmental organizations active in the states during its period of office. While some of these did a good job, the New South Wales Minister for Planning and Environment, Sir John Fuller, said afterwards, others were "mere fronts of the ALP ... in stirring up groups on a political basis."[3]

The states, moreover, each had their own mixtures of policy priorities. The placing of environmental issues on policy agendas has depended on a number of factors, including requirements for economic development, decreased unemployment, the promotion of trade and the attracting of investment; the make-up of the main economic sectors of the states; and the ideological and policy preferences of different parties. To the extent that strong environmental agencies were viewed as detrimental to the pursuit of other policy goals, pressure from outsiders in Canberra — especially outsiders controlled by a rival political party — had to be resisted. Many states were slow during the 1960s and 1970s to establish environmental departments in government. Departments, once established, varied considerably in their roles and powers. Some simply joined a variety of other government ministries which also shared some environmental policy functions. Premier Bjelke-Petersen of Queensland defended his government's record against attacks by environmentalists in 1974 by pointing out that Queensland was the first state to set up an environmental control administration, a lead which other states had since followed. He as premier, moreover, was head of the government's environmental activities and exercised coordinating responsibilities.[4] Despite the variety from state to state, all governments by the 1980s had set up departments of environment or conservation (New South Wales, Victoria, South Australia, Western Australia and Tasmania) or else had subsumed these areas under the work of bodies with general coordinating powers (the Co-ordinator-General's Department in Queensland and the Department of the Chief Minister in the Northern Territory).[5]

A comparative overview of the workings of these policy mechanisms is outside the scope of the present study. The level of state authority is central, however, in that it comprises the bulk of environmental activities by governments in Australia; many aspects of federal policy, particularly in relation to international agreements, depend for their effective implementation on political will and administrative resources in the states; through the joint federal-state machinery, state officials are engaged in a wide range of international policy matters; and the states can, to a certain extent, take actions of their own on international environmental issues.

State governments can and do send representatives to international meetings as set down in the rules governing the composition of Australian delegations to such forums. Some governments have used opportunities to present their views directly, as did the government of New South Wales in overtures to Washington in 1974 in connection with the bilateral exchanges between Australia and the US on restriction of the kangaroo trade. States, or some state government agencies or officials, may have their own informal contacts with international organizations. A number of state bodies, such as the National Parks and Wildlife Service of the government of Queensland, have joined IUCN as members. They have also benefited from international connections. Research on endangered species in Tasmania, for example, has been carried out with funding from the World Wildlife Fund.[6] Several state governments decided to work on their own versions of the IUCN-UNEP-WWF *World Conservation Strategy* of 1980 rather than rely exclusively on Canberra's lead in producing an Australian strategy that might have limited relevance to their needs. The government of Western Australia, for example, made use of the services of a former FAO official who had taken part in IUCN deliberations which culminated in the 1980 document.[7] When the government of South Australia was preparing legislation on deposits on non-returnable drink containers in the early 1970s, it used as a guide legislation then operating in the state of Oregon; its Director of Environment and Conservation was sent on a mission there to evaluate conflicting reports of its effectiveness.[8]

These kinds of examples, it should be emphasized, do not add up to a concerted and consistent policy on the part of state governments to take over parts of the international responsibilities of the Commonwealth. Apart from the constraints, constitutional and otherwise, state governments in practice have not aspired to international roles. They are drawn into international policy matters more as a form of insurance. At this level the Commonwealth is active in leadership roles, so costs as well as benefits can accrue to states bent on intervention. Before turning to the setting of federal-state encounters, we must first look at the evolution of the Commonwealth's interest in the environment.

Policy process at the Commonwealth level

The Commonwealth's role as an environmental actor began to take shape in 1969. Commonwealth and state authorities held discussions that year on measures to protect Australian fauna. The issues, in a series of Australian Fauna Authorities Conferences, overlapped with many of the questions on emerging environmental policy agendas. Discussions in two Senate committees, dealing respectively with air and water pollution, led Australians to begin questioning the adequacy of the Commonwealth's role. The Department of Health convened an inter-departmental committee on the environment, which held its first meeting in July 1970. A working party was set up "to enquire into and advise the conference on the most appropriate methods of approach for the national resolution of the problems of the Australian environment."[9] Following a report prepared for a further meeting in October, an Office of the Environment was established as a division of the Prime Minister's Department in December 1970. The office was not designed to initiate new programmes, but rather to advise the Commonwealth on matters under its control.[10]

The fate of the new office was threatened by a fresh look at the budgetary implications of its work from early 1971. At the same time, however, public pressure was mounting on the Commonwealth to provide some tangible evidence of its commitment to play a role in shaping Australia's environment policies. The office was eventually re-located in the new Department of Environment, Aborigines and the Arts. Existing programmes carried out by various federal departments, on top of the prior roles of the states, made it difficult to carve out a distinctive and agreed niche for environmental policy. The federal Cabinet gave the matter its first serious look in November 1971.[11] Although the Commonwealth was coming relatively new to this policy area, it was clear to Howson, as minister, that further developments on the Commonwealth side would have to wait until the states had also set up counterpart machinery.[12] Discussions with state governments proceeded slowly during 1971; an important Commonwealth-state environment ministers conference held in September highlighted organizational weaknesses at both levels of government. Thus pressures within the context of relations with the states, and expectations arising from Australia's preparations for UNCHE, both pointed in the same direction towards the requirement of more effective organization and coordination between the federal and state governments. The Labor opposition, led on this issue by Whitlam and Uren, took the Commonwealth to task for having failed to bring this about. An integrated system similar to that in the US was needed, they argued, not the ad hoc and piecemeal approach to be found in Australian government.[13]

In April 1972, Howson singled out three areas in which the federal department had responsibilities: coordination of federal action, cooperation with the states and international aspects.[14] We will look shortly at the emergence around this time of more institutionalized cooperation between Canberra and the states. It was the government's case that its more cautious approach was more likely to generate cooperation with the states than would the impatient stance of the Labor opposition, that it was more responsibly restrained fiscally, and also that its policies were based on a sounder appreciation of the negative impact that environmentalism could have on Australia's economic growth if given a free rein.[15] Within government, several departments handled environment questions: the Department of Education and Science (which had responsibility for relations with UNESCO, for example in connection with the 1968 biosphere conference); the Department of the Interior, which also had a small conservation office; the Department of Transport and Shipping, which dealt with marine pollution and ocean dumping; the Department of Primary Industry, which had regulatory authority in connection with pesticides; and the Departments of Health, Works and National Development, all of which carried out significant programmes. This complexity made for delays in the government's production of its first major policy statement on the environment, which finally appeared towards the end of May 1972.

The Stockholm conference in June produced more calls for the injection of greater vigour into Commonwealth policies and organization. The House of Representatives Select Committee on Wildlife Conservation recommended in October the establishment of a Commonwealth nature conservation authority. The Labor government, which took office at the end of 1972, lost no time in getting down to business. As part of its widespread government reorganization, it established a Department of Environment and Conservation.

The new department, with Dr. Moss Cass as minister (Tom Uren, who had spearheaded Labor's attacks on the previous government's record, went to Urban and Regional Development) and Dr. D.F. McMichael as Secretary, underwent rapid expansion during Labor's term. In a sense, it pursued the same three goals set for its predecessor: coordinating the federal machinery, negotiating with the states, and representing Australia internationally. Cass emphasized that the new Department was not to be seen as an arbiter in difficult choices facing Australians; it would, however, be concerned with "policy-making coordination and review."[16] Among its immediate tasks were to develop policy on environmental impact statements, establish an Australian national parks and wildlife service, define national pollution criteria, rationalize land use policies, and develop the Commonwealth's role in assisting the states in formulating and executing their own environment policies. From the outset, the internationalist orientation of the department was flourished with gusto. Its job was to "increase Australian activity in the international environmental arena." While many environmental issues were the responsibility of state and local governments, the Commonwealth had "responsibility for this sector of the globe for international aspects and must, by leadership and cooperation at home, encourage all to play their part in the successful resolution of environmental problems."[17]

The need for appropriate enabling legislation, and the increasing sense of alarm of state governments, however, acted as constraints in several areas. Organizational development was viewed as the means for removing obstacles from whichever quarter they appeared. The department grew in size: to more than 70 officers by mid-1973, with a projected doubling the following year. Cass observed in June that the department had "come a long way from the one-man Office of the Environment within the Prime Minister's Department" of mid-1971.[18] Expenditures increased rapidly: to $3.1 million in 1973-74, and to $18.2 million in 1974-75.[19] A significant restructuring was announced in June 1973; a Bureau of Environmental Studies was created in the department in September; and in April 1975, the name was changed to the Department of Environment so as better to indicate that conservation "was in fact a major component of the Government's total environmental policy" and not something separate from it.[20] The Commonwealth also acted to enhance its capabilities by expanding the previous government's advisory body. Despite an earlier Cabinet decision to the contrary, the Prime Minister had been converted to this idea in December 1971; an advisory three-person committee was established in May 1972, under Professor R.J. Walsh of the University of New South Wales.[21] Labor took this initiative much further.

101

The Australian Advisory Committee on the Environment (AACE) was expanded and reorganized in 1974, and fifteen members had been appointed by mid-1975.[22]

Establishment of an Australian National Parks and Wildlife Service (ANPWS) was an important Labor goal from the start. The Commonwealth's absence from this area had long been commented on, for example in a 1968 survey of Australia's parks and nature reserves by the Australian Academy of Sciences, and in the October 1972 report of the House Select Committee on Wildlife Conservation.[23] Following enabling legislation, the Service was established in March 1975, and gradually expanded from the small nucleus staff inside the environment department.[24]

The hectic pace of institution-building, government reorganization, legislative change and programme creation, was abruptly halted with the dismissal of the Labor government by the Governor-General in the crisis of 1975. Following the return of the Liberal-National Country coalition in the election at the end of the year, the pace slowed. State sensitivities were respected; the principles of cooperative federalism became again the slogan of the day. As a signal of change, environment responsibilities in the federal government were again altered, and at the end of 1975 re-emerged in a new Department of Environment, Housing and Community Development. Conservation and environment were listed by Fraser in December 1976 as the third of the new department's functions (after housing and the building industry, and issues of community development); and a new Secretary, R.B. Lansdown, was brought in from the Department of Urban and Regional Development.[25] It appeared to critics that the government was making a conscious effort to diminish the environmental role of the Commonwealth, and to recognize again the implications of the constitutional paramountcy of the states in this area.[26] The government also undertook major reviews of existing environmental legislation later in the 1970s.

None the less, there was also a significant line of continuity between the early and the late 1970s. The post-1975 Liberal coalition altered course, but did not reverse engines. The Commonwealth kept its environment department, though in a number of different institutional guises; the ANPWS and Australian Heritage Commission were later joined by the Great Barrier Reef Marine Park Authority; and during the 1970s the two main federal-state institutions, the Australian Environment Council and the Council of Nature Conservation Ministers, settled down to regular examinations of substantive, and frequently non-controversial questions.[27] The government did, however, keep the process of change well under control after 1975. Organization was also affected by the government's reviews. The review of the functions of the ANPWS was carried out following Liberal election commitments that, in government, it would ensure that environment and conservation policies would in future be shaped in full consultation with the states. As a result of the review the definition of the Service's role was re-defined in August 1976, and the ANPWS finally became an effective working organization in 1977 after approval of the creation of new positions.[28] Minor organizational revisions were made later. Federal environment and science responsibilities were amalgamated in 1978; a new Department of Home Affairs and Environment was created in a reorganization of 1980.[29] Although all these changes took their toll in public service morale, and in the confidence of environmental groups in the government's intentions and capabilities, federal government institutions retained much of the character defined for them in the early 1970s. More particularly, it was the environment department which in the late 1970s had "overall responsibility for Commonwealth participation in international environmental activities."[30]

Labor returned to power in 1983. The Tasmanian dam crisis, however, culminating in the High Court decision of 1983 that confirmed the constitutional propriety of Commonwealth measures to halt work on the dam, had the longer-term practical consequence of ruling out a return to expansionist environmentalism. The Tasmanian issue aside, the atmosphere of the mid-1980s was in any case much altered from that of the early 1970s. Especially at the state level, Labor had had a prolonged opportunity to digest environmentalist arguments and to weigh them against older economic goals. Often they were found wanting. Some new steps were taken. The Hawke government carried out a general review of programmes in the natural heritage area, and set in motion plans to establish an environmental contaminants authority; a new environment advisory council was also planned to report to the minister "on any matter relating to the environment and conservation responsibilities of the Commonwealth".[31] Following the December 1984 election, a government reorganization led to the creation of a Department of Arts, Heritage and Environment, but the main environment responsibilities were unchanged.[32] In general the Hawke administrations appeared to be at pains to signal that this was a changed party, firmly committed to putting the Australian economy on an even keel. Environmental issues played little role in the 1987 general election, and Labor distanced itself from the ones that did surface.

The Commonwealth's role in relation to environmental policy has also influenced, and been affected by, developments in a number of related and specialized areas. Science policy has been connected at a number of points. Many aspects of environment policy rely on good data and methodologies, even though their presence may be as weak a guarantee of the political acceptability of policies as their absence is a deterrent to their advocacy. Establishment of a science council was part of the ALP's platform in 1972, and the Minister of Science, W.L. Morrison, later introduced an important discussion paper on the subject.[33] In general, the focus of such debates was not so much the environment as the practical uses of science in industry, agriculture, health policy and communications. They therefore inevitably entailed appraisals of CSIRO, set up in 1949 as a development of a Commonwealth body created in 1916. Criticism has been directed towards the quality and relevance of its research, its place in the wider network of Australian research bodies, and other matters. The study by the OECD in 1974 of Australian science and technology found problems with the CSIRO's dominant position and "monolithic image"; a continuing series of reappraisals has included a major enquiry in 1977, and one conducted by the Australian Science and Technology Council (ASTEC) in 1985.[34] One strand of this extended debate has been the contribution to environmental knowledge and policy made by the CSIRO. Early 1970s critics maintained that the organization was insufficiently geared to these objectives; the CSIRO denied the charge, arguing that two-thirds of its divisions were engaged in environment-related research, much of it started before the environmental revolution.[35] In practice, though, its work tended to be tangential to the environmental policy requirements of government, despite pertinent work on various wildlife species, insect pests, atmospheric pollution, or the criteria for selecting natural areas for inclusion on the Register of the National Estate.[36] A major restructuring took effect in 1986-87 and led to research tasks being carried out in six CSIRO institutes, one of which was devoted to natural resources and the environment.

More directly related to conservation aspects of environment policy were the Commonwealth's efforts to add to its capability for research and data-gathering in relation to biological resources. An Australian Biological Resources Study (ABRS) Interim Council was created in 1973. This followed pressure from the scientific community for a large-scale ecological survey, and support for such work by the House of Representatives Select Committee report on wildlife conservation in 1972; the National Estate committee was also enthusiastic about the potential of this kind of research.[37] The succeeding government announced its intention to go ahead in 1977, though with more carefully circumscribed goals, and an organizational framework linked to the Department of Science and Environment was in place by 1979.[38] The centrepiece of its research effort for the next two decades was work on a multi-volume *Flora of Australia*.[39]

The continuing sequence of government reorganizations in 1970-84 was in part a product of buffeting by larger movements in government, but in part it also reflected a series of only partially resolved disagreements about the priority to be accorded environmental policy objectives. Creation of a federal environment department did not imply the subordination to it of other departments whose responsibilities touched on environmental questions. Environment agencies have ebbed and flowed in their capacity for influence in government; administrations, and Prime Ministers, have differed substantially in their approach to, and investment in, environmental policy.

The problem of coordination within the federal government was both eased and complicated by the invention of an environment department. The need for more effective coordination was recognized, and environmentalist viewpoints were granted some say on how this might be achieved. Other departments, however, were reluctant to share their respective slices of the environmental pie. In the late 1960s, the science department had good claim to be regarded as the most central. The science branch of the Department of Education and Science, established in 1966, played a key role in the federal-state discussions of 1969-70 which led to the creation of the AEC and CONCOM; and the secretariat of the main body of this period, the Australian Fauna Authorities Conference, was located in the department.[40] The department also had responsibility in relation to the MAB Programme, which grew out of the 1968 biosphere conference convened by UNESCO.[41] Similarly, important responsibilities for Antarctic conservation matters have continued to lie with the Antarctic Division, first in Foreign Affairs and later in the science department, though on some questions, such as management of the Agreed Measures system, the environment department took the lead. When the ANPWS was first established, it immediately confronted the problem that many of the areas in which its senior officials hoped to make an impact were handled elsewhere in government: for example, in the Bureau of Customs (on the implementation of CITES), the Department of Transport (on questions involving some of Australia's islands, and also aspects of the Japan convention on migratory birds), the Department of Administrative Services (in relation to Australia's external territories, especially Norfolk and Christmas Islands, where the Service had a special interest in endangered species), the Department of Science (on Antarctic matters), the Attorney-General's Department (with regard to international conventions generally), the Department of Primary Industry (which dealt with some questions involved with marine conservation goals), and, finally, the Department of Foreign Affairs (on international questions generally, and on questions connected with UNCLOS III in particular).[42]

Coordination at the federal level has been approached by way of general policy made by the Cabinet, in the light of federal-state exchanges, through definitions of the respective roles of various departments, and in the process of inter-departmental consultations. Inter-departmental committees (IDCs) have played an important role. IDCs, Hawke said in Parliament in 1984, are "just one method of inter-departmental consultation and alone do not provide a true indication of the on-going level of communication and consultation among departments. They do, however, represent a legitimate administrative function of governments and are directed to the preparation and oversight of government programmes and policies."[43]

Because of the nature of the issues involved, IDCs have been part of environmental policy-making from the early days of Commonwealth involvement in this area. The original Office of the Environment was established as a result of the work of the environment IDC convened by the Director-General of Health in 1970. Labor's environment and conservation department recognized that it had to "concern itself with a wide range of matters which lie within the administrative responsibility of other departments." It could best achieve its objectives, therefore, by "vigorous participation in inter-departmental committees."[44] By 1975 the department was chairing several IDCs, for example on Australia's participation in the WMO-UNEP plans for a global network of pollution monitoring stations, and on the marine environment.[45] This activity overlapped with coordinating work involving state agencies and NGOs. In the late 1970s, for example, the department was national coordinator for Australian involvement in the IOC's International Coordination Group for the Southern Oceans; the coordinating body for Australian participation in the IOC generally, however, was chaired by the Department of Foreign Affairs.[46] In 1984, the environment department was acting as chairman of six IDCs, on issues such as nuclear codes of practice, the OECD Chemicals Programme (though, similarly, the general IDC on policies in the OECD, on which the department was not represented, was chaired by Foreign Affairs), and the National Conservation Strategy for Australia. Its officials also were members of the Antarctica IDC and those on the Law of the Sea, the Torres Strait, radionuclide wastes, atomic energy legislation, Southwest Tasmania, and aboriginal affairs.[47] The ANPWS has had representation at various time on IDCs on Antarctica, the Law of the Sea, the Torres Strait, and the National Conservation Strategy.[48]

The ability of environment officials to shape Commonwealth policy through such means has varied. If chairmanships, and memberships, of IDCs are taken as an indicator of overall clout, the department has tended to occupy a modest position compared to the Commonwealth heavy-weights. In 1984, for example, the Prime Minister's and Cabinet Department was participating in 58 and chaired another 15. For the Department of Finance, the figures were respectively 47 and 2, for the Department of Trade 31 and 7, for the Attorney-General's Department 28 and 6, and for Treasury 19 and one.[49]

In relation to environmental policy questions that have some international aspect, the department has also had to accommodate itself to the position of the Department of Foreign Affairs. The Department has been an active participant in inter-departmental arrangements by virtue of its general coordinating responsibility for Australia's external relations. Numbers are difficult to calculate because of variations in definitions; for example, the National Conservation Strategy committee just noted was properly an inter-departmental Working Group. According to one estimate, in 1975 the Department was represented on 49 IDCs, and was the convening department for 13. According to the Secretary of the Department, N.F. Parkinson, in testimony to a Senate committee, Foreign Affairs was participating "in more than 130 interdepartmental committees in Canberra" in 1978; he added that he was "surprised, in fact, that it is not higher."[50]

Some of the dynamics of IDC processes, including decisions on their formation and composition, also appear to work against the interests of specialized organizations such as environment departments. For example, it had representation on the IDC on South-west Tasmania set up by Hawke in 1983 ("to examine proposals for the creation of alternative employment as a consequence of the cessation of the Gordon-below-Franklin dam project"), but the matter was of such high importance, and delicacy, that this body was chaired from the Prime Minister's and Cabinet Department.[51] The participation of environment officials in OECD questions has generally been restricted to specialized topics, such as toxic chemicals policy.[52] As part of its own continuing case for paramountcy in any international area, the Department of Foreign Affairs has taken the lead over the environment department on a number of key questions. Tensions were evident between Foreign Affairs and environment officials in the run-up to UNCHE in 1972. More generally, the Department of Foreign Affairs has been criticized by other departments for exaggerating the international or "political" aspects of issues in order to provide itself with entry permits.[53] Its defence has rested partly on a theoretical appeal to the coherence and interrelatedness of the subject-matter of international relations, and partly on pragmatic observations: that in practice, IDCs constrain Foreign Affairs' power by decelerating deliberations, absorbing officers' time and energy, and allowing other departments to defend entrenched positions. The Department of Foreign Affairs has taken steps to expand its capabilities in specialized areas. It was Foreign Affairs, for example, not the Attorney-General's Department, that led policy processes in relation to UNCLOS III; there was a significant growth in its oceans expertise during the 1970s, and also to some extent on Antarctica. Its International Organizations division handled relations with UN technical agencies, the UN itself, and multilateral organizations, while the UN economic agencies, and also the OECD, fell under its Economic branch. In addition, the Department established the position of Adviser on Science, Technology and the Environment.[54]

The influence of the environment department within the Commonwealth bureaucracy has also been affected by the broader political structures of government. In the early 1970s, both under the Liberals and Labor, environment policy was a direct concern of prime ministers, as it was again in the late 1970s and early 1980s, both before and after the change of government in 1983. In terms of government organization, environment policy at the federal level began in 1970 as part of the Prime Minister's Department. Gorton intervened on a number of occasions later to put his stamp on this evolving area, for example, in relation to the composition of the advisory body on the environment. In April 1972 he told the minister, Howson, that the draft of his forthcoming statement on the environment was "still not positive enough" and that he "had not seized enough of the glamour of this subject of the environment."[55] After the 1972 election, Whitlam was both Prime Minister and Minister of Foreign Affairs; his involvement in the general shaping of environment policy, particularly in its international aspects, was made plain on many occasions. More generally, key questions of environmental policy have been resolved finally only in Cabinet decisions, such as those on the overall shape of policy in November 1971, on Australia's adherence to various international conventions during 1973-75, and later on the government's reappraisal and review of federal environmental legislation and institutions, on Antarctic policy questions, and on South-west Tasmania.

The politics and mechanics of federal-state collaboration

The states, however, remained the chief actors in many environmental matters. A narrow interpretation of the Commonwealth's role gave it authority only in Australia's external territories, the Northern Territory, the ACT, and small areas under federal control in some states. Constitutionally, a wider role was contingent on other kinds of powers, for example in relation to Australia's external relations, international trade, assistance to the states, aborigines, or taxation. The main initiative for change came from the federal level. It reflected rising public attention to environmental questions in the late 1960s. The issues that emerged — threats to endangered wildlife, protection of the natural heritage, chemicals, the global ecological balance, as well as specific questions at state or local levels — increasingly took the debate to the Commonwealth. Here were matters that appeared to call for national action of a kind the states could not provide.

A first tentative step was taken in 1969, when Commonwealth and state ministers met to discuss the question of possible collaboration on wildlife conservation. They decided a need existed for continuing machinery, and that the Commonwealth should provide a secretariat to facilitate future meetings of ministers and working groups. The secretariat would collect information on conservation activities being carried out in Australia and overseas, and would establish and maintain liaison between Commonwealth and state agencies.[56] It was set up in the science branch of the Department of Education and Science in 1970, and assisted meetings of the biennial Australian Fauna Authorities Conference, held that year in Darwin, and of the Australian Committee on Waterbirds in Townsville.[57] At this time, as we have seen, the Commonwealth had no environmental policy body, apart from the small Office of the Environment. Only a few states, including South Australia and New South Wales, had environment departments,[58] though all had related agencies handling specific questions such as national parks or wildlife.

Thus the process of effecting federal-state collaboration took place side by side with the simultaneous creation by both Commonwealth and state governments of environment organizations. The Australian Environment Council (AEC) had its origins in meetings held in 1971. At the time, Labor was criticizing the federal government for procrastination in the establishment and staffing of the Office of the Environment. Plans for a federal-state council were seen by the government as part and parcel of the overall environmental effort. In the Prime Minister's view in 1971, the Council would "deal with matters which, because of their very nature, tend to transcend State boundaries."[59] The pace of developments picked up during the year. At the important meeting in Canberra in September, Howson was able to secure a qualified acknowledgment by the states that the Commonwealth had some role to play. The meeting recognized state governments had "already been active in a wide range of fields, including national parks, wildlife, water, soil and forest conservation; and control of water and sewerage systems and air, water, oil and noise pollution." However, it was also agreed there was a "continuing need to combat pollution and to improve the quality of the environment."[60] This clause implied that the Commonwealth had to be more assertive. Even so, Howson was clearly also worried that the federal side was forcing the pace and that there were limits to its persuasive power.

This process was delayed by continuing difficulties on the part of the states in setting up environmental policy bodies.[61] More important, it was still less than clear what the Commonwealth's role should be. The 1971 meeting had discussed "the means of continuing Federal and State consultation and the degree to which uniformity of approach was desirable,"[62] but no consensus emerged. The AEC was none the less agreed to in February 1972 as a body intended "to achieve effective consultation and coordination between Commonwealth and State Governments on appropriate environment matters."[63] Its area of competence was limited. It was to work towards production of a statement of requirements for environmental research at the national and state levels, and also undertake a survey of programmes in operation. Discussions were to follow about the best method of liaising with existing bodies. In sum, it was to underline the general principle of state authority. Recognizing the reality, and the desirability, of decentralized control was also in tune with federal Liberal, and especially National-Country, sympathies generally. It was agreed, Howson said in April 1972 in connection with the AEC's first meeting in Sydney, that "the great majority of environmental problems come within the jurisdiction of the States." At this meeting the Commonwealth and state delegations confirmed their acceptance of the "merits of decentralization as a means of environment improvement."[64]

For Labor, questions of the environment were too important to be left in the parochial bailliwicks of state politicians. In addition to developing the Commonwealth's role, ministers worked to establish a leadership role within a more dynamic AEC. Meeting in Melbourne in 1973, ministers also agreed to establish the Council of Nature Conservation Ministers (CONCOM), which held its first meeting the following January.[65] Its aims were described as being to further the development of coordinated policies for nature conservation, and especially for the reservation and management of adequate areas of land for conservation of Australian wildlife.[66] CONCOM's main Standing Committee was also set up in 1974. A number of specialized Working Groups were created to deal with birds, law enforcement, kangaroo management and other questions, and a number of ad hoc groups, for example on training and education, endangered flora and endangered fauna, supplemented this evolving structure.[67]

The AEC and CONCOM became the main institutional mechanisms for Australia-wide policy-making on environmental issues in the 1970s. They acted as a buffer between the conflicting positions of state and federal officials on many questions. Much of their work, too, was in areas that only a short while earlier would have been regarded as incontestibly within the jurisdiction of the states. These bodies were therefore vulnerable to shifts in state definitions of the boundary of acceptability of Commonwealth activity. After the 1975 change of government, the ANPWS and the AHC were reviewed and their functions redefined to reassure state governments that the Commonwealth understood their concerns. Even so, particular questions, such as planning for Kakadu National Park or the negotiations on the Great Barrier Reef Marine Park, often brought underlying conflicts into the open. Even where the Commonwealth's role was clearer, as in the Northern Territory, federal officials could find themselves being charged with proposing a "complete takeover of all national parks and wildlife functions" in Australia.[68]

109

An important aspect underlying change in the federal-state relationship in environmental policy has been financial. The availability of Commonwealth funds has been at various times a significant instrument in Canberra's attempts to mould state policies. State governments have, however, also been alert to the political potential of accusing the federal authorities of using such means to encroach on areas of state jurisdiction. Following passage of the *States Grants (Nature Conservation) Act* under the Labor government in 1973, the Department of Environment and Conservation became the body administering a funding programme which centred on transfers for purchase of land of conservation value. The Commonwealth used guidelines for protected areas developed by IUCN to assess the "suitability" of land the states proposed to acquire under the scheme.[69] Grants were made, for example, to allow the Queensland government in 1978 to acquire land which was the habitat of the near-extinct bridled nail-tailed wallaby, and to assist the Tasmanian government in its 1979-80 survey of the Southwest.[70] During 1975 alone, the value of land acquired under the Act was around $6 million.[71] There were a number of related federal programmes. The National Estate Grants Program was administered jointly by the Commonwealth and the states, with technical and policy advice provided by the AHC and state heritage bodies. From 1973-74 until 1980 a total of about 1400 projects were funded to the value of $20 million.[72]

Consensus could also be reached between state and Commonwealth governments about the requirement for, and political acceptability of, federal data-gathering activity. Such work was needed in connection with several of the international conventions signed by Australia in the 1970s. For the Man and the Biosphere Programme of UNESCO, the federal government also needed to engage in ecological mapping work to facilitate the creation of a network of biosphere reserves in Australia according to internationally defined criteria. A total of twelve biosphere reserves had been set up by 1983.[73] Scientific bodies had long pressed for a wide-ranging survey of Australian ecological resources. The work of the ABRS has already been noted; related data-collection activity geared to ecological surveys, for example in relation to Australia's wetlands, continued during the 1970s and 1980s.[74]

Acceptance by the states of a policy role for the federal government has not been smooth. However, since the early 1970s there has been a cautious mutual acknowledgment of respective spheres of responsibility, and also of the need for joint action in defined areas. Liberal coalition governments in particular, as in 1971[75] or in relation to South-west Tasmania in 1980-82, have been careful to spell out clearly their recognition that most environmental policy questions come within the jurisdiction of the states. Many of these, however, also called for national and trans-state boundary solutions. At an important meeting in June 1982, the first of its kind, the AEC and CONCOM jointly agreed on a Declaration reaffirming the collective commitment of Australian governments to environmental policy objectives. Continuing efforts would be made:

- to control all forms of pollution of the environment . . .;
- to prevent the extinction of Australian species of flora and fauna and to protect their habitats;
- to incorporate, at an early stage, environment and nature conservation considerations in government decision-making;
- to encourage and provide opportunities for constructive public participation on decisions with potentially significant environmental consequences;
- to ensure that the costs of preventing and controlling pollution are borne by the polluter;
- to support environmental education and to promote community awareness of environment and nature conservation issues;
- to contribute to international activities directed towards safeguarding and improving the global environment; and
- to improve arrangements for monitoring and reporting on the major indicators of the state of the Australian environment.[76]

Much of the statement affirmed continuing policies and procedures. The "polluter pays" principle had long been a familiar one in both OECD guidelines and Australian approaches, as had the general commitment of state and federal governments to combat pollution, collaborate in the protection of Australian fauna and flora, and promote data-gathering and reliable environmental statistics. The studied vagueness of some of the provisions also reflected past disputes. Both levels of government had in practice made distinctions earlier between environmental groups on the criterion of the "constructiveness" of their role in public debates and decision-making, for example in connection with government funding programmes. Cooperation between the Commonwealth and state authorities on international environmental matters had likewise been a practice of several years' standing; its enshrining as an important principle of the Hobart Declaration was nonetheless a significant symbolic step in the process of legitimizing the part state governments ought to play in such matters.

Cooperative federalism and the environment

The Declaration of 1982 confirmed the understandings that had come to support federal-state cooperation on environmental and nature conservation policies during the previous decade. While the Liberal coalition government of the day was ideologically more predisposed than the ALP had been in the 1970s to defend the participatory rights of states, it is significant that the transition to the Labor government of Prime Minister Hawke in 1983 did not lead to any deflection of the course set in the Declaration. The machinery established in the early 1970s was limited, however, in its capacity to reconcile serious clashes of interest between the federal and state governments. Other institutions of federalism, such as the annual meetings of the premiers, had a role to play when environmental conflicts could not be contained within the AEC-CONCOM framework. This framework was nonetheless a vital part of environmental policy-making on such matters as the workings of international conservation agreements, data collection, and programmes dealing with toxic chemicals, flora and fauna protection, and related topics.

The machinery was significant also for the role it played in legitimizing the claims of the federal government in the environmental area. State interests were not threatened by these developments. Indeed state governments had a number of incentives to sustain the level of collaboration entailed. Commonwealth legislation provided several sources of funding for state programmes in environmental and heritage areas; since the federal government was accepted as the lead player on international matters, the joint machinery afforded states access to decision-making at this level; and cooperation with Canberra could sometimes be a useful way for a state to prove to local pressure groups that it had a national vision too. A series of events from the controversies surrounding the Whitlam government's policies in 1972-75 to the Tasmanian dam issue and its resolution in 1983 also underlined the point that Canberra had to operate within a milieu of cooperative federalism, and that unilateralism and expansionism on its part were high-cost enterprises.

At times equally problematic was the task of coordination within the federal government itself. "Environmental" policy is notoriously a difficult area to pin down conceptually and administratively. Several federal departments, including Health and Science, had responsibilities in what later became environmental policy areas once an environment department was established. Formulation of policy within inter-departmental committee or working group settings was in any case a norm of Australian government in the 1970s and 1980s, and the diverse character of the environmental policy field ensured that this pattern would evolve there too. From the outset, other departments had to be assured that the new environmental bodies would not be vested with a powerful coordinating role. Later experience showed that environmental officials were in practice constrained by the facts of departmental power in Australian government. Departments such as Finance, the Treasury, Foreign Affairs, and Trade, and the Prime Minister's and Cabinet Department, could set limits to the freedom of manoeuvre of environment departments and agencies. In relation to external policies, the broader coordinating responsibility of the Department of Foreign Affairs was at times a significant constraint. Given these circumstances, the existence of an environmental constituency outside government, the subject of Chapter 9, represented an addition to the capability of environmental bureaucracies inside government to influence the course of policy-making.

Notes for Chapter 6

1 *The Howson Diaries: The Life of Politics,* ed. Don Aitkin (Ringwood: Viking Press, 1984), p. 770.
2 *New South Wales, Parliamentary Debates,* Vol. CL (Session 1979-80), 15 November 1979, p. 3079, (Hon. D.P. Landa).

[3] *New South Wales, Parliamentary Debates,* Vol. CXII (Session 1975-76), 18 March 1976, p. 4453.

[4] *Queensland, Legislative Assembly,* Vol. 265, 31 July 1974, p. 11.

[5] See G.M. Bates, *Environmental Law in Australia* (Sydney: Butterworths, 1983), p. 23; Douglas E. Fisher, *Environmental Law in Australia: An Introduction* (St. Lucia: University of Queensland Press, 1980), p. 39.

[6] *Tasmania, Journals and Printed Papers of the Parliament of Tasmania,* Vol. 204, Pt. I, 20 October 1981, p. 201 (Adams). The species were the Orange-bellied Parrot, Forty-spotted Pardalate, and Thylacine.

[7] *Western Australia, Assembly,* Vol. 241, 17 November 1982, p. 5695 (Laurance).

[8] *South Australia, House of Assembly,* Session of 1973, Vol. I, August 1, 1973, p. 131 (Hon. G.R. Broomhill).

[9] The committee was chaired by the Director-General of Health. The Departments represented were: Education and Science, External Affairs, Civil Aviation, Health, Interior, Primary Industry, Labour and National Service, National Development, Shipping and Transport, Supply, and the Prime Minister's Department; also represented were CSIRO and the National Capital Development Commission (NCDC). See Sen. Dame Annabelle Rankin, *Senate,* 45, October 1970, p. 1035.

[10] *Senate,* 47, 15 February 1971, p. 342; exchange between Whitlam and Gorton, *House of Representatives,* 71, 24 February 1971, p. 559, and 10 March, 1971, pp. 820-1.

[11] *The Howson Diaries: The Life of Politics,* ed. Don Aitkin (Ringwood, Victoria: The Viking Press, 1984), p. 796.

[12] Howson, *House of Representatives,* 74, 26 October 1971, pp. 2509-10.

[13] *House of Representatives,* 74, 13 October 1971, p. 2294. The Minister was of course well aware of these problems; see Howson at 74, 26 October 1971, pp. 2509-10.

[14] *House of Representatives,* 77, 26 April 1972, p. 2060.

[15] These kinds of arguments also took place in the public service, particularly in light of Uren's pro-environment, anti-development speeches. "Partly the argument between the government and the opposition environmentalists is an argument between two generations of behind-the-scenes ideas men in the Commonwealth public service": Peter Samuel, "The Environmental Line," *Bulletin,* October 28, 1972, pp. 19-21.

[16] Cass, statement of 24 June 1973, *AGD,* 1(2), 1973, p. 585; DEC, *Report for Period December 1972 to June 1974* (Canberra, 1975; PP 298), pp. 1-2; Whitlam, on the first World Environment Day, *AFAR,* 44(6), June 1973, p. 423.

[17] DEC, *Report for Period December 1972 to June 1974* (Canberra, 1975; PP 298), pp. 3-5.

[18] Cass, *AGD* 1(2), 1973, p. 585; ninety-seven new positions were added between December 1972 and March 1974 (*House of Representatives,* 88, 21 March 1974, p. 799).

[19] Cass, statement of September 24, *AGD* 2(3), 1974, p. 677.

[20] *AGWD* 1(1975), p. 109; DEC, *Report for Period December 1972 to June 1974* (Canberra; 1975: PP 298), p. 44.

[21] *Howson Diaries,* pp. 807, 832, 855, 867. The matter was resolved in Cabinet. At the Prime Minister's insistence Prof. Walsh became Chairman, rather than the earlier choice of Prof. Len Weickhardt, Chancellor of the University of Melbourne.

[22] Cass, statement of 1 August, at *AGD* 2(3), 1974, p. 673; DOE, *Report for Period July 1974 to June 1975* (Canberra, 1976; PP 139), p. 28; Cass, *House of Representatives,* 90, 19 September 1974, p. 1646. Initial reports were prepared on DDT, PCBs, supersonic transport, and later, land use.

[23] Recommendation 30 of the Report of the House of Representatives Select Committee on Wildlife Conservation pointed to the need for a Commonwealth authority in the field of nature conservation. The ideas was approved by the ALP caucus in September 1973 (*AGD,* 1(3), 1973, p. 1009).

[24] ANPWS, *Report for Period 13 March 1975 to 30 June 1976* (Canberra, 1976), pp. 107; DEC, *Report for Period December 1972 to June 1974* (Canberra, 1975; PP 298), p. 6. An Executive officer was recruited to oversee preparations, and McMichael acted as secretary of the resulting three-person committee in the Department, with help from an advisory council. Support for the

113

heritage concept also added weight to this development; see *National Estate. Report of the Committee of Inquiry* (Canberra, 1975; PP 195), para 8.73, p. 239.

[25] DEHCD, *2nd Annual Report 1977* (Canberra, 1978; PP 308), p. 1; the initial definition is at DEHCD, *1st Annual Report, 1975-6* (Canberra, 1977; PP 398), pp. 1-6. Lansdown had been permanent head of Urban and Regional Development.

[26] See criticisms by Dr. Jenkins, *House of Representatives,* 105, 27 May 1977, p. 2028.

[27] Summary at ASTEC, *Science and Technology in Australia,* Vol. 2 (Canberra, 1978; PP 106), Ch. 36, pp. 583-610.

[28] DEHCD, *1st Annual Report, 1975-6* (Canberra, 1977; PP 398), p. 12; Newman, *Commonwealth Record,* 1(6), 9-15 August 1976, p. 315; ANPWS, *Report for the Period 1 July 1976 to 30 July 1977* (Canberra, 1977), p. 2.

[29] DSE, *Annual Report 1978-9* (Canberra, 1979; PP 349); DSE, *Annual Report 1979-80* (Canberra, 1980; PP 357), p. 61; DHAE, *Annual Report 1980-1* (Canberra, 1982; PP 35).

[30] DHAE, *Annual Report 1982-3* (Canberra, 1983; PP 345), p. 9. The international functions were primarily the responsibility of the Environmental Coordination Branch; this, together with the Environmental Studies Branch, and the Environment Legislation Branch, constituted the Environment Division of the Department (*ibid.*, p. 65).

[31] Cohen, *Weekly Hansard, House of Representatives,* No. 1, 1984, 28 February 1984, pp. 93-5; *Senate,* No. 1, 1984, 28 February 1984, pp. 73-4.

[32] *AEC Newsl.,* 4(4), December 1984; and the text of Prime Minister Hawke's announcement, *Canberra Times,* December 12, 1984. The minister (Cohen) now had as an important part of his tasks assisting the Prime Minister in preparations for the 1988 Bicentennial celebrations.

[33] *Towards an Australian Science Council, A Discussion Paper issued by the Hon. W.L. Morrison, MP, Minister for Science, March 1974* (Canberra, 1974; PP 74), p. 1.

[34] OECD, *Examiners Report on Science and Technology in Australia* (Canberra, 1975; PP 177), p. 16; *Independent Inquiry into the CSIRO, August 1977* (Chairman, A.J. Birch) (Canberra, 1978; PP 283); on the ASTEC review, see *Australian,* 15 March 1985. The Act of 1949 was substantially amended in 1978.

[35] CSIRO, *25th Annual Report for the Year 1972-73* (Canberra, 1974), p. 8. The research programme was described as becoming more "people-oriented" as against "industry oriented."

[36] CSIRO, *35th Annual Report* (Canberra, 1983), p. 151.

[37] This was "... responsible for stimulating the study of the taxonomy, distribution and ecology of Australia's biological resources and for assessing the long-term national requirements in this and related matters": ABRS Interim Council, *Report for 1973-74* (Canberra, 1975; PP 263), pp. 1-3; DOS, *Report for Year 1973-74* (Canberra, 1975; PP 269), p. 87.

[38] An advisory committee, chaired by Prof. Sir Rutherford Robertson, was set up in December 1978; and a new branch of the Department of Science and Environment to coordinate activities in December 1979. Also included was the Bureau of Flora and Fauna, and the ABRS Participatory Programme, the agency designed to administer grants to institutions: *ABRS, 1973-78* (Canberra, 1978; PP 354), pp. 1-6, 8, 9: ABRS, *Report March 1979 - June 1980* (Canberra, 1981; PP 214), pp. 102.

[39] *Ibid.,* p. 23; Sen. Webster, *Commonwealth Record,* 4(14), 9-15 April 1979, p. 447; and reports, *ibid.,* 5(33), 18-24 August 1980, p. 1281, and 7(42), 18-24 August 1982, p. 1467. Volume I (largely introductory) was published in 1981, Vols. 8 and 29 in 1982, and vol. 22 in 1984. A total of 50 volumes are planned.

[40] DES, *Report for 1969* (Canberra, 1970; PP 178), p. 36; *Report for 1970* (Canberra, 1970; PP 130), p. 72.

[41] DES, *Report for Year 1967 and 1968* (Canberra, 1970; PP 172), p. 2; *Report for 1971* (Canberra, 1973; PP 116), p. 58, App. 4, p. 103; *Report for 1972* (Canberra, 1974; PP 272), pp. 55, 105.

[42] ANPWS, *Report for Period 13 March 1975 to 30 June 1976* (Canberra, 1976), pp. 1-7.

[43] *Weekly Hansard,* House of Representatives, No. 7, 1984, 30 May 1984, pp. 2387-8.

[44] DEC, *Report for Period December 1972 to June 1974* (Canberra, 1973; PP 298), p. 2.

[45] *House of Representatives,* 90, 23 August 1974, p. 1185; DEC, *Report for Period December 1972 to June 1974* (Canberra, 1975; PP 298), pp. 24, 29.

[46] DSE, *Annual Report 1978-79* (Canberra, 1979; PP 349), p. 10.

[47] Cohen, *Weekly Hansard,* House of Representatives, No. 3, 1984, 27 March 1984, p. 884; No. 10, 1984, 4 September 1984, p. 577.

[48] ANPWS, *Report for Period 1 July 1976 to 30 June 1977* (Canberra, 1977), p. 10; Cohen, *Weekly Hansard,* House of Representatives, No. 10, 1984, 4 September 1984, p. 577.

[49] See Hawke at *Weekly Hansard,* House of Representatives, No. 7, 1984, 30 May 1984, pp. 2387-8; and the respective ministers at No. 8, 7-8 June 1984, pp. 3183-4; No. 3, 29 March 1984, p. 1106; No. 7, 30 May 1984, p. 2407; and No. 6, 7 May 1984, pp. 1987-8.

[50] Senate, Standing Committee on Foreign Affairs and Defence, *Australian Representation Overseas — the Department of Foreign Affairs* (Canberra, 1978), Vol. 2, pp. 1490, 1501.

[51] Hawke, *Weekly Hansard* (House of Representatives), No. 7, 1984, 30 May 1984, pp. 2387-8.

[52] See references at n. 49 above.

[53] See Geoffrey Hawker, R.F.I. Smith and Patrick Weller, *Politics and Policy in Australia* (St. Lucia: University of Queensland Press, 1979), pp. 207-26.

[54] Alan Watt, "Australia," in Zara Steiner, ed., *The Times Survey of the Foreign Ministries of the World* (London: Times Books, 1982), pp. 46-7.

[55] *Howson Diaries,* pp. 807, 855, 867.

[56] DES, *Report for 1969* (Canberra, 1971; PP 178). p. 36.

[57] DES, *Report for 1970* (Canberra, 1972; PP 130), p. 50; Sen. Wright, *Senate,* 45, 19 August 1970, p. 29.

[58] *Senate,* 53, 24 August 1972, p. 417. Sen. Keeffe noted South Australia's Minister for Conservation, and the New South Wales Minister for Environmental Control; the Premier of Western Australia was also Minister for Environmental Protection.

[59] Gorton, *House of Representatives,* 71, 24 February 1971, p. 559, and 10 March 1971, pp. 820-1.

[60] *House of Representatives,* 74, 6-7 October 1971, p. 2003 (Howson).

[61] The September 1971 meeting had earlier been postponed because of this (Howson, *House of Representatives,* 73, 26 August 1971, pp. 750-1), and the meeting then planned for Perth in November took place the following February.

[62] *House of Representatives,* 74, 6-7 October 1971, p. 2003 (Howson).

[63] *House of Representatives,* 76, 23 February 1972, p. 179.

[64] Howson, *House of Representatives,* 77, 26 April 1972, pp. 2057-8. This was in line with the general approach of the government, following particularly a report by Commonwealth and state officials on decentralization in government.

[65] *House of Representatives,* 87, 5 December 1973, p. 4363, and 88, 3 April 1974, p. 975.

[66] DEC, *Report for Period December 1972 to June 1974* (Canberra, 1975; PP 298), p. 64. There is a slightly different definition of its aims at ANPWS, *Report for Period 13 March 1975 to 30 June 1976* (Canberra, 1976), p. 10.

[67] ANPWS, *Report for Period 1 July 1976 to 30 June 1977* (Canberra, 1977), pp. 18-19; *Report for Period 1 July 1978 - 30 June 1979* (Canberra, 1979), pp. 32-34. Others included groups on professional training, marine parks and reserves, and youth.

[68] This was denied by Cass; *AGWD,* 1, 1975, p. 240.

[69] DEC, *Report for Period December 1972 to June 1974* (Canberra, 1975; PP 298), p. 6.

[70] DSE, *Annual Report 1979-80* (Canberra, 1980: PP 357), p. 80; *Commonwealth Record,* 3(24), 19-25 June 1978, p. 744.

[71] *AGWD,* 1, 1975, p. 894. The budget included $9 million to assist states in the acquisition of land for nature conservation purposes, and $8 million for related grants to states *(House of Representatives,* 90, 17 September 1974, p. 1281).

[72] DHAE, *Annual Report 1980-81* (Canberra, 1983; PP 35), pp. 34-5.

[73] Australian National Commission for UNESCO, *Australia's Biosphere Reserves: Conserving Ecological Diversity,* by B.W. Davis and G.A. Drake (Canberra, 1983), pp. 9-43.

[74] The Ecological Survey of Australia was designed to survey Australian ecosystems "directed towards identifying those areas worthy of preservation and which are best suited for preservation as National Parks or Nature Reserves. Whilst much has been done by individual States in the reservation

115

of areas of nature conservation, representative samples of all the significant ecosystems in the Australian environment have not yet been protected" (DEC, *Report for Period December 1972 to June 1974* [Canberra, 1975; PP 298], p. 15).

[75] *House of Representatives,* 77, 26 April 1972, p. 2057.

[76] *AEC Newsl.,* 2(2), June 1982, pp. 5-6; DHAE, *Annual Report 1981-82* (Canberra, 1982: PP 263), pp. 2, 17, 67, App. 10; AEC/CONCOM, *Australian Achievements in Environment Protection and Nature Conservation, 1972-1982* (Canberra, 1982), pp. 31-32.

CHAPTER SEVEN

Federal-state Diplomacy and International Institutions

The use of government to manage resource and environmental problems in Australia is not new. The colonial authorities went to considerable lengths to combat the most notorious threat of the nineteenth century — the waves of destruction inflicted by rabbits — and offered substantial rewards to anyone who could come up with the answer.[1] In the 1960s, demands for action by both federal and state governments on matters of environmental policy expanded in degree and kind. To these were increasingly added expectations arising from outside the country, in a variety of international forums such as the meetings of parties to international treaties. The Commonwealth and federal-state machinery discussed in the last chapter was thus both a basis for the formulation of international environment policy and a means of responding to domestic pressures. For Australia to participate fully in international developments, it had to give thought to government organization and programmes; and for domestic regimes to be effective, it had to pay attention to the workings of international institutions and conventions. After an uncertain start, federal-state diplomacy became an important feature of the formulation of external policies. In addition, the departments of the federal government gradually adjusted to the changing patterns of policy-making required to manage the country's growing external environmental relations.

The states, the Commonwealth and international institutions

Lack of a sure Commonwealth or federal-state guide for steering Australia into these relationships explains some of the awkwardness and uncertainty that characterized its early approaches to UNCHE. The newness of the federal environment department, and the still controversial nature of the Commonwealth's role domestically, compounded the dilemma. Disagreements over the composition of the Australian delegation to Stockholm were eagerly grabbed by the Labor opposition. Uren complained in October 1971 that the new environment department was "fighting with the Department of Foreign Affairs about who has the responsibility to place Australia's mediocre contribution before [UNCHE]."[2] Officials from the departments of Health, Trade and Industry and National Development, and the CSIRO, were eventually included, in addition to representatives from Foreign Affairs and the environment department. Of these, ironically, all but the environment department had good claims arising out of past activities to speak for Australia in Stockholm. Given the tentative character

117

of federal-state experimentation in 1971-72, it was also incumbent on the Commonwealth to bring the states into the picture. In October 1971, Howson asked state governments to advise him "on the attitude they want to take towards the Stockholm conference."[3] State representatives were added to the delegation, as the Prime Minister put it, "in view of the important role of the States in environmental matters."[4] The governments of New South Wales and Victoria sent two officials each, and other state governments sent one each. The states were also consulted with regard to the brief for the Australian delegation. At Stockholm, Howson emphasized the "spirit of cooperative federalism" that inspired the Australian approach to environment policy.[5]

The scope for state influence, however, was restricted. Australia's was only one voice in conference processes. Its main priorities — ensuring a continuing role in the future organization, encouraging moves to check marine pollution, responding to the twists and turns of the nuclear tests issue — were predominantly Commonwealth matters. The first of these, more particularly, could be closely identified with the thinking of the Department of Foreign Affairs, and the last was decided by the federal Cabinet in Canberra. Questions of pollution, however, were indeed a concern of some state governments, especially New South Wales. Some were determined — as were the federal departments of Trade and Industry, and National Development — to qualify concern for environmental protection with an emphasis on the requirements of economic development. State governments ensured they were involved in assessing the results of UNCHE. The AEC met in Canberra in July 1972 to consider its outcome. Particular importance was attached to its recommendations on air, water and noise pollution. More significant in the long run, though, was the conclusion drawn by the states that Stockholm confirmed the requirement of continuing cooperation between the Commonwealth and themselves on both domestic and international environmental policy. The ministers recommended "a continuing participation by the States in the preparations for and business of future international actions and conferences on environmental matters that might affect the States."[6]

In practice, however, many items on UNEP agendas during the 1970s were of interest primarily to federal government agencies. This was reinforced by pressures from Australian NGOs, which tended to see in a stronger Commonwealth role the natural complement to more effective international cooperation. Steadily declining attention to UNEP over the decade, some repetitiveness in its calls for action, and shifts of government priorities after the 1975 change of government, combined to make routine Australia's cooperation with UNEP. For the lower-level technical activity of the post-Stockholm period, the environment department, rather than Foreign Affairs, was regarded as the appropriate actor.[7] Thus federal environment officials followed through and coordinated Australian responses to the Global Environment Monitoring System (GEMS) and INFOTERRA. Feasibility studies on the establishment of an Australian baseline station for atmospheric monitoring were undertaken by the Commonwealth environment and science departments, in association with the government of Tasmania.[8] Indeed closely related coordinating work was done by federal science officials, for example in relation to Australian participation in the World Meteorological Organization (WMO), especially in the World Weather Watch (WWW) from the early 1970s, and in the Global Atmospheric Research Programme (GARP), organized by WMO in collaboration with the International Council of Scientific Unions (ICSU).[9] This division of Commonwealth responsibilities matched the division at the international level, and followed from prior Australian definitions of the functional separability of the two areas.

Stockholm set more of a precedent for international environment conferences attended by Australia. The extensive preparations for the 1976 Habitat conference centred around a task force inside the environment department, which coordinated the Australian response; an inter-departmental committee of Commonwealth officials; a federal-state liaison committee; and a national advisory committee of fifteen members. The identity of the two key federal players — the environment department and the Department of Urban and Regional Development — was dictated by the agenda. States were represented through the liaison committee, and also by means of the advisory body, which was chaired by a senior officer of the South Australian Housing Trust. Environment officials, however, took the main role in international preparatory work, for example in preparatory committee meetings in New York in January 1975 and at a regional conference a few months later in Tehran.[10] The Australian approach also reflected changes in government organization resulting from the return of the Liberal coalition in 1975, which led to a restructuring of environment policy responsibilities within the new, and more development-oriented, Department of Environment, Housing and Community Development.

The desertification conference similarly fostered and rested on federal-state cooperation, particularly in light of what was seen at both levels of government as an opportunity to project internationally distinctive Australian expertise in arid lands management. The Department of Foreign Affairs came to be more actively involved in the outcome, however, because of the unexpected eruption of the desertification fund issue, which transformed the question into a broader foreign policy one affecting the wider interests of western countries, and moved environment officials away from the controlling levers. Foreign Affairs staff were also involved, with federal environment officials, in later exchanges with state governments on implementation of the International Plan of Action to Combat Desertification.[11] Australian activity, however, was constrained by relative immobility within the UN system on desertification.

Questions related to these developments occasionally arose in the AEC and CONCOM frameworks, though other international matters tended to take priority. The Council established a subcommittee to coordinate responses to UNEP's tenth anniversary celebrations in 1982. The joint AEC-CONCOM session in Hobart in June 1982, and the declaration on environmental policies which resulted, was also in part an Australian response to these events.[12]

119

The environmental activities of other UN bodies had repercussions for the machinery of Australian federal-state cooperation. The MAB Programme, which had its origins in the 1968 UNESCO conference on the biosphere — the Australian contribution to which was organized by the federal Department of Education and Science[13] — was of interest to state governments on several counts. Non-governmental institutions across the country were involved, and, more significantly, the Programme had as a goal the creation of a global network of biosphere reserves, a question affecting land use, therefore touching on state jurisdiction. Exchanges with the states on this matter were channelled through the AEC and its Standing Committee. In May 1976 the Council finally approved Australian participation in the relevant part (Project 8). Strictly speaking, this approval was not required, since the MAB Programme rested ultimately on contributions by scientific institutions; but the decision gave the Programme useful backing from federal and state governments, and facilitated the participation of official bodies. The ANPWS was responsible for advising state governments on the pertinent criteria for the biosphere network, seeking nominations from them, and, in general, coordinating the Australian response. The Australian National Commission for UNESCO, however, which had in the early 1970s been closely involved with MAB developments, remained the body formally responsible for forwarding to UNESCO Australia's nominations for proposed reserves.[14] The international arrangements thus encouraged interlocking between Australian organizations. The Australian UNESCO Committee for MAB was established in the context of preparatory moves in the early 1970s to launch the Programme, and also of a general restructuring of the Australian UNESCO Commission itself in 1971-72.[15]

Listing implied no enforcement capability for UNESCO. It was presumed, however, that national authorities would undertake protection, management and research tasks. Aided by the international contacts of key individuals,[16] the nomination process went surprisingly quickly. This occurred despite the fact that these matters fell very much on the periphery of the concerns of state governments, and that some states were especially hesitant at the prospect of tying up parcels of land in international red tape. In 1976-77, the first year of the Programme's operation, UNESCO approved five Australian reserves; another six were added during 1977-78.[17] Several criticisms arose. On scientific grounds, doubts were expressed whether proposals from the states necessarily reflected the most appropriate sites from a national point of view. The absence of systematic nation-wide studies of Australia's biogeographical provinces, and the continuing international debate on criteria for the selection and size of biosphere reserves, added to these fears. Further, after the first round of promptings by the Commonwealth, nominations from the states tended to be intermittent.[18] Thus by 1983, Australia had only twelve designated biosphere reserves. These were Uluru (Ayers Rock-Mount Olga) National Park, Danggali Conservation Park (South Australia), Kosciusko National Park (New South Wales), an unnamed park in South Australia, Yathong Nature Reserve (New South Wales), Croajingalong National Park (Victoria), Macquarie Island Nature Reserve (Tasmania), South-West National

Park (Tasmania), Hattah-Kulkyne National Park and Murray-Kulkyne Park (Victoria), Prince Regent River Nature Reserve (Western Australia), Fitzgerald River National Park (Western Australia), and Wilsons Promontory National Park (Victoria).[19] The biosphere reserve network lacked much potential to mobilize public opinion. These were designed as areas for scientific research and conservation, not for public access (unless, as in several cases, the designations overlapped with other categories); the criteria for selection, moreover, tended to be more esoteric than those deployed in public conservation debates.

Participation in intergovernmental organizations (IGOs) is often constrained by financial considerations. In times of budgetary restraint, government departments often had to work hard to justify activities. In the early 1980s, Australian environment officials were in any case placing new emphasis on the need to improve financial management within UNEP,[20] partly in response to criticism at home that Australia's contribution was not being well spent. The Department of Foreign Affairs was itself under increasing pressure in the late 1970s to minimize expenditures involved in international conferences, particularly in view of the proliferation of new organizations;[21] restrictions imposed through Treasury also affected the ability of the environment department to participate fully in international activities. In relation to the OECD, to which we now turn, Australia's participation as Chairman of the Environment Committee in the early 1980s was for a time threatened by criticism of the expense involved in using Canberra-as opposed to Paris-based staff.

The political economy of chemicals regulation

The OECD's interest in pollution in the early 1970s was welcomed by both state and Commonwealth agencies in Australia. In 1972, the AEC set up a research committee to establish priorities for a five-year environmental research programme in the area.[22] Several OECD meetings of this period, for example that of May 1972 on air pollution, had productive connections with Australian interests. Several federal departments were involved. For example, the Department of Transport chaired the national Committee on Motor Vehicle Emissions (COMVE); officials from the atmosphere section of the environment department took part in its work.[23] In general, Australian approaches and responses to OECD environmental activities were coordinated by the environment department, especially in relation to the important programmes of the late 1970s and early 1980s on toxic chemicals. Senior environment officials viewed the OECD in an increasingly important light during the 1970s, a reflection, perhaps, of diminishing expectations concerning UNEP. The Deputy Secretary of the department, H.J. Higgs, had long experience of OECD work, serving for several years as Vice-Chairman of its Environment Committee; the Chairmanship was taken over by McMichael, then Secretary of the department again, in the early 1980s.

The strengthening of federal-state consultative mechanisms during the 1970s allowed state governments more opportunity to express preferences. As a result, greater Australian emphasis was placed inside OECD forums on matters the states had indicated were of particular concern to them: hazardous chemicals, for example, noise abatement policies and environmental economics.[24] There were a number of instances of OECD-related federal-state cooperation. Australian work in the OECD's Air Management Sector Group on photochemical smog problems in the early 1970s was based largely on data collated by the New South Wales air pollution control authorities. In connection with the objectives of the OECD's Water Management Sector Group in the mid-1970s, two bodies — the Engineering and Water Supply Department of the government of South Australia, and the Sydney Metropolitan Water Sewerage and Drainage Board — took part in surveys of water pollution problems through studies of eutrophication in two Australian reservoirs.[25] Australia did not have the luxury, however, of being able to take part in any OECD programme that happened to look promising. Sensitive to potential criticism in the more budget-conscious early 1980s, environment officials emphasized that participation in OECD environment programmes was "highly selective according to the limited resources available."[26]

Toxic chemicals management problems became a high-priority area of concentration in the late 1970s. This followed AEC proposals for joint federal-state efforts in the area, and Commonwealth recognition in 1976 of the need for comprehensive federal and state measures in relation to environmentally hazardous chemicals.[27] A number of highly publicized pollution incidents guaranteed wider public support for such moves. The AEC sponsored the creation of a National Advisory Committee on Chemicals (NACC) in 1977; this body, on which both Commonwealth and state officials sat, met for the first time early in 1978. One aim was to produce an initial list of hazardous chemicals. Particular attention was paid at first to alkyl mercury compounds and to problems associated with the use of mercury in some mining operations. While the NACC commenced work on a national action programme on environmentally hazardous chemicals, the AEC continued work on its own report on these substances.[28]

From the outset this activity had an important international dimension. Talks were held with IRPTC officials in 1978-79 on ways to improve cooperation.[29] In general, however, this Geneva venture was considered less directly pertinent to Australia's needs than OECD work. It tended to move slowly, for example, and Australian officials were in practice interested in only a handful of chemical groups on which more efficient data collection could be done inside Australia. As indicated in Chapter 4, Australia in the late 1970s was moving towards introduction of an interim notification and assessment scheme for new industrial chemicals. The groundwork was laid by the NACC and AEC in 1978-80, with evaluations of procedures for assessing the potential environmental effects of chemicals, a review of existing Australian practices for monitoring chemicals in the living environment, and study of problems associated with the transport and handling of dangerous chemicals. Plans for the interim scheme were completed in 1980-81, and it was announced by the AEC in October 1981. Under the scheme, chemicals referred to the government were assessed by a new body, the Chemicals Review Subcommittee (CRSC), which reported to the NACC and through it to the AEC's Standing Committee. By June 1982, a total of forty chemicals had been referred to the federal environment department.[30] Environment officials openly acknowledged the scheme's indebtedness to OECD work.[31] The government progressively incorporated other aspects into its chemicals policy. Australia endorsed two key OECD decisions of 1982, relating to the acceptability among member-states of each others' test data on chemicals, and the minimum pre-marketing data required as the basis for initial assessment of new chemicals. These approaches were grafted on to the existing notification scheme.[32]

One obstacle was a natural wariness on the part of chemical companies. From an industry perspective, these tentative, and voluntary, beginnings, contained the hidden threat of a much broader regulatory strategy. In evaluating the impact of the scheme, officials therefore began to suggest reforms that would ensure wider participation by industry associations, so that the transformation of the interim arrangements into a fully, mandatory scheme could be achieved with minimal difficulty. For some advocates of more stringent regulation of the chemical industry, the scheme's restriction to newly marketed chemicals was also a significant weakness. During 1981 the NACC identified a number of existing chemicals it thought required further study, and produced profiles of a short list of twelve of these.

Chemicals received more publicity, and more high-level government attention, following the 1983 election. In July 1983, the AEC's Standing Committee set up a Chemicals Consultation Committee of federal and state representatives to liaise with industry, the trade unions and other organizations. Also included on the committee were representatives of the Chemical Importers and Exporters Council of Australia, the Confederation of Australian Industry, the Australian Council of Trade Unions, the Australian Conservation Foundation, and the Royal Australian Chemical Institute.[33] Attention to developments in OECD meetings continued to form a central strand of the policy process. Toxic chemicals were generating more public alarm. UNEP's choice of "chemicals" as the theme for the 1984 World Environment Day was taken up in media commentary and by environmental groups, and a major conference on hazardous chemicals in the Australian environment was held at the University of Sydney in August.[34] The AEC released a discussion paper on a proposed permanent scheme in July 1984, drawing on the experience provided by the interim notification scheme. Planned to start operations in 1985, the scheme required manufacturers and importers of all new chemicals, and of selected chemicals already in use, to submit information on their properties, uses and likely health and environmental effects.[35] In addition to the specific contributions of OECD discussions and recommendations to the Australian scheme, Australian officials also made extensive use of data collected for OECD purposes as a basis for general policy development.[36]

123

Towards a National Conservation Strategy

Australia's membership of IUCN tended to fall considerably lower than the OECD in its ordering of priorities among international organization memberships. Few of the issues on its agendas had echoes over a wide field of public policy. The mixed character of its membership, too, moderated the Australian government's perception of its importance. Australia, like many other western countries, was a member, but so also were a large number of non-governmental bodies; though within its sphere of environmental conservation IUCN increasingly during the 1970s acted like an inter-governmental organization, it was still shaped in many ways by its earlier history as an association of non-governmental groupings. Thus while virtually any activity of the OECD in the environmental policy area was regarded as significant and worth further study, at least in areas that happened to be of interest to Australia, the same was not true of IUCN. The Union did, however, enjoy a special place within the workings of Australian environmental policy-making, not least because of the multiple contacts which a number of officials, and various conservation groups, had with it.

These relations were generally coordinated through the environment department in Canberra, the budget of which bore the cost ($25,000 per annum by 1980) of membership.[37] Other related coordinating tasks were carried out by the ANPWS, and, from the late 1970s, by the Australian Committee for IUCN. As a rule, too, the environment department had responsibility for the composition of Australia's delegations to IUCN General Assemblies or other meetings. A constraint on the department was posed by the fact that a variety of Australian bodies — federal agencies such as the AHC, conservation agencies in some state governments, and environmental pressure groups — also at different times had their own separate memberships of the organization and these, for procedural purposes, tended to be grouped together by IUCN secretariat officials as "the Australian delegation." Depending on the constitutional rules in force at any given time, these other members also had voting powers of various kinds in Assemblies. The structuring of Australian delegations was also affected by budgetary constraints. Rather than send an officer from Canberra for this purpose, for example, or rely exclusively on environment personnel, a regionally based foreign service officer led the Australian delegation at the 1984 Assembly in Madrid.[38]

Specific kinds of expertise formed an additional source of Australian links with IUCN, both before and after the government's decision in 1973 to apply for full state membership of the organization. Thus an officer of the ANPWS was selected as a member of the specialist marsupials group of the IUCN's Survival Service Commission when this was established in the mid-1970s. The IUCN roles of some leading Australian environment and nature conservation officials were referred to in Chapter 2. Following Australian membership, the federal government's task in the transmission of data to the organization gradually expanded. Thus federal officials included amongst their responsibilities the collating and forwarding to IUCN of information on Australian endangered species required for the periodic updatings of the Union's *Red Data Book*.[39] The Australian ability to carry out this role improved during the 1970s and 1980s, particularly in light of the work of CONCOM. The CONCOM Working Group dealing with species of flora in the CITES appendices, for example, increasingly from the late 1970s re-defined this mandate into a more general exploration of ways to achieve flora conservation objectives in Australia.[40] This activity was in turn reinforced by the greater emphasis placed by IUCN at this time on endangered flora through its London-based Threatened Plants Committee.

For the most part, then, Australian interest in IUCN tended to be limited to the relatively small enclaves of federal and state officials, or members of environmental groups, who were professionally or politically engaged in the subjects it treated. In turn, IUCN interest in Australia has focussed primarily on those of its threatened species or areas that happen to be of wider international concern to its varied membership, such as tortoise or turtle species, threatened species on Christmas Island, or problems confronting the conservation of the Great Barrier Reef.[41] Two kinds of processes have given these links greater political salience. First, in response to conservationist criticism voiced by members, particularly though not exclusively NGOs, Australia has been the target of criticism for its treatment of some species, especially some crocodile species. Secondly, Australian members have also been able to use the authority of IUCN's standing in the international conservation world as a means of attempting to pressure Australian governments, state or federal, into taking action on particular issues. In 1972, for example, IUCN formally intervened by writing to the governments of both Australia and Tasmania and appealing to them to take steps to preserve the Lake Pedder area, because of its unique scientific importance.[42] The workings of these relationships will be explored more fully in the next chapter.

However, IUCN achieved significant public visibility in Australia only in relation to one question: the *World Conservation Strategy* that it published, in conjunction with UNEP and WWF, in 1980. Even before the official launch of the *Strategy* in Australia by Prime Minister Fraser, environment officials, in line with IUCN's goals, had begun to think in terms of its implications for Australian policies. Work on a national strategy document "would seek to develop for Australia the world theme of wise management of resources and harmonious balance between development and the protection of the environment."[43] There were a number of substantial obstacles to such an enterprise. First, in spite of — or perhaps because of — several re-drafting exercises by IUCN in the 1970s, the ideas expressed in many parts of the *World Conservation Strategy* were couched in very general terms. Different conclusions could be reached in practical efforts to translate its provisions into policy recommendations. Secondly, although the final 1980 version reflected critical contributions to the task of drafting made by more development-oriented organizations than IUCN tended to be, it still was a document which emphasized the conservation, or wise use, of resources, not their exploitation as part of broader strategies of economic development. On several points, therefore, such as problems of dealing with pesticides and other hazardous chemicals, its spirit clashed with economic interests. Charges of fuzziness and misguided

125

economic thinking left the unconverted skeptical. Its supporters, by contrast, saw in the *Strategy* a variety of innovative blends of environmental and developmental objectives.

Later in 1980, the Prime Minister announced plans for a National Conservation Strategy, based on the statement of goals and guidelines present in the IUCN document. This was to be a cooperative federal-state-territory venture. He wrote to the other heads of government with proposals for collaboration.[44] Mr. Thomson, the environment minister, said that for the first time in Australia a consensus was being sought between the Commonwealth and state governments on a comprehensive range of matters involving environmental protection, nature conservation and living resource management.[45] This high level of response was a result of several factors: prodding inside government from environment, nature conservation and heritage officials, especially those closely familiar with IUCN work; a perception that Australia should not be left out of what appeared to be a significant multilateral initiative; the enthusiasm of non-governmental bodies, such as the Australian Conservation Foundation; and, not least, a desire on the part of the government to respond conclusively to criticism of its handling of environmental policy priorities since 1975. In a sense, too, support for the IUCN *Strategy* was an obligation of membership. Australia had not participated directly in the drafting exercises of the 1970s, though a number of officials had been indirectly involved as a result of deliberations in IUCN Assemblies or contributions to its advisory Commissions.

Early estimates of the capacity of this momentum to generate consensus on a National Strategy were exaggerated. As a result of federal-state discussions in 1980, it was agreed that two things were required: a review of the development objectives of Australian governments in the light of the *World Conservation Strategy*, including an assessment of the extent to which its goals were being, or could be, achieved in Australia; and development of a "programme of possible measures, to be implemented by governmental and non-governmental bodies, including Commonwealth, State and Northern Territory administrative and legislative measures, for achieving the three main objectives of the World Conservation Strategy."[46] An institutional structure was created. It consisted of plans for a series of national seminars, a task force located in the federal environment department, and, later, a consultative group comprising equal numbers of conservation and industry representatives. The states, then, were partners in the project from the start. Several were in any case familiar with IUCN and the Strategy as a result of attendance of officials at IUCN Assemblies.[47] State governments also had some form of representation on the Australian Committee for IUCN, set up in 1979. This included federal and state bodies and other interested members, and was chaired by Don Johnston, Director of the New South Wales national parks and wildlife service.[48]

The National Strategy process took some time to get under way. It was accompanied by occasional parliamentary complaints of unnecessary delays.[49] Meeting in June 1981, the steering committee approved the main outline, and this, following reviews of draft sections by officials and non-governmental experts, was discussed at a national seminar held at the end of 1981 in Canberra. Afterwards, the large number of proposals for modifications, many of them conflicting, the distraction of environmentalists' attention by the South-west Tasmania question, and the intervention of the 1983 general election, delayed a national conference on the Strategy until June 1983. The draft document that emerged from this meeting, "A National Conservation Strategy for Australia" (NCSA), was then circulated to state governments and the government of the Northern Territory for consideration before final approval.[50]

The states had interests of their own to protect during this lengthy process. Many tended to be responsive to economic interests and private sector concerns, and were inclined to be suspicious of many elements in the draft Strategy. Some, like New South Wales, also listened to environmental groups operating at state and local levels. Nevertheless, state governments quickly put their support on record. The Hobart Declaration of June 1982 later noted federal and state ministers' appreciation of the "important contribution that the National Conservation Strategy for Australia can make in identifying priority areas for action."[51] Most governments, however, were reluctant to see the Commonwealth dominate the process. Western Australia took an early lead in 1982 in opting instead for a state Strategy. This, its environment minister staid, was "completely different from the national strategy being produced in Canberra. It has different objectives in that it will examine State resource management policies in the light of the World Conservation Strategy. In that sense, it will have a more practical application."[52] A former FAO official with close links to the internal IUCN process that led to the 1980 document was retained as a consultant to prepare the state's Strategy paper.[53] The result, "A Conservation Strategy for Western Australia," was released for public discussion by the government in March 1984.[54] The government of Victoria was also at this time working on a state version of the *World Conservation Strategy*.[55] The first state openly to endorse the NCSA was South Australia, in May 1984. It did so, however, with the significant qualification that this step implied only endorsement of objectives and principles agreed at the 1983 national conference, rather than of the detailed path taken later by the document.[56]

Fears on the part of state authorities that the National Strategy could become another vehicle for expanded Commonwealth influence thus slowed down developments at the national level. In the early 1980s this process was suffering too from some of the inherent ambiguities and other difficulties presented by the IUCN *Strategy*. Agreement could be reached on some of its basic tenets — such as the goal of integrating conservation and development, or of retaining options for future use — only at a high level of generality which defied detailed implementation. The NCSA tended to find its most vigorous support among non-governmental bodies such as the Australian Conservation Foundation, and the various conservation and heritage organs of the federal government. The Australian Heritage Commission was particularly vocal in its enthusiasm. In response to

127

critics, the AHC pointed out that the Commonwealth had a legitimate role in relation to the *World Conservation Strategy*. The NCSA "should be the nation's blue-print for the next century and, as such, no effort should be spared in achieving broad support for it." The Commission "must continue to be vitally concerned that the Strategy is developed quickly, that the Commonwealth Government inject purpose and resources into its development, and that the strategy is effectively promoted and explained." The Strategy was "of the utmost importance to mankind. What Australia does is a fundamental insurance for the future well-being of its own citizens and an example for the rest of the world."[57]

As a result of the South-west Tasmania crisis, the Labor administration that took office in 1983 was reluctant to appear to be using the NCSA to promote the role of the Commonwealth as opposed to those of the states. Federal-state wounds inflicted by those events had to be healed by silence, caution and a more realistic approach to peaceful coexistence. In addition the Hawke government came to office with a commitment to economic, rather than to environmental, policy objectives. In the mid-1980s public interest in the NCSA waned significantly. The NCSA mechanism was trimmed down and re-structured after the 1983 conference;[58] consultations during 1984-86 produced two reports for the attention of the federal environment minister and a final report on the shape and details of the Strategy.[59]

Institution-building at the international level

The management of Australia's relations with international environmental institutions, then, brought a variety of actors into play. These international activities also had consequences for domestic policies and programmes and the organization of government. The early 1970s was a time of flux. It was far from clear which governmental body would be the main player in international developments. Older and more powerful departments, particularly Foreign Affairs, contested the right of the new environment department to undertake this role; others were concerned lest Australia be led down a path of international regulation by environmental agencies, in which case economic development priorities might suffer. Later in the 1970s matters became more routine. Programmes such as those initiated by UNEP were mainly in the preserve of environment departments and agencies. Yet this authority was subject to clearly defined limits. Australian policies towards the UN, or particular Specialized Agencies and the OECD, were often determined within inter-departmental arenas in which the influence of environmental officials was minimal or from which they were excluded.

State governments varied in the degree of interest they showed in international institutions. Even if they lacked appreciation of how such developments might be relevant to their concerns, however, the federal-state machinery centring on the AEC and CONCOM allowed them access to Australian decision-making in these areas. Some of the more important international programmes to which the Australian government was committed, moreover, required for their effective working some form of active contribution by the states. The MAB Programme, for example, had among its objectives the creation of a global network of protected biosphere reserves; Australia could be an active participant in this work only if state authorities were drawn into the process. The formulation of national guidelines on the registration, marketing and use of toxic chemicals in the 1980s similarly depended on cooperation between the two levels of government concerned. In this case, international institutions were directly useful. OECD decisions arrived at collectively with other western countries were instrumental in shaping Australian regulatory programmes on chemicals notification and assessment.

The mixed inter-governmental and non-governmental character of IUCN expanded the scope for engagement by Australian organizations. As well as federal bodies, agencies of state governments and environmental pressure groups have at various times been included in its membership. As we shall see in the next two chapters, this has enhanced the ability of groups to mobilize international opinion to promote goals related to international conventions. A background of support for IUCN objectives from environmental officials and non-governmental bodies provided the *World Conservation Strategy* with a ready-made Australian constituency in the 1980s. The generalities contained in many parts of the document, however, as well as the more controversial conservationist views underlying some of its provisions, meant that a direct translation into the Australian context was problematic. The protracted exercise of negotiating its implementation also highlighted the unwillingness of some state governments to accept the concept of national environmental planning, and their preference for state-based alternative strategies. The federal government's interest in this process waned early: in the case of the Liberal coalition before 1983 because of philosophical hesitations about interfering with state programmes, and in the case of Labor afterwards because of changing policy orientations and the fall-out from the Tasmanian issue.

Notes for Chapter 7

[1] Quoted in *Scientific American,* 257(6), December 1987, p. 10.

[2] *House of Representatives,* 74, 13 October 1971, pp. 2294-5; Howson, *House of Representatives,* 79, 17 August 1972, p. 455; *CNIA,* 43(3), March 1972, p. 100.

[3] Howson, *House of Representatives,* 74, 26 October 1971, p. 2510.

[4] McMahon, 14 May, in *CNIA* 43(5), May 1972, pp. 229-30.

[5] *UNCHE, Stockholm, June 1972. Summary Report of Australian Delegation* (Canberra, 1973; PP 143), App. 1, pp. 13-14; "UNCHE," *CNIA* 43(6), June 1972, pp. 301 ff.

[6] Howson, *House of Representatives,* 79, 17 August 1972, p. 455.

[7] The Australian delegation was led by McMichael, the environment department Secretary, who took Australia's role as Vice-President of the Governing Council and Chairman of Committee II (on financial and budget matters). See DCE, *Report for Period July 1974 - June 1975* (Canberra, 1976; PP 139), p. 19.

[8] *Ibid.,* pp. 15-16; *Commonwealth Record* 1(8), 23-9 August 1976, p. 491.

[9] DOS, *Report for Year 1973-74* (Canberra, 1975; PP 269), pp. 22, 43; ASTEC, *Science and Technology in Australia,* vol. 1B (Canberra, 1978; PP 105), p. 127.

[10] *AGWD*, 1, 1975, pp. 207-8 (statement by Cass and Uren, May 12); DCE, *Report for Period July 1974 to June 1975* (Canberra, 1976; PP 139), p. 20; DEHCD, *1st Annual Report, 1975-76* (Canberra, 1977; PP 398), p. 13.

[11] DECHD, *3rd Annual Report, 1977-78* (Canberra, 1978; PP 433), p. 4; DOE, *Annual Report 1978-79* (Canberra, 1979: PP 349), pp. 64-5.

[12] *AEC Newsl.*, 2(1), March 1982, P. 3; *AEC Newsl.*, 2(2), June 1982, p. 4.

[13] DEC, *Report for Years 1967 and 1968* (Canberra, 1970; PP 172), App. IV, p. 64.

[14] ANPWS, *Report for Period 13 March 1975 to 30 June 1976* (Canberra 1976), p. 15; ANPWS, *Report for Period 1 July 1976 to 30 June 1977* (Canberra, 1977), p. 23. The Australian MAB Committee was itself responsible for coordination in the early 1970s, before the ANPWS was created.

[15] DOS, *Report for 1971* (Canberra, 1973; PP 116), p. 58; DOS, *Report for 1972* (Canberra, 1974; PP 272), p. 54.

[16] Prof. Slatyer, for example, was Chairman of the Australian Committee for MAB, and both member and Chairman of the MAB International Coordinating Council; before heading the new ANPWS, Prof. Ovington served also as a member of the Australian National Commission for UNESCO and of the MAB Committee, well as in various IUCN capacities.

[17] ANPWS, *Report for Period 1 July 1976 to 30 June 1977* (Canberra, 1977 p. 23; ANPWS, *Report for Period 1 July 1977 to 30 June 1978* (Canberra, 1978), pp. 23-4; ANPWS, *Report for Period 1 July to 30 June 1979* (1979), pp. 25-8.

[18] B.W. Davis and G.A. Drake, *Australia's Biosphere Reserves: Conserving Ecological Diversity* (Australian National Commission for UNESCO, Canberra, 1983), pp. 3-4, 9.

[19] *Ibid.*, pp. 9-42; *ACF Newsl.*, 15(10), November 1983, p. 30.

[20] DHAE, *Annual Report 1980-81* (Canberra, 1982; PP 35), pp. 23-4.

[21] Senate, Joint Committee on Foreign Affairs and Defence, *Australian Representation Overseas: the Department of Foreign Affairs* (Canberra, 1978); vol 2, p. 1502 (Campbell).

[22] *House of Representatives*, 81, 24 October 1972, pp. 3111-2.

[23] DEC, *Report for Period December 1972 to June 1974* (Canberra, 1975; PP 298), pp. 27-8.

[24] DHAE, *Annual Report 1980-81* (Canberra, 1982; PP 35), pp.22-4.

[25] DEC, *Report for Period December 1972 to June 1974* (Canberra, 1975; PP 298), pp. 27-8, 41.

[26] DHAE, *Annual Report 1980-1* (Canberra, 1982; PP 35), pp. 22-4.

[27] *Commonwealth Record*, 1(10), 6-13 September 1976, p. 580.

[28] *Commonwealth Record*, 2(31), 8-14 August 1977, p. 1022; DOE, *Annual Report 1978-79* (Canberra, 1979; PP 349), p. 68; DSE, *Annual Report 1979-80* (Canberra, 1980; PP 357), p. 64; *Australia and New Zealand Environmental Report*, 3 (1978), p. 77. Other Commonwealth bodies included the Australian Agricultural Council, National Health and Medical Research Council, and the Air Transport Advisory Council. The secretariat was located in the environment department.

[29] DOE. *Annual Report, 1978-79* (Canberra, 1979; PP 349), p. 69; DSE, *Annual Report 1979-80* (Canberra, 1980; PP 357), p. 64.

[30] *AEC Newsl.*, 1(1), September 1981, p. 5; *AEC Newsl.*, 1(2), December 1981, pp. 1-3; DSE, *Annual Report, 1979-80* (Canberra, 1980; PP 357), p. 66; DHAE, *Annual Report, 1980-81* (Canberra, 1982; PP 35), p. 13; DHAE, *Annual Report, 1981-82* (Canberra, 1982; PP 263), pp. 2, 9. During the first year of the scheme, 58 chemicals were notified, but only two were considered "new" to Australia and assessed accordingly (*AEC Newsl.*, 2(4), December 1982, p. 3).

[31] Officials from the US Environmental Protection Agency also acted as consultants on the design of the inventory of existing chemicals in a report considered by a working group of Commonwealth and state officials with industry representatives. See DHAE, *Annual Report 1982-83* (Canberra, 1983; PP 345), p. 6; *AEC Newsl.*, 1(2), December 1981, pp. 2-3.

[32] OECD, "Decision of the Council concerning the Minimum Pre-marketing Set of Data in the Assessment of Chemicals," Doc. C(82) 196, 1982; OECD, *Good Laboratory Practice in the Testing of Chemicals* (Paris: OECD, 1982); *IRPTC Bull.*, 5(1983), pp. 11-12; *AEC Newsl.*, 2(4), December 1982, p. 4.

[33] *AEC Newsl.*, 3(2), August 1983, pp. 2-3; *Commonwealth Record*, 8(27), 4-10 July 1983, p. 978.

[34] *ACF Newsl.*, 17(1), February 1985.

[35] *AEC Newsl.*, 4(1 & 2), August 1984.

[36] DHAE, *Annual Report 1982-83* (Canberra, 1983; PP 345), p. 17.

[37] DSE, *Annual Report 1979-80* (Canberra, 1980; PP 357), p. 63.

[38] In this case Mr. C.R. Ashwin, Ambassador to West Germany (*AEC Newsl.*, 4(4), December 1984, p. 4).

[39] Specialist groups on these issues functioned under the IUCN's Survival Service Commission (SSC). See ANPWS, *Report for Period 1 July 1976 to 30 June 1977* (Canberra, 1977), p. 22. Among Australians active in IUCN activities (see Chapter 3), Prof. Ovington had long experience, for example through the IUCN national parks and ecology commissions. On his convening of the first IUCN Ecology Commission meeting in Australia, see *IUCN Bull.*, 10(11), November 1979, p. 96.

[40] ANPWS, *Report for Period 1 July 1978 to 30 June 1979* (Canberra, 1979), p. 32.

[41] E.g., *IUCN Bull.*, 2(5), October/December 1967, p. 37, and 7(10), October 1976, p. 56 (Great Barrier Reef); *IUCN Bull.*, 2(6), Jan./March 1968, p. 48, and 2(9), Oct./Dec. 1968, p. 65 (tortoises and turtles); and *IUCN Bull.*, 1(8), July/Sept. 1968, p. 59 (Christmas Island).

[42] *IUCN Bull.*, 3(5), May 1972, p. 19; H. Luther and J. Rzoska, *Project Aqua: A Source Book of Inland Waters Proposed for Conservation* (Oxford: Blackwell, IBP Handbook No. 21, 1971).

[43] DSE, *Annual Report 1979-80* (Canberra, 1980: PP 357), p. 61.

[44] DHAE, *Annual Report 1980-81* (Canberra, 1982; PP 35), p. 20; and more generally *IUCN Bull.*, 11(4), March 1980, p. 33.

[45] *Commonwealth Record*, 5(39), 29 September - 5 Oct. 1980, p. 1599; *The National Estate in 1981. AHC Report, June 1981* (Canberra, 1982; PP 96), pp. 93-4.

[46] *Senate*, 88, 26 March 1981, p. 860.

[47] *AEC Newsl.*, 4(4), Dec. 1984, p. 4, on the 1984 Madrid Assembly.

[48] AHC, *4th Annual Report, 1979-80* (Canberra, 1980; PP 33), p. 16.

[49] E.g., Sen. Missen, at *Senate*, 90, 4 June 1981, p. 2609.

[50] On the background see *Senate*, 91, 20 August 1981, p. 230. The 1981 conference attracted more than 200 participants; for reports see DHAE, *Annual Report 1981-82* (Canberra, 1982; PP 263), pp. 2, 17; and *Commonwealth Record*, 6(48), 30 Nov. - 6 Dec. 1981, p. 1634. On the 1983 conference, chaired by Sir Rupert Myers, with more than 150 delegates, and the draft NCSA, see DHAE, *Annual Report 1982-83* (Canberra, 1983; PP 345), pp. 1-2; and *Commonwealth Record*, 7(4), 6-31 December 1982, p. 1805. Important intervening meetings were held in February 1982 in Canberra of both the steering committee and consultative group (*Commonwealth Record*, 7(8), 22-8 February, 1982, p. 174), and the NCSA Task Force released the papers from the 1981 conference *(Towards a National Conservation Strategy)* in May 1982.

[51] DHAE, *Annual Report, 1981-82* (Canberra, 1982; PP 263), App. 10, p. 67; *AEC Newsl.*, 2(2), June 1982, pp. 5-6; AEC/CONCOM, *Australian Achievements in Environment Protection and Nature Conservation, 1972-1982* (Canberra, 1982), pp. 31-32.

[52] *Western Australia, Assembly*, vol. 241, 17 November 1982, p. 5695.

[53] *Ibid.* Mr. Riney was a member of the Executive Committee of IUCN in 1964-73 as a representative of FAO.

[54] *AEC Newsl.*, 4(1 & 2), August 1984.

[55] *ACF Newsl.*, 15(9), October 1983, p. 8. The Western Australian and Victorian approaches were criticized by national organizations for ignoring important parts of the NCSA (Murray Wilcox, "The Future of the National Conservation Strategy," *ACF Newsl.*, 12(4), 1984, p. 6).

[56] *AEC Newsl.*, 4(1 & 2), August 1984.

[57] Though the AHC recognized that the Strategy would not be a panacea, and that there would be "some conflicts over land use that will require sensitive decision-making at the appropriate level of government": AHC, *5th Annual Report 1980-81* (Canberra, 1981; PP 242), pp. 1-2; and *The National Estate in 1981. AHC Report, June 1981* (Canberra, 1982; PP 96), pp. 93-6.

[58] The reorganization centred on the replacement of the consultative group and steering committee by the Consultative Committee for NCSA (*Weekly Hansard,* Senate, No. 1, 1984, 28 February 1984, pp. 73-4).

[59] *AEC Newsl.,* 4(4), December 1984, p. 3.

CHAPTER EIGHT

The Management of International Conventions

International conventions are closely connected with the institutional components of regimes. Many were born in the UN's Specialized Agencies; others have given rise to complex institutional webs designed to secure their objectives in light of the interests of their parties. Environmental conventions have at times stimulated prolonged, intense and widespread political activity in Australia. They have concrete provisions; they are potentially binding on governments; and, as part of a country's external milieu, are capable of being exploited by domestic groups for their own purposes in their dealings with governments. The terms of the World Heritage convention, for example, were central to the politics of the South-west Tasmania case. By interacting with broader trends in the character of interest group activity in Australia, the convention helped groups to exert influence over the course of national policies and, not least, to attract publicity. As Whitlam had observed in 1970, "Quite small and ineffectual demonstrations can be made to look like the beginning of a revolution if the cameraman is in the right place at the right time."[1] This domestic political context of policy will be examined in the next chapter; in this chapter, the focus is the policy process in Australia in relation to the key international agreements on conservation, pollution and Antarctica.

The negotiation and impact of international agreements

The trade in Australia's wildlife and wildlife products was an issue in federal-state exchanges before signature of CITES in 1973. This background forms an important part of the context into which the Australian CITES process later fitted. Questions of kangaroo culling and the trade in kangaroo products have been a long-standing irritant in federal-state relations. Controversy over cull quotas became more heated during the 1960s. In 1969-71 criticism in Parliament increasingly focussed on the government's handling of exports.[2] Trade regulation fell constitutionally under the Commonwealth's jurisdiction. As the federal government began to take on more environmental policy responsibilities in the early 1970s, environmental officials became more involved in trade matters. Requests to export native fauna were routinely referred to them by Customs staff. Potential endangerment then constituted the primary criterion for a negative recommendation, in line with "a continuing policy of prohibiting export of any native fauna except under special circumstances and where the animals will be cared for."[3]

133

Early in 1973 the US Secretary of the Interior, Roger Morton, announced the addition of seventeen kangaroo and wallaby species to the US Endangered Species List. The move in effect banned the import of kangaroos and related products. Shortly after the CITES conference, Canberra imposed a total ban on the export of kangaroo skins. The Labor government clearly hoped that the various exceptions provided for in the US and Australian moves would appease domestic critics. The US action, Cass pointed out, was not a blanket ban, and provisions were made for culling for legitimate scientific purposes.[4] Both the substance and the style of the Commonwealth decision, however, provoked strong reactions from the states. Several had their own kangaroo management programmes based on permitted culling and links with the export trade. The government of New South Wales led the attack. Kangaroos were an asset and resource, ministers argued, to be used and managed like any other, and culled when they assumed pest proportions. Tom Lewis, who as Minister of Lands had drawn up the state's *National Parks and Wildlife Act* in 1967, objected strenuously to federal Labor interventionism. In imposing the 1973 ban, Canberra was trying to meddle in state affairs for "emotive and political purposes."[5] Lewis took the government's case directly to Washington in 1974, where he argued, in meetings with officials of the Interior Department, that the Commonwealth authorities had nothing to do with fauna protection in Australia.[6] The apparent abruptness of the change exacerbated tensions. Though Cass, as federal environment minister, defended the ban as a tightening of previous loopholes, the decision appeared to be more a product of the impatience of the Minister for Customs and Excise, Senator Murphy, who, according to some accounts, did not consult his Cabinet colleague on this question.

Even so, though the constitutional division of labour was fairly clearly defined — the states managed the resource, the Commonwealth regulated international trade — it was evident that management schemes that had worked in the past were in need of renovation. The approach to mutual accommodation was assisted by administration of CITES. The Commonwealth had given a graphic demonstration of its ability and will to use its international trade powers to intervene in a sensitive question of resource management; both sides moved to ease tensions by agreeing to the procedural strategy that states could resume exports if they submitted management plans deemed satisfactory by the Commonwealth. State officials took part in decisions on the criteria reached through the CONCOM framework in 1973-74.[7] Plans submitted by New South Wales and South Australia were soon approved; the ban on exports from Queensland and Western Australia was lifted in 1975, and for Tasmania shortly afterwards.[8] The five states that harvested and exported kangaroos and kangaroo products were thus brought back into line with a Commonwealth-sanctioned set of guidelines, and face was saved on both sides. Federal officials reiterated their view that kangaroo control "should be an ordered operation, and as far removed from pest or vermin destruction as possible." The Commonwealth encouraged a viable kangaroo industry, "providing it was properly managed."[9]

Kangaroo and wallaby species were not for the most part of central importance in CITES, though some rarer ones were included in Appendices. The heat of the question in Australia owed more to extra-convention considerations of their symbolism, especially to city-dwellers, and of their impact on economic activities. In the administration of CITES from 1973, the consultation between environment and customs officials established earlier became consolidated.[10] New *Customs (Endangered Species) Regulations* became operative with the entry into force of the convention in October 1976, following Australian ratification in July. The timing of the step owed much to the forthcoming first meeting of the parties, scheduled for November in Berne, and which Australia could now attend as a full party. Officials of the ANPWS, which coordinated Australian implementation, tended to emphasize continuity from previous practices: Australian wildlife trade controls were already strict, but CITES then extended and strengthened the protection accorded to rarer species.[11]

CITES in general raised few high-level questions for state governments. State officials attended the 1973 Washington conference as members of the Australian delegation, but not the Berne meetings in 1976.[12] By this date, state interests were also being protected more systematically through the workings of CONCOM. More than a hundred flora and fauna species were listed in CITES Appendices by 1976, most of them with habitats in state territory. CONCOM meetings regularly included CITES items on their agendas. This was particularly the case immediately following ratification, when Australia wanted to bring about revisions in the Appendix listings. Australia, and other countries, proposed amendments at Berne, but discussion was for the most part postponed until the Special Working Session scheduled for 1977. In the interim, the ANPWS reviewed all fauna listings in the Appendices, in conjunction with continuing deliberations in CONCOM's ad hoc Working Groups on Endangered Fauna and Endangered Flora.[13] Thus by the late 1970s, federal-state cooperation on CITES questions had become regularized. Many of the questions tackled at meetings of the parties, moreover — the trade in feral species, preparation of an identification manual for customs officers, standardization of the taxonomy used to compile the Appendices — could either be handled by federal officials, or else settled without significant controversy in the CONCOM framework. The *Wildlife Protection (Regulation of Exports and Imports) Act* of 1982, a product largely of work by the ANPWS, then aimed to make CITES implementation more effective "and give legislative recognition to Australia's strict policy on export of native wildlife."[14] The Act set the seal on existing federal-state consultative procedures, and also served to confirm recognition of the wildlife trade as a distinct administrative area within the federal government, rather than as one for which customs officers had primary responsibility.

The external setting of policy, of which CITES was now a significant part, both helped and hindered Australian governments. The change in the US position on import of certain kangaroo species in the early 1980s, which we noted in Chapter 3, represented a trade liberalization measure encouraged by Canberra.

Data collated through CONCOM indicated the species concerned were not threatened with extinction, and this formed the basis of the detailed Australian submission to the US Fish and Wildlife Service towards the end of 1982 on the desirability of a relaxation of trade restrictions.[15] In some cases, however, the external constituency created by CITES conflicted with Australia's wider interests. Australian policy on crocodile farming provoked extensive criticism in IUCN and CITES meetings in the early 1980s. At its June 1982 meeting, CONCOM acknowledged that estuarine crocodiles needed continued protection, but made clear Australia's view that provisions should be made in CITES for its growing interest in crocodile farming. More particularly, federal and state ministers endorsed a report which underlined the significant danger crocodiles in northern Australia were now posing, because of their numbers, to tourists and residents.[16]

The 1970s and 1980s saw a gradual adaptation of rules and practices to other international conservation agreements. Apparently innocuous in themselves, provisions in some could be controversial in practice because of their implications for land use policies in the states.

The low-key nature of many of the issues, however, and the fact that large-scale implementation called for initial data-gathering efforts that were politically tolerable, minimized the risk of confrontations. Under the terms of the wetlands convention, Australia was committed to the designation and protection of at least one wetland of international importance. The Cobourg Peninsula had the dual advantage of meeting the Ramsar criteria — it was a key habitat for rare waterfowl, including the Magpie Goose — while avoiding the need to step on sensitive state toes. Even so, some of the federal government's state critics saw in such moves an implied longer-term threat to their interests. Management plans for the area were developed by the ANPWS in conjunction with the Department of the Northern Territory.[17] The Ramsar convention also sharpened Australian requirements for data on the country's wetlands. This work moved slowly during the 1970s. Because of the paucity of existing knowledge, the policy functions of the Wetlands Survey of Australia — providing data on which programmes for the management and conservation of waterbird populations could be formulated and implemented — took shape in a more desultory fashion. The states themselves initiated research. In 1984, for example, a Wetlands Coordinating Group was set up in Western Australia, comprising representatives from government, conservation groups, farmers associations and other bodies.[18] Data collection was also needed in relation to the Japan convention. One of the first steps taken by the ANPWS was to commission studies on the status of migratory birds and their habitats, particularly in relation to Australia's offshore islands and the external territories.[19]

The Japan convention, however, led to conflict with New South Wales. Towra Point, near Botany Bay, was an area of mangrove and salt-marsh environments, freshwater meadows and sand dunes in an urban area, and habitat for a number of birds, including 33 species listed in the Japan treaty. The Commonwealth acquired a first parcel of just over 200 hectares in June 1975.[20] Towra Point as a result became one of the two issues — the other was the environmental enquiry concerning Fraser Island — which in 1975 prompted court challenges of Labor's environmental policies. The federal response to the New South Wales case was to cite the national responsibilities of the Commonwealth, which in international matters took precedence over state practices. As Whitlam argued, he "was certainly not attracted to the proposition that the Australian Government, having regard to its status as a national Government, cannot acquire a national park or national nature reserve under an enactment of the national Parliament."[21] The proximity of urban and tourist developments was part of the reason for the strong stand taken by New South Wales. To deflect some of its specific concerns, Commonwealth officials argued that federal action would directly assist the state, since rapid degradation of parts of the foreshore of Botany Bay was held to be related to damage occurring at Towra Point.[22]

State fears that such conventions could become a Trojan Horse for federal forces were to some extent alleviated with the change of government of 1975, and the return of a less environmentally precocious administration. It took several years for appropriate state and Northern Territory legislation to come into being. Governments were encouraged by the federal authorities to introduce laws that would allow Australia as a whole to implement the terms of the agreement with Japan. Both the ANPWS and the Attorney-General's Department provided officers to assist the states with the preparation of legislation.[23] Federal-state exchanges on related questions meanwhile proceeded within the CONCOM framework, particularly through its Working Group on Birds. Regulations covering areas under Commonwealth jurisdiction, particularly the External Territories, were introduced more easily.

These problems were barely perceptible irritants compared with the magnitude of the federal-state confrontation that erupted over the Franklin dam in Tasmania. Because of the mounting volume of demands for action by the Commonwealth government in the early 1980s, and the international obligations argued to have been created by Australia's adherence to the UNESCO World Heritage convention, more specifically by the Australian and Tasmanian governments' nomination of the area for inclusion on the World Heritage List in November 1981, the issue of the role of the federal government emerged as a central focus of the politics of the dam.

Natural heritage conservation in Australia in the 1970s was a policy area with significant domestic and international aspects. Much activity, however, reflected Commonwealth initiatives. The Australian government, Whitlam stated in 1973, was "committed to the preservation and enhancement of the national estate."[24] The committee set up under Mr. Justice Hope, of the Supreme Court of New South Wales, generally emphasized the need for Commonwealth leadership; indeed both the states, as the main constitutional players, and the federal government should maintain heritage lists.[25] The role of the states, however, was recognized to be dependent on funding. The committee recommended that the Commonwealth "ensure that adequate funds are made available to the States and local government" for heritage protection.[26] It was undeniable that the states had the authority in

137

this area. "Some parts, and indeed important parts, of the National Estate are in the Territories, or, although within the States, are owned by the Commonwealth, but the greater part of the National Estate is within the States and so is subject to the general legislative control of the States." A national programme could, however, be organized around the combination of state needs and authority, and federal capabilities. The limitations of the powers of the states were "generally not legal limitations: they are limitations such as the shortage of money; the lack of skilled personnel; the difficulty of doing some things on a State as opposed to a national basis." Central to the federal role, finally, was its international presence. Indeed in the view of the Hope committee, "In the case of areas accepted as of world significance, the question of cost should hardly need to be considered against the background of world responsibility."[27]

The main goal of the Australian Heritage Commission, set up by legislation of the mid-1970s, was thus the compiling of the national Registry of heritage sites in Australia. Initially it supported exploratory research in some states, for example a Queensland study of criteria and methods for rapid site selection, a survey of wilderness areas in eastern New South Wales and south-eastern Queensland, and a study of heritage conservation problems affecting the Victoria coast-line.[28] The AHC also had responsibility for vetting proposals for foreign investment sent to it by the Foreign Investment Review Board, an onerous task involving several hundred referrals a year. As far as natural sites in the registry were concerned, the Commission developed four main sets of criteria: representativeness in terms of geological and biological history, rare or outstanding natural phenomena, the habitats of endangered species, and selected areas that were worth conserving because they were accessible to the public.[29] A first list was completed by the end of 1980. It contained a total of 6,707 sites, in all states, of which 1,034 were natural environment listings.

Several constraints affected the efficacy of this work. One problem was that of satisfactorily integrating the variety of criteria that went into site selection. Attempts were made to build on international classifications developed by IUCN of biogeographical provinces and landscapes. States were the main actors: in the final analysis, listing could aspire only to moral and persuasive influence; it lacked enforcement capability. The AHC also encountered frustrations with the National Estate Grants Programme: long delays in finalizing the programme, a lack of consultation by some states, the funding of projects in some cases outside programme guidelines, lack of evaluation of completed projects, and the "virtual impossibility" of funding a truly national project.[30] Later in the 1970s, other problems arose, including budgetary restraint, uncertainty and criticism from within government. Major reviews of the legislative basis of Commonwealth environment and heritage policies were carried out. Limited staff and resources restricted the Commission's ability to counter the heritage costs of the eastern Australian drought of the early 1980s, or, perhaps, to resist the injection of politically determined criteria — such as pressure for labour-intensive projects as job-creation schemes — into its approaches to the choice of sites. This work had longer-term implications for the international aspects of Australia's heritage policies. The AHC became an articulate proponent of the view that important obligations and responsibilities fell to the Commonwealth — over the heads of state governments if necessary — as a result of the World Heritage convention.

The process of selecting areas for submission to the World Heritage Committee was designed as an exercise in cooperative federalism. Strictly speaking, this was not a concern for the Committee. According to Article 34(a) of the convention, the obligations of a federal government "shall be the same as for those states parties which are not federal states." The Commonwealth, through consultations primarily among officials of the AHC, the ANPWS and the environment department, considered a first list of places proposed by state governments in 1977-78. This followed an invitation from Prime Minister Fraser to state premiers to put forward nominations on a continuing basis. This led, as we saw in Chapter 3, to the nomination of the Great Barrier Reef region and the Alligator Rivers Region.[31] The stringent World Heritage Committee guidelines[32] led to withdrawal later of the nomination of the Sydney Opera House and its adjacent areas, which had been put forward following strong pressure from the state government and Sydney municipal authorities.

As in the earlier Tasmanian case surrounding development plans for the Lake Pedder area, conservationist concern over the Tasmanian government's plan to pursue hydroelectric power generation schemes in the South-west was at first restricted to groups in the state, together with sympathetic bodies outside, such as the Australian Conservation Foundation. The crucial differences of opinion within the state, and between the federal and state governments, centred on the appropriate balance between wilderness protection values and development activities, particularly dam construction and forestry. For much of the debate, the key issues hinged on demarcation of the precise area to be afforded protection, whether by Tasmanian, Australian, or world instruments. Parts of the area under contention were protected at the state level as a result of the 1976 creation of the South-west National Park, an extension of Lake Pedder Park, and the setting up of the Wild Rivers National Park in 1980. A large area of South-west Tasmania was also added to the Register of the National Estate in 1980.[33]

These issues proved unresolvable through the normal heritage policy channels. Tasmanian plans were already becoming a target of national environmental debate in the mid-1970s. After 1975 the federal government was retreating from many of the vantage points staked out by its predecessor, and reappraising the Commonwealth's environmental policy role in light of state complaints of federal duplication and intervention.[34] Tasmanian conservation issues began to surface in Parliament. In 1977 Senator Carrick spoke of "the magnificent wilderness area capacity of south-west Tasmania" amid mounting criticism of the extension by forestry interests of roads into proposed conservation areas.[35] The issues dominated Tasmanian agendas in the late 1970s. The requirement of the state, one of the poorest (and the coolest) in Australia, for expanded electrical power generation capability was articulated vigorously by the state Hydroelectric Commission (HEC), which, it was later alleged, even withheld information from the government which would damage its case. Of the various options presented by the Commission, one contained in a 1979 report was accepted by the state government. This combined plans for construction of a dam on the Gordon River, above the junction with the Olga River, with creation of a Wild Rivers National Park. This last, a concession to the preservation argument, was designed to protect the Franklin River catchment area. Analysis of the issues in this state, and later national, debate is largely outside the scope of this study. They centred on the degree of destruction likely to be caused by construction of the proposed dam, the overall addition it was likely to make to Tasmania's electricity needs, projections of those needs for future years, the numbers of jobs involved in construction projects and later work, the impact of related activities such as forestry development, and the actual and potential effects of a variety of alternative options, including expanded tourism development.[36]

Various international options were also central to these debates. The Liberal election campaign statement in 1975 declared a future government objective as being to "assist the Tasmanian Government in establishing a National Park of world significance in South-west Tasmania to include a substantial wilderness area." The Tasmanian South-west Advisory Committee, set up in 1975, reported in 1978 with a recommendation that the state government "should submit a case to the Commonwealth Government for substantial annual funding for South-west Tasmania on the basis that the area is of world heritage status and is a uniquely national asset."[37] This led to the Tasmanian government's decision to declare part of the area a national park, but to designate the whole of the region as a special conservation area. The Commonwealth government continued to express support for a world park, in accordance with the 1975 platform. In 1977 it allocated an initial grant of $75,000 towards an inventory of the natural, recreational and cultural resources of the region.[38]

The use of varied phrasings reflected an underlying agenda of dispute over the constitutional position. Thus reference to "world heritage" status restricted options to those in the UNESCO convention. Talk of a "park of world significance" did not. The latter could be de-coded to mean Commonwealth non-involvement (except in advisory and funding capacities) and a lead from the state level, consistent with the Australian tradition of state "national parks." The former language, however, tended to recur more frequently after Australia's membership of the World Heritage Committee, set up in 1976, brought the convention more and more into the Tasmanian controversy. This, in turn, directed more attention towards the Commonwealth, and, inexorably, towards the conclusion that the Commonwealth was the only player on the stage who had some room for manoeuvre. The federal government maintained consistently "that decisions on the development of the State-owned area of South-west Tasmania are the responsibility of the Tasmanian Government."[39] After the Commonwealth and Tasmanian nomination of the area for inclusion on the World Heritage list, the Commonwealth appeared to shift its ground a little. Expressing the hope that the submission would be successful, Prime Minister Fraser in April 1981 said that he believed "that it is an issue which is largely for the Government of Tasmania."[40] Thus pressure for direct Commonwealth intervention was resisted throughout this period. All states, Fraser commented in February 1982, "would object vigorously if the Commonwealth were to impose its decision-making on the normal programs of the States. These are matters on which the States must carry responsibility."[41]

Constitutional arguments were mustered on all sides. Or rather, the political positions being developed increasingly resorted to constitutional interpretations. In this process, debate on the Commonwealth's external affairs power loomed large. This was simultaneously a significant factor in a 1982 High Court decision *(Koowarta v. Bjelke-Petersen)* which upheld the validity of the *Racial Discrimination Act* of 1975 in part on the basis of the Commonwealth's signature of the International Convention on the Elimination of All Forms of Racial Discrimination. The connection with Tasmanian issues was not lost on advocates of Commonwealth intervention.[42] The general question had earlier been explored by the National Estate committee, which noted the existence of several relevant international conventions: "If the Australian Government has the power, through appropriate legislation, to implement the provisions of these conventions, the somewhat limited powers which it has in respect of the National Estate within the States could be greatly enlarged."[43] If these were ratified by Australia, and brought into force internationally, "they would all attract the provisions of S.51(xxix) and give the Parliament legislative power."[44] Various forms of the argument reappeared in relation to the South-west. As the AHC put it in general terms in 1980, Australia "as one of the first signatories . . . and as a member of the World Heritage Committee since its inception, has a special responsibility to play a part in the development of the Convention."[45] The federal Attorney-General's Department, in an opinion of July 1982, thought the question was open to different answers. There was a "substantial argument" that the Commonwealth under the external affairs power could legislate to carry out the obligations of Articles 4 and 5 of the World Heritage convention. The Court would have to decide whether the convention dealt with matters of sufficient "international concern" to bring it under Commonwealth jurisdiction; it would also be open to the Court to hold that the mere existence of the treaty obligation was sufficient to support Commonwealth legislation under this power.[46]

Section 51(xxix), however, was not the only basis for federal action. Also in Section 51 were the Commonwealth's trade and commerce powers, its "inherent" power as the national government, the racial powers provision, and powers in relation to the funding of state programmes. In addition, Commonwealth legislation of the 1970s put some aspects of heritage protection under federal jurisdiction. Powers granted to the federal authorities under these acts could be used, critics argued, in the Tasmanian case. For example, the Commonwealth had earlier used its export control powers to halt sand-mining on Fraser Island for environmental reasons, and had gone on to use federal funding powers to compensate a state

141

disadvantaged as a result. Similar kinds of strategies, it was argued, could apply in the South-west. As the Attorney-General summed up the position in 1982, the Commonwealth had "substantial constitutional powers" that could be used to preserve South-west Tasmania. "Any decision not to intervene must therefore be based on political grounds, not on any constitutional impediment."[47]

The federal government, then, had as a result of the 1975 Liberal election platform what could be interpreted as a commitment to aid Tasmania in the creation of a park of "world significance" in the South-west. This general position, coupled with emphasis on state powers, and avoidance where feasible of discussion of precise boundaries, was reiterated in the years following. Initial overtures concerning the world heritage option were made to Hobart in 1978 in light of the Cartland Committee's report that year. This was formalized late in 1980 when the Commonwealth approached Tasmania "with the suggestion that South-west Tasmania be considered for possible nomination for the World Heritage List."[48] Early negotiations failed, however, as the Tasmanian government's preferred area failed to meet the Commonwealth's, and international, interpretations of the world heritage criteria. Exchanges continued, and met with success by September 1981.[49] The Prime Minister earlier, in April, specifically expressed his support for world heritage listing.

In the resulting submission to UNESCO, of November, the Tasmanian government and the AHC, on behalf of Australia, put forward the Western Tasmania Wilderness National Parks for inclusion in the World Heritage list. This identified Tasmania as both "owner" and "agent responsible for preservation/conservation," and the Commonwealth as the national government formally responsible for the nomination.[50] The rationale for inclusion cited cultural property, particularly the existence of significant Aboriginal archaeological sites, and natural property. On the last point, the region comprised "most of the last great temperate wilderness remaining in Australia and one of the last remaining in the world." All four criteria for the nomination of natural sites were held to be satisfied: (i) the region was "representative of a major stage of the earth's evolutionary history and contains the most glaciated area in Australia"; (ii) it was "an outstanding example of one of the few remaining temperate areas which is of sufficient size for natural processes to continue"; (iii) it "contains unique, rare and superb natural features and areas of exceptional natural beauty"; and (iv) the region "contains a diversity of habitats where populations of rare and endangered species of plants and animals still survive."[51] Most of the points had been rehearsed at length already; indeed the possibility of world heritage listing had itself spurred on archaeological work and studies of threatened flora and fauna. Australia formally submitted the nomination in January 1982.[52]

But this did not mean that the path to actual listing, approved by the World Heritage Committee in December 1982, was free of obstacles. The area defined in the nomination contained some stretches that would be affected by dam construction. In November 1981, moreover, the then Labor premier of Tasmania, Doug Lowe, was deposed in a party coup, and resigned from the party. The new premier, Harry Holgate, wrote to Fraser asking for the nomination to be withdrawn. In view of the climate of opinion in Australia at that time, and the Prime Minister's own stated preferences, this was not a viable option; constitutionally, moreover, it was concluded that the Commonwealth had no obligation to accede to the Tasmanian request.[53] Further, there were still proponents at the federal level of the view that the proposed area was insufficient. After the decision of December 1982, for example, the AHC expressed its belief that "consideration should be given to the revision of boundaries of the nomination to include a wider area."[54]

During 1982 the Commonwealth continued to maintain that matters of land use fell within the jurisdiction of state governments. Tasmania insisted that Tasmanians had themselves voted for the dam in a referendum (one that environmentalists retorted was not a true test of Tasmanian opinion), that the state needed energy, and that cessation of hydroelectric schemes would significantly increase unemployment.[55] Debate grew more bitter, particularly from September, when road construction work indicated renewed pursuit of the dam project. Hobart elevated the matter into a symbol of the constitutional rights of states; at one point the premier referred to Tasmania's "sovereignty" and "autonomy" in these matters.[56] He also addressed these concerns direct to the World Heritage Committee, which Commonwealth officials viewed as a significant overstepping of the state government's authority in Australian constitutional law and international law.[57] While making it clear that the nomination (and another for Lord Howe Island) would go ahead,[58] the Commonwealth also agreed to a Tasmanian request for representation at the December meeting. This was "subject to the conditions which normally apply to State representatives on Australian Government delegations."[59]

The World Heritage Committee's decision in December 1982 to approve listing was more an expression of the politics of hope than a formal acknowledgment that all criteria had been met fully. Tasmania was still proposing to construct a dam in the nominated area; and Commonwealth-Tasmanian negotiations to minimize the damage had not been concluded, and it was even uncertain what the nature of the consultative relationship between the two governments should be.[60] The federal authorities, moreover, still opposed the idea of intervention. It was the government's contention, McVeigh said in Parliament on December 14 "that the mere existence of potential legal powers is not in itself a reason demanding Commonwealth action on any particular issue."[61] After December, the pressure intensified. Inside the Commonwealth, the AHC's views on world heritage matters, and Tasmania in particular, were well-known. Its Chairman, Kenneth Wiltshire, wrote to the environment minister to seek his "urgent support and action to protect" the area, citing Australia's obligations under Articles 4 and 5 of the UNESCO convention.[62] More important was the altered domestic political situation. By December 1982 anti-dam organizations were making increasing calls for campaigns of civil disobedience and the physical disruption

143

of dam construction activity. The law and order aspect was high on the agenda of the Premiers Conference in Canberra that month.

How the issue might have been resolved in the absence of a general election is a moot point. In December and January the Commonwealth tried to force the issue of compensation, Prime Minister Fraser proposing that the federal government should pick up the full capital costs of constructing a coal-fired power station on the island. Tasmania, however, was not interested in serious negotiations on any item that would imply concession on the main point of principle. The federal ALP's position, developed in July 1982, was to oppose dam construction, assist the Tasmanian government to diversify means of electricity production, and help it to expand its tourism industry. Later in 1982 the party was increasingly vulnerable to sniping from the Australian Democrats, who were less unequivocal than Labor in their anti-dam stance. One of the first actions of the Hawke government after the 1983 election was to bring in the *World Heritage (Western Tasmania Wilderness) Regulations* to halt construction of the dam. This was followed by the World Heritage Properties Conservation Bill, introduced in April amid opposition fury over "the introduction of the jackboot into the Federal system of government,"[63] protests about reconnaissance overflights of Tasmania by RAAF aircraft, and alarm at the longer-term implications of the Commonwealth's resort to the external affairs power.

These steps were followed by the government's successful defence of its actions in the High Court, which confirmed their constitutional validity in July 1983.[64] Yet the actions were taken more in the hope that the issue would then go away, and not mar Labor's return to power as it had the last year of the previous government's term. Three supporting courses of action were adopted in connection with this damage-control strategy. First, ministers and officials went to considerable lengths to argue that use of the external affairs power as one basis of Commonwealth action did not imply an open-ended pursuit by Labor of intervention rights in policy areas that happened to be covered by international conventions. Secondly, Tasmania had to be compensated, and alternative forms of energy and sources of jobs found. The question still contained the potential for heading the Commonwealth into a general confrontation with the states, or for releasing an unending stream of irritants across federal-state encounters on any issue. Negotiations on compensation and the design of a management authority for the South-west moved very slowly.[65] A third, more short-term, device was the imposition of a policy of silence on federal officials, including particularly environment and AHC staff, with the objective of minimizing the risks of still greater friction in relations with the states. In the longer term, Tasmania was one of a number of factors — internal factional debate inside the ALP, the emergence of unavoidable economic policy issues, and a desire to distance the party from memories of Whitlamism, were among others — that led to a steady demotion of the rank of environmental and heritage questions in the party's policies during the 1980s.[66]

Finally, the dam controversy inside Australia had a significant external audience. This was most evident in the context of the transnational links of

Australian environmental groups and scientific bodies, and the generation of media attention overseas. In addition to its formal advisory role in relation to the World Heritage convention, IUCN also attempted at various junctures directly to influence the course of events in Australia. This was in line with its earlier appeals to the Australian and Tasmanian governments to take steps to preserve the Lake Pedder area.[67] In 1979 the organization emphasized the unique wilderness values of the Lower Gordon and Franklin catchments. The IUCN Director-General, David Munro, also wrote to Prime Minister Fraser, reminding him that Australia was a member of the World Heritage Committee and pointing out that the convention was "intended to be a powerful weapon in the fight for the conservation of both natural and cultural areas." Natural area applications, however, had lagged behind applications on the cultural side. He urged the nomination of a member to the Committee with "deep understanding" of natural areas, adding that "We would greatly welcome a nomination from Australia of an outstanding site."[68] Awareness of this outside constituency had a differential impact within government, and counted for most with the AHC. It also entered into the federal and Tasmanian authorities' calculations during 1981 about UNESCO's receptiveness to a Southwest nomination, and meant that the future path of any application was more predictable.

Jurisdiction in the marine environment

The question of jurisdiction over coastal waters and the seabed is an old one in Australian constitutional history. It re-emerged in the 1960s in the form of disputes over offshore oil resource development. Negotiations between the Commonwealth and state governments concluded in 1967 with an agreement to set aside the constitutional issue, and provided for so-called "mirroring" legislation by both levels of government operating from low water mark to the edge of the continental shelf.[69] However, neither this, nor the more controversial *Seas and Submerged Lands Act* (1973) of the Whitlam government, offered a longer-term pacific settlement. The last was in line with Labor's "national" viewpoint, and claimed for the Commonwealth sovereignty over territorial waters, the adjacent seabed and the superjacent air space. The Commonwealth, more specifically, also secured rights to exploit continental shelf resources. The legislation was finally upheld by the High Court in 1975 following a lengthy battle initiated by the government of New South Wales. The majority view of the Court was that the sections of the Act asserting Commonwealth sovereignty over the territorial seas were justified by the external affairs power; Australia had signed and ratified various international conventions, particularly the Convention on the Territorial Sea and Contiguous Zone, which recognized coastal state sovereignty over the territorial sea, and, in this context, this meant the federal government. A minority opinion found the Act to disturb state rights over the territorial sea and seabed inherited from pre-federation days.[70]

145

In practice, however, the states rather than the Commonwealth were in many respects the main actors. It was this situation that the ALP government was proposing to change in the legislation being planned by the government in 1975 before its dismissal. After 1975, the course was re-set in the direction of cooperative federalism. Negotiations culminated in an agreement in 1979 which recognized state legislative power within the three-mile limit and over intra-state shipping, while the Commonwealth retained primary responsibilities outside that limit, together with authority over inter-state and some types of international shipping. Two coastal waters acts of 1980 confirmed the terms of the settlement in legislation.[71] The Fraser government also extended the scope of cooperative federalism within the international sphere. In 1977, the federal and state governments reached agreement in general terms that the federal government would consult with states at an early stage of treaty negotiation; that it would give them the option of implementing treaties on topics traditionally regarded as falling within their competence; that it would include state representatives in Australian delegations at international meetings for the negotiation of treaties; and, finally, that it would press for inclusion of "federal clauses" in such conventions where appropriate.[72]

State governments tended to be less assertive in relation to the UNCLOS III negotiations than these achievements in the definition of the federal-state balance might have indicated. Nor was there much in the way of parliamentary or public attention, a reflection, perhaps, of the traditional self-image of Australia as a nation with a vast interior but little connection with the seas. State governments thus tended to accept that most law of the sea questions lay within Commonwealth jurisdiction, particularly since the difficult issues in the UNCLOS III sessions centred on problems of seabed control beyond national jurisdiction. There was little inclination on the part of the states to suspect that a future Law of the Sea convention would in practice lead to a curtailing of state powers, despite the precedent set by the High Court's recognition of past law of the sea agreements as a legitimate basis for the Commonwealth's earlier enhancement of its authority in the 1973 Act. After 1975, both Prime Minister Fraser and the foreign minister, Andrew Peacock, assured the states that their rights were not affected by the UNCLOS III negotiations. The 1977 agreement also established the federal principle as a more solid factor in Australia's approach. Fraser stated in 1980 that as state governments had prime carriage of coastal matters, formation of specific policy on coastal management had always been a state rather than a Commonwealth responsibility.[73] The implication was that pursuit by Australia of stronger coastal state power, especially as regards marine pollution, in the future convention was a matter of readjusting international arrangements, and did not presage change in the division of labour through which Australian governments themselves managed the coastal zone.

The Law of the Sea negotiations, however, did raise some jurisdictional problems within the federal government. The Department of Foreign Affairs strengthened its position vis-à-vis other departments in the early 1970s. Complaints about its predilection for intervening in the affairs of others surfaced regularly during the decade.[74] In the context of UNCLOS III negotiations, the department was able to overcome the argument that, as legal counsel for all government bodies, the Attorney-General's Department ought to take a more prominent role in formulating the Australian approach.[75] Central to the delegation's goals in UNCLOS III sessions were policy matters that touched the concerns of other departments. Marine pollution was one. One Senator criticized the government in 1979 for allowing important Australian priorities to be neglected at the talks. Marine environment questions were being handled by "junior officers" of the Department of Foreign Affairs, instead of by staff from the Department of Science and Environment. Speaking for the government, Senator Webster said that the law of the sea was a matter for negotiation by the Minister of Foreign Affairs and the Attorney-General; when the negotiations were concluded the environment department would be "well forward" in seeking to protect Australia's interests in those areas.[76] In fact, it was already represented in inter-departmental UNCLOS III consultations, through the pertinent IDC, and an officer of the environment department was included in the Australian delegation to each negotiating session. The ANPWS was involved more sporadically, and on more specific questions such as marine mammal conservation.[77] Even so, environmental officials tended to be weakened in this framework by the interrelatedness of UNCLOS III issues, especially in the context of negotiations on integrated texts. Its voice sometimes appeared to be more influential than it was, because of the coincident pursuit by Foreign Affairs of coastal state pollution control powers as a crucial Australian objective.

State, public, and parliamentary attention to the issue of marine pollution was channelled more towards the international conventions in the area. Labor came to power in 1972 in an impatient mood. As Snedden said in 1972, "Every time international conventions are brought forward for ratification, particularly those dealing with maritime matters, we run into the problem of the states having the responsibility for the introduction of complementary legislation and of the measures being delayed unnecessarily."[78] The federal government had, in fact, been active in a number of areas, for example in the 1970 extension of oil pollution prevention powers, and the pursuit through IMCO of the Great Barrier Reef amendment. In the view of the ALP, however, what was needed was greater Commonwealth dynamism both within and outside Australia. Thus in 1975, as we have seen, the government was engaged in preparing a comprehensive package of legislation designed to give the Commonwealth the power to control all aspects of marine pollution.[79] Its successor was more circumspect.

Federal-state exchanges failed to move expeditiously, however, regardless of which party was in power in Canberra. A long-standing reason was the requirement to ensure that state legislation and administrative capabilities were in place, and the convention itself in force internationally, before the Commonwealth took steps to pass appropriate legislation and move towards ratification. Many of the assumptions underlying this approach were criticized during the

1960s and 1970s. Another factor was the growing pace of international marine pollution work during this period, which, together with the expansion of public interest, led to seemingly unavoidable delays at the state level. Thus, as we saw in Chapter 4, the 1954 oil pollution convention (Oilpol) did not secure the required state legislation until 1962. A similar time-lag followed Commonwealth signature of the 1962 amendments. Tasmania passed corresponding regulations in 1967, and measures for New South Wales, Victoria and South Australia came into force in 1969.[80] The pressure of events then intensified. State premiers were sent details of the two 1969 conventions in July of that year; in August they were consulted by the Commonwealth about the proposed amendments of that year to Oilpol, and were sent details of these the next year.[81] Federal-state discussions followed about the goals of Australia in UNCHE, during which pursuit of the oil dumping convention emerged as a high priority; the 1972 London dumping conference and the 1973 marine pollution convention both called for input by state governments. These were questions, moreover, which affected the interests of all states: no Australian state is land-locked, and one (Tasmania) is an island.

Cooperation between the Commonwealth and state governments on a variety of matters connected with these conventions became more institutionalized during the 1970s. The need for this change was recognized in the early 1970s. As Bowen pointed out in 1972, in the context of the Australian aim of strengthening international dumping and pollution provisions, each state had its own laws regulating the circumstances in which ships might discharge oil in the territorial sea and internal waters.[82] The AEC became a main forum. It established a Working Group on the National Plan to Combat Pollution of the Sea by Oil, which dealt with questions such as guidelines on the use of dispersants to control oil spills. Representatives of state governments also took part, together with federal officials and industry representatives, in the policy-making structures set up to prepare the National Plan.[83] Applications for dumping, within the framework of the 1972 convention and existing laws, were routinely handled by state authorities. The determination of monitoring requirements, similarly, was largely a matter for the states, in consultation with officials of the federal environment department; a joint federal-state body was created specifically with the aim of establishing a national marine monitoring network.[84] Other institutions of federalism were involved. In relation to the 1973 marine pollution convention (Marpol), for example, and its amendments of 1978 and 1980, mechanisms for consultation included the AEC, the Solicitors-General Committee, the Standing Committee of Attorneys-General, and the Premiers Conference.[85]

In 1978 Peacock reported that discussions with the states on the various conventions and amendments were continuing, and expressed the hope that suitable legislation would be prepared shortly.[86] By this time thinking had moved towards a package approach to Commonwealth legislation. An important step was taken in 1980. Agreement was then reached on the general divisions of responsibility in the coastal zone between the two levels of government. As part of this understanding, the states would control discharges into the territorial sea, while the Commonwealth remained responsible for discharges beyond that area.[87] Commonwealth legislation was then drafted. The bills contained provisions "preserving the operation of State law"; however, "in the absence of such State or Northern Territory legislation the Commonwealth Acts will apply."[88] The process of accepting the main conventions was also assisted by two developments of the 1970s. First, the 1973 marine pollution convention was regarded in Australia as a significant improvement over that of 1954. This earlier instrument was based on a zonal approach. This failed to meet Australian needs for such areas as the Great Barrier Reef, its scope, for example, being defined in terms of the "nearest land"; it also tended to be out of line with the best industry practices; and enforcement was retained by flag states.[89] The 1973 agreement, among other things, extended responsibility for enforcement beyond flag states; and, with the addition of the 1978 Protocol, allowed countries greater flexibility in the timing and application of its provisions.

Thus the Fraser government introduced two bills in October 1982 designed to give effect to Marpol. Bills similar in essentials were brought forward by the new Labor government in 1983. Protection of Australia's coastline was vital, the government stated. It was "fundamentally important that we be able to demonstrate to ourselves and the international community that we take our responsibility for this national and global resource seriously and that we are committed to its protection."[90] Initially, however, Australia implemented only the compulsory Annexes of Marpol; operation of other provisions was delayed for three years (as permitted under the 1978 Protocol). The delay was primarily to ensure that adequate reception facilities for the discharge of tank washings and sludge were provided at Australian ports.[91] These and other matters were still being examined in various federal settings, particularly the Marine and Ports Council of Australia, a body comprising federal, state and Northern Territory officials. In its general approach, the Council adopted the traditional practice of recommending that complementary Commonwealth, state and Territory legislation be enacted before Australia could go ahead with ratification.

Antarctica and the Australian policy process

By contrast, matters concerning the Antarctica regime fell firmly within federal jurisdiction (though Tasmania retained some residual responsibility in relation to some areas touched on in Antarctic policy). The Commonwealth exercised powers for two reasons: it was the Australian government responsible for external territories, including the AAT; and it was also Australia's representative as far as the international legal framework of Antarctica was concerned. State involvement was for the most part incidental. Local employment and other interests were at issue in the proposal of the early 1970s to move the Antarctic Division from Melbourne to Hobart,[92] and both Tasmania and Hobart had a stake in the decision to site the AMLR convention machinery there.

The formulation of policy on Antarctica took place in a close-knit group of institutions surrounding the main Commonwealth authorities. Australian interest in the continent revived after 1945. In 1947 the Commonwealth established the Australian National Antarctic Research Expeditions (ANARE) as the basic organizational unit for carrying out scientific activities. The following year, the Antarctic Division was set up in the then Department of External Affairs as the Commonwealth agency responsible for providing administrative and logistic support for the ANARE. Under its first Director, Dr. Phillip Law, the Division oversaw major expansion of Australian Antarctic work.[93] The relationship between the federal science department, which later absorbed the Antarctic Division, and Foreign Affairs, which handled the coordination of Australian policies in the multilateral framework of Antarctic parties' meetings, contained some inherent potential for tension. This was magnified by the relative secrecy that has usually surrounded Antarctic decision-making, both internationally and within Australia, and by the tendency for these bodies to exclude others from an effective say in the shaping of policy. Scientists' complaints of neglect and insufficient funding of Antarctic research have also shaped the context in which policies have been developed.

The reviews of the 1970s brought a number of changes, beginning with the White Committee report of 1974 and the discussion paper published by the federal science minister in 1975.[94] During the decade, a fresh round of debate took place on Antarctic research priorities. The Australian Science and Technology Council (ASTEC) argued strongly in favour of a heavier concentration on marine biology, a research area considered vital for future policy requirements.[95] Debate again centred on the Antarctic Division, the functions of which remained the administration and logistic support of ANARE, and the carrying out of approved programmes in various fields of scientific research in Antarctica.[96] Critics argued that the Division was insufficiently responsive to the ideas and viewpoints of the scientific community, as represented by specialist bodies of the Australian Academy of Sciences (AAS) and the Australian components of International Council of Scientific Unions (ICSU) Antarctica organs. As we saw in Chapter 5, this higher profile of Antarctic policy during the decade from about 1974-75 drew the political parties, environmental groups and others into discussion of future options. Further administrative review in 1983-84 produced new proposals for the organization of the Antarctic Division designed to make it a more effective supervisor and supporter of ANARE activities.

The role played in Antarctic policy by the Department of Foreign Affairs has led some Australian critics to suspect that trade-offs and the bargaining of high politics may have damaging consequences. The removal of the Antarctic Division from the Department represented a rationalization of government activity, generally welcomed on the grounds that this detailed work could best be carried out in Melbourne or Hobart within the federal government's main scientific arm. Antarctic expertise, however, remained a significant element in the structure of the Department, primarily in the 1980s through the Law of the Sea and Antarctic

Section.[97] Even if Australia had no sovereign claim in Antarctica, we can surmise that this preeminent role would still have been maintained to protect Australia's interests as an Antarctic treaty signatory nation. Antarctica is an arena of world politics in which Australia can exert influence. However, as Bruce Davis has argued, it is "unlikely to head the list of Australia's international priorities. Moreover, Antarctic initiatives must sometimes be viewed as merely one of the cards to play in the broader spectrum of external relations."[98]

The central importance of Foreign Affairs in the workings of the Antarctic policy process, including its role in the Antarctica IDC, gives us a useful perspective on the specific area of environmental policy. As with the UNCLOS III negotiations, the influence of environmental bodies inside government is difficult to isolate since environmental conservation objectives have been crucial to Australian foreign policy in this area.[99] Thus at the time the Agreed Measures were formulated in 1964, the Commonwealth did not have an environmental agency; responsibility for overseeing this aspect of the treaty system fell to Antarctic Division and Department of Science officials. Through membership of Australian delegations, and representation at inter-departmental sessions in Canberra, environment officials have none the less promoted the argument that environmental protection should remain a core Antarctica goal, and also that international cooperation encouraged by Australian leadership was a primary means for securing this.[100] More specifically, the environment department was responsible in the early 1970s for Australian commitments under the Antarctic seals convention of 1972,[101] and, together with representatives of the ANPWS, it played an important role in the Working Group set up to advise the inter-departmental committee with respect to the region's marine living resources in preparations for the CAMLR.[102] Because of the broader functioning of the Antarctic treaty system, however, and of the Australian approach to its deliberations, Antarctic policy has generally not been an area in which the environment department's working relations with various NGOs has in turn facilitated their access to policy-making. This dimension is examined in the next chapter.

The politics of international conventions

International conventions in the environmental area have thus impinged on the interests of the Australian states at several points. In order to set the workings of cooperative federalism on a more even keel after the controversies of the first half of the 1970s, there was consensus under the Liberal coalition government later in the decade to allow state participation at early stages in the negotiation of international agreements in any sphere. As far as possible, the federal government would also try to secure the inclusion of federal clauses in such conventions and by this means to obtain wider international acknowledgement of the distinctive character of Australian constitutional practices. This general principle was apparent in approaches to international conservation agreements during the later 1970s and 1980s. The fact of state jurisdiction in environmental policy areas assured governments access to such questions, both in direct bilateral exchanges with the federal government and in collective bodies such as the AEC and CONCOM. Cooperation with state governments was crucial to the Commonwealth's negotiation of the implementation of international marine pollution agreements, not least because it was at the state level that the key decisions were made concerning the provision of physical facilities necessary for Australia to be able to discharge its obligations under these conventions. In relation to the World Heritage convention, the federal government lacked enforcement power regarding the protection of sites, and its relevant agency, the AHC, for various reasons provoked state government suspicions that it was an instrument imbued with excessively interventionist thinking.

Conservation conventions also had some less immediately observable effects. Several highlighted weaknesses in Australia's capacity to work as an effective partner in treaty settings. Gaps in marine science capabilities were evident in relation to the Antarctica treaty and also the UNCLOS III negotiations, and the need for these to be remedied formed an important element in internal policy debates of the 1970s. Other agreements spurred the search for policy-relevant data, for example on wetlands and other habitats in relation to the Ramsar and Japanese conventions. The World Heritage convention similarly served to reinforce research on the archeological and other features of the South-west to ensure the World Heritage Committee's criteria would be indisputably met. Work by Australian scientific bodies and environmental groups in these contexts will be examined in the chapter following.

The development of a body of international conservation law has created some problems of jurisdiction within the federal government itself. Earlier post-1945 disputes on Antarctica policy were partially resolved by placing responsibilities under the federal Science Department rather than Foreign Affairs. The main foreign policy community retained a key role, however, because of the importance of Antarctic issues to core Australian interests and by virtue of the inter-governmental setting in which Antarctic regime decisions were made after 1959. Further, although environmental issues were generally high on Antarctic treaty agendas, and especially so from the mid-1970s, this did not necessarily entail a prominent role in the policy process for federal environmental bodies in Australia. Environment policy was instrumental in the pursuit of Antarctic policy; primary environmental policy goals, for example in connection with the AMLR convention, tended to be developed and articulated by Foreign Affairs. Where the wider considerations of Australia's general interests in the international community were more distant, as in relation to CITES, the environmental bureaucracy was able to take more of a lead role. This included the formulation and negotiation internationally of policies on which other agencies could agree, such as those in the controversial areas of kangaroo management and culling, and crocodile farming. One ally of the environment department and related bodies in such encounters was the Australian environmental constituency. There were occasional public and parliamentary grumbles that diplomats, as instinctive compromisers, would be less likely than environmental officials to protect Australian interests vigorously in settings such as the UNCLOS III negotiations. To these broader domestic contexts of policy we now turn.

Notes for Chapter 8

1 Stephen Murray-Smith, ed., The *Dictionary of Australian Quotations* (Richmond: Heinemann, 1984), p. 280.

2 E.g., Sen. Mulvihill, *Senate*, 44, 18 June 1970, p. 2608; and 45, 19 August 1970, p. 29.

3 DEC, *Report for Period December 1972 to June 1974* (Canberra, 1975; PP 298), p. 10.

4 *AGD*, 1(1), 1973, pp. 159-60, statement by Cass of 17 January 1973.

5 Brian Hoad: "Wildlife: Sense vs. Sentiment," *Bulletin*, 16 March 1974, pp. 30-2.

6 *Ibid.*

7 On CONCOM meetings on these issues and recommendations by the Ministerial Working Party for the management and conservation of kangaroos, see *House of Representatives*, 90, 23 August 1974, pp. 1212, and 90, 24 September 1974, p. 1746.

8 DOE, *Report for Period July 1974 to June 1975* (Canberra, 1976; PP 139), p. 10. ANPWS, *Report for Period 13 March 1975 to 30 June 1976* (Canberra, 1976), p. 4; on Queensland and Western Australia see *AGWD*, 1 (1975), p. 666; and on Tasmania, *Commonwealth Record*, 1(1), 1-11 July 1976, p. 15.

9 Announcement of 21 August 1975, *AGWD*, 1 (1975), p. 666.

10 DOE, *Report for Period July 1974 to June 1975* (Canberra, 1976; PP 139), p. 10; on the ratification of CITES see also *Commonwealth Record*, 1(12), 20-6 September 1976, p. 711 (statement by Howard and Newman of 24 September).

11 ANPWS, *Report for Period 1 July 1976 to 30 June 1977* (Canberra, 1977), pp. 14-15.

12 CITES, *Proc. First Meeting of the Conference of the Parties, Berne, 2-6 November 1976* (Morges; IUCN, 1977), p. 167, Doc. 1.4 (Final). The delegation at Berne consisted of officials from the ANPWS, the Import-Export Control Section of the Bureau of Customs, and the Australian Embassy in Berne.

13 ANPWS, *Report for Period 1 July 1977 to 30 June 1978* (Canberra, 1978), pp. 19, 28, 37-38; *Report for Period 1 July 1979 to 30 June 1979* (Canberra, 1979), p. 32.

14 See the statement by Mr. Moore (Business and Consumer Affairs) and Mr. Wilson (Home Affairs and Environment), of 1 September 1981. In the interim existing controls would be strictly enforced. Amendments to the *Customs (Endangered Species) Regulations*, the ministers stated, would ensure Australia's commitment to CITES (*Commonwealth Record*, 6(35), 31 August - 6 September 1981, p. 1076, and *Gazette*, 182, 31 August 1981). On preparation of the legislation see also DHAE, *Annual Report 1980-81* (Canberra, 1982; PP 35), p. 21; *Annual Report 1981-82* (Canberra, 1982; PP 263), pp. 15-6; and *Annual Report 1982-83* (Canberra, 1983 PP 345), p. 15; *AEC Newsl.*, 2(3), September 1982, p. 10; and *Commonwealth Record*, 7(49), 6-31 December 1982, pp. 1805-6.

15 *Commonwealth Record*, 5(21), 26 May - 1 June 1980, p. 763; and 7(47), 22-8 November 1982, p. 1713.

16 *Commonwealth Record*, 7(22), 31 May - 6 June 1982, p. 676.

17 DEC, *Report for Period December 1972 to June 1974* (Canberra, 1975; PP 298), pp. 12-13; DOE, *Report for Period July 1974 to June 1975* (Canberra, 1976; PP 139), pp. 11-12; ANPWS, *Report for Period 13 March 1975 to 30 June 1976* (Canberra, 1976), p. 16.

18 *AEC Newsl.*, 4(1 & 2), August 1984.

19 ANPWS, *Report for Period 13 March 1975 to 30 June 1976* (Canberra, 1976), p. 17; and *Report for Period 1 July 1977 to 30 June 1978* (Canberra, 1978), p. 19.

[20] DOE, *Report for Period July 1974 to June 1975* (Canberra, 1976; PP 139), pp. 9-10.

[21] *AGWD*, 1(1975), pp. 554-5.

[22] *AGWD*, 1(1975), p. 731.

[23] ANPWS, *Report for Period 1 July 1977 to 30 June 1978* (Canberra, 1978), p. 19.

[24] *House of Representatives*, 84, 17 May 1973, pp. 2263-4.

[25] *Report of the Interim Committee on the National Estate* (Canberra, 1976; PP 139), p. 20.

[26] *National Estate. Report of the Committee of Inquiry* (Canberra, 1975; PP 195), p. 30.

[27] *Ibid.*, pp. 31, 206.

[28] AHC, *1st Annual Report 1976-77* (Canberra, 1978; PP 238), p. 16.

[29] AHC, *4th Annual Report 1979-80* (Canberra, 1980; PP 330), App. A, pp. 20-21.

[30] AHC, *Annual Report 1982-83* (Canberra, 1984; PP 39), p. 1.

[31] AHC, *Annual Report 1977-78* (Canberra, 1978; PP 350), p. 12.

[32] This was particularly after the Luxor meeting of the World Heritage Committee, chaired by Prof. Slatyer, which resolved to tighten criteria for the assessment of places for inscription on the list. See AHC, *4th Annual Report 1979-80* (Canberra, 1980; PP 330), p. 16.

[33] AHC, *5th Annual Report 1980-1* (Canberra, 1981; PP 242), pp. 1-2.

[34] E.g., questions at *Senate*, 67, 3 March 1976, p. 359.

[35] *Senate*, 73, 27 May 1977, p. 1529.

[36] E.g., testimony of the Tasmanian Wilderness Society, in Senate, *Select Committee on South-west Tasmania* (Canberra, 1982), Vol. 1, esp. pp. 34-41. The 1975 party document is cited in Vol. 2, p. 1332. There was support for Tasmanian energy development plans at the federal level, from national development officials (*ibid.*, vol. 1, pp. 139-40). The Tasmanian Chamber of Industries thought the Gordon-below-Franklin option "qualifies as the only scheme which will meet the needs of Tasmania in the 1990s" (*ibid.*, vol. 2, p. 1399).

[37] Quoted by Andrew Lohrey, former minister, *ibid.* vol. 1, pp. 296-7.

[38] *Ibid.*

[39] *House of Representatives*, 119, 17-18 September 1980, p. 146. Some such statements appeared to leave doors open for possible future intervention in undefined circumstances. For example Thomson earlier said "I do not believe that the Commonwealth Government should interfere in these matters — certainly not at this stage" (*House of Representatives*, 117, 27 March 1980, p. 1308).

[40] Fraser, *House of Representatives*, 122, 8 April 1981, p. 1431.

[41] Fraser, *House of Representatives*, 126, 23 February 1982, p. 42.

[42] E.g., testimony of the Australian Conservation Foundation, in Senate, *Select Committee on South-west Tasmania*, vol. 4, pp. 3743-4.

[43] *National Estate. Report of the Committee of Inquiry* (Canberra, 1975; PP 195), pp. 207-9, para. 7.8, 7.13.

[44] *Ibid.*, para. 7.14.

[45] AHC, *4th Annual Report 1979-80* (Canberra, 1980; PP 330), p. 1.

[46] *House of Representatives*, 129, 19 October 1982, pp. 2215 ff.

[47] Senate, *Select Committee on South-west Tasmania*, vol. 2, p. 1318 (Sen. Peter Rae) and p. 1580 (Tasmanian Wilderness Society, Canberra branch); *House of Representatives*, 129, 19 October 1982, pp. 2216 ff., para. 28.

[48] *Senate*, 87, 5 December 1980, p. 444 (Sen. Peter Baume). On the Prime Minister's 1978 letter to Premier Lowe suggesting consideration of world heritage status for the South-west, see *House of Representatives*, 123, 10 June 1981, pp. 3428-9.

[49] The area nominated was Cradle Mountain-Lake St. Clare Park, the Frenchman's Cap Park, the Franklin Wild Rivers Park, and the South West National Park, a total area of 769,355 h. See remarks by Andrew Lohrey and Douglas Lowe (the former premier) at Senate, *Select Committee on South-west Tasmania*, vol. 1, pp. 296-8, and vol. 4, pp. 3603 ff.

[50] *Nomination of Western Tasmania Wilderness National Parks by the Commonwealth of Australia for Inclusion in the World Heritage List* (Tasmanian Government and AHC, November 1981), pp. 1, 10.

[51] *Ibid.*, pp. 14-16, 19-21.

The Management of International Conventions

52 Announcement by the Minister of Home Affairs and Environment, 24 January 1982. This was anticipated in the remarks by the Prime Minister earlier to the World Heritage Committee meeting in Sydney in October 1981. For a summary, see testimony of the Australian Council of National Trusts, in Senate, *Select Committee on South-west Tasmania,* vol. 2, p. 1695.

53 Opinion of the Attorney-General's Department, 1 July 1982, quoted in *House of Representatives,* 129, 19 October 1982, p. 2216. In addition Prime Minister Fraser's inclinations may have been against reversal; Lowe later described him as a "closet greenie" (*Australian,* 30 November 1984).

54 AHC, *Annual Report 1982-83* (Canberra, 1984; PP 39), p. 3.

55 Premier Holgate, to the Senate *Select Committee on South-west Tasmania,* vol. 2, pp. 1199 ff.

56 *House of Representatives,* 129, 19 October 1982, pp. 2216 ff. (para. 28).

57 *House of Representatives,* 130, 26 October 1982, p. 2496.

58 E.g., Fraser, *House of Representatives,* 130, 28 October 1982, p. 3698; statement by McVeigh, 130, 8 December 1982, p. 3085.

59 *Ibid.,* p. 3086.

60 *Ibid.*

61 *Ibid.;* and *House of Representatives,* 130, 14 December 1982, p. 3411.

62 Quoted *ibid.,* p. 3408.

63 Tuckey, *House of Representatives,* 131, 4 May 1983, p. 218, on second reading. The Australian Democrats' bill was introduced in the Senate the previous December, but the government moved to defer debate on the second reading in the House (*House of Representatives,* 130, 14 December 1982, p. 3498).

64 Four main heads of power in the Constitution were used in the Commonwealth's case in the High Court: external affairs, national, corporate and racial. For a brief summary, see K.W. Ryan, ed., *International Law in Australia,* 2nd ed. (Sydney: Law Book Co., 1984), p. 52.

65 The process was begun by Hawke in a letter to Premier Gray of 30 March 1983 offering assistance in developing energy alternatives (*House of Representatives,* 130, 5 May 1983, p. 293). Negotiations followed on compensation and the constituting of a management authority for the area. Plans for the latter were increasingly criticized as inadequate by conservation groups on the grounds that too much power was being conceded to Tasmanian interests, including HEC opinion. See *Canberra Times,* 18 March 1985; and Bruce Montgomery, "Conservation bodies 'black' Franklin plan," *Weekend Australian,* January 19-20, 1985.

66 Matters were approached with cautious formality in the December 1984 election. Labor's position was that it would "consider nominations" from the states of sites for world heritage listing, while the Liberals emphasized the need for promotion of federal-state cooperation (*Australian,* 30 November 1984). The world heritage and other questions were further played down in Labor's approach to the 1987 federal election.

67 "Unique Tasmanian area may be lost to science," *IUCN Bull.,* 3(5), May 1972, p. 19.

68 Tasmanian Wilderness Society (Canberra branch), Senate, *Select Committee on South-west Tasmania,* vol. 2, p. 1496; *ACF Newsl.,* 11(2), March 1979, p. 11.

69 R.D. Lumb, "Australian Coastal Jurisdiction," in Ryan, ed., *International Law in Australia,* p. 370.

70 *Ibid.,* p. 371.

71 *Ibid.,* p. 372.

72 Henry Burmester, "The Australian States and Participation in the Foreign Policy Process," *Federal Law Review,* 9, 1978, p. 280.

73 *House of Representatives,* 118, 13 May 1980, pp. 2611-2. This was in a communication to the House Standing Committee on Environment and Conservation in connection with its work on Australia's coastal zone.

74 *Royal Commission on Australian Government Administration, Report* (Canberra, 1976), p. 335, para. 10.4.17.

75 Geoffrey Hawker, R.F.I. Smith and Patrick Weller, *Politics and Policy in Australia* (St. Lucia: University of Queensland Press, 1979), pp. 207-26.

76 *Senate,* 80, 3 April 1979, pp. 1202-3

[77] DEHCD, *First Annual Report 1975-76* (Canberra, 1977; PP 398), p. 8; *2nd Annual Report 1977* (Canberra, 1978; PP 308), p. 23; ANPWS, *Report for Period 1 July 1978 to 30 June 1979* (Canberra, 1979), p. 37. Prof. Ovington, Director of the Service, had related responsibilities for the International Whaling Commission.

[78] *House of Representatives*, 81, 25 October 1972, pp. 3207-8.

[79] P. Brazil, "The Protection of the Marine Environment: Restraints on Environment Harm," in Attorney-General's Department, *Environmental Law: The Australian Government's Role* (Canberra, 1975), pp. 40-1; Henry Burmester, "Australia and the Law of the Sea — The Protection and Preservation of the Marine Environment," in Ryan, ed., *International Law in Australia*, pp. 439-40.

[80] *House of Representatives*, 69, 18 September 1970, pp. 1410-11 (McMahon, responding to a question from Whitlam).

[81] *Ibid.*

[82] *House of Representatives*, 78, 25 May 1972, p. 1391.

[83] DOE, *Report for Period July 1974 to June 1975* (Canberra, 1976; PP 139), p. 17; DEHCD, *2nd Annual Report 1977* (Canberra, 1978; PP 308), p. 24. The plan became operational in late 1973, with implementation tasks shared by federal and state authorities. Stockpiles of dispersants were maintained at several sites, through funding by a levy on the shipping industry.

[84] This was the joint AEC-Australian Fisheries Council Joint Technical Working Group on Marine Pollution. See DEHCD, *2nd Annual Report*, (Canberra, 1978; PP 308), p . 24.

[85] *House of Representatives*, 122, 14 May 1981, pp. 2442-3.

[86] *House of Representatives*, 109, 9 May 1978, p. 2093.

[87] Department of Home Affairs and Environment, cited by Burmester, "Australia and the Law of the Sea," p. 442.

[88] Hunt, *House of Representatives*, 127, 6-7 May 1982, p. 2496.

[89] At the 1954 conference, Australia was in favour of a general prohibition rather than a zonal approach, but was unsuccessful in attempts to secure this. See R.M. McGonigle and M.W. Zacher, *Pollution, Politics and International Law* (Vancouver: University of British Columbia Press, 1979), p. 90; Burmester, "Australia and the Law of the Sea," p. 445.

[90] *House of Representatives*, 131, 25 May 1983, pp. 939-40.

[91] *Ibid.*

[92] Lloyd, *House of Representatives*, 87. 20 November 1973, pp. 3532-3. On the Hobart decision see DOS, *Report for Year 1973-4* (Canberra, 1975; PP 269), p. 59.

[93] For a short summary of ANARE see "Australian Involvement in Antarctica," in *Australians in Antarctica* (Canberra: Antarctic Division, 1981), pp. 14-19. See further P.G. Law, *Antarctic Odyssey* (Melbourne: Heinemann, 1983).

[94] *Towards New Perspectives for Australian Scientific Research in Antarctic. Discussion Paper presented by the Hon. W.L. Morrison, MP, Minister for Science, March 1975* (Canberra, 1975; PP 54).

[95] E.g., ASTEC, *Annual Report, 1978-79* (Canberra, 1979; PP 223), App. 13, p. 12, para. 9; and ASTEC, *Towards a Marine Sciences and Technologies Program for the 1980s*, May 1981 (Canberra, 1981; PP 168), pp. 80 ff.

[96] DOS, Antarctic Division, *Report for Year 1972-73* (Canberra, 1974; PP 251), p . 1.

[97] See the organizational account in relation to the functions of ARPAC at DST, *Annual Report 1982-3* (Canberra, 1983), pp. 86-7.

[98] Bruce Davis, "Australia and Antarctica: Aspects of Policy Process," in Stuart Harris, ed., *Australia's Antarctic Policy Options* (Australian National University: Centre for Resource and Environmental Studies, 1984), p. 348.

[99] See for example the report by the Department on the 8th Antarctica Treaty meeting, Oslo, 1975 at DFA, *Annual Report for 1975* (Canberra, 1976; PP 142), pp. 14-15.

[100] DEHCD, *2nd Annual Report 1977* (Canberra, 1978; PP 308), p. 25. Officials from the environment department were present for example on the delegation to the Canberra Special Meeting of the Parties of February-March 1978 (DEHCD, *3rd Annual Report 1977-78* (Canberra, 1978; PP 433), p. 6).

[101] DEC, *Report for Period December 1972 - June 1974* (Canberra, 1975; PP 298), p. 14.

[102] ANPWS, *Report for Period 1 July 1977 - 30 June 1978* (Canberra, 1978), p. 41.

156

CHAPTER NINE

Domestic Contexts: Environmental Constituencies in Australian Politics

Controversy in Australia on environmental issues has been coloured by economic, partisan and ideological factors. During the 1970s and 1980s demands by environmental groups provoked various sources of opposition: from farming, industrial, mining and other interests affected by the consequences of regulatory innovation; from critics who saw in environmentalism little more than a disguised form of left-wing assaults on established approaches; and from defenders of the rights of states, allegedly threatened by the growing federal power entailed in the search for national environmental policies. Among conservationists themselves, gradualists were often stern critics of radicals. Compromise was inevitable, Sandford Clark wrote in 1974. "The utter intractability of some adherents to the [conservation] movement immediately puts them out of sympathy with the politician to whom compromise is, necessarily, a way of life."[1] Debates have tended to surround domestic rather than international questions. Many issues, such as the development of Black Mountain in Canberra,[2] have been highly localized. Some have spawned blueprints for national campaign architecture: for example, the woodchips industry, uranium mining, or whaling.

Environmentalists' arguments have been only one source of pressure on governments. State governments have often proved more responsive to economic interests, to the case that the state economy requires more, not less, favourable conditions for the development of forestry, tourism, farming, or hydroelectric power. Federal governments have been at times acutely sensitive to the political implications of the constitutional division of powers in Australia, which puts responsibility for many of these questions into the hands of the states. This consideration, together with pressure from mining and other interests adversely affected by earlier environmental impact legislation,[3] led to retrenchment and wariness in the second half of the 1970s. The strategies of environmental groups have varied in part with the answers they have found to some classic dilemmas: can influence be wielded more effectively through the politics of confrontation and publicity, or by way of quiet behind-the-scenes diplomacy? Does pursuit of the second lead to dependence and a vulnerability to manipulation? Should funding from powerful actors be viewed as fuel for the engine or a foot on the brake?

International questions, however, have on closer inspection never been very far from the centre of environmental politics. Some issues, such as protection of the Great Barrier Reef, or crocodile farming, or wilderness preservation in South-west Tasmania, have been objects of concern for external constituencies. Some of these, including sympathetic international bodies, could be coaxed into exercising their own persuasive talents inside Australia. A number of groups, moreover, are organizationally, and in terms of the self-image of members, the national segments of larger transnational networks. Appeals for action have sometimes been grounded in part in definitions of global, rather than Australian, needs. Such arguments have federalist corollaries. Since the Commonwealth has responsibility for Australia's international relations, many environmental groups have been drawn to the view that it, rather than the states, should also be the primary actor in environmental policy. Some critics of parochialism, fragmentation and antipathy towards the environment at the state level have reached the same conclusion; others, repelled by perceptions of the bureaucracy, excessive caution, isolation, or geographical and psychological remoteness of Canberra, have preferred to concentrate their energies on state politics. To assess the significance of these domestic contexts of policy formation, we will examine here the character of environmental groups, their roles in relation to international questions, the part they have played in the politics of some of the major issues studied in earlier chapters, the activities of scientific organizations, and the interactions between these bodies and party and parliamentary politics.

The evolution and character of the environmental movement

Despite the sense of newness and urgency that was an essential part of the politics of environmental conservation during the 1970s, many groups could probably have traced their ancestry back to the national trusts, philosophical societies and naturalists groups of the nineteenth century. Some leading individuals, such as Myles Dunphy in New South Wales, had careers in conservation politics that spanned several decades from the 1920s.[4] Groups of this period were influential in the spread of the national parks movement, and the setting up of national park and wildlife services by state governments. In the more radical and politicized atmosphere of environmental politics in the 1970s, however, genealogy did not guarantee legitimacy. The Australian Conservation Foundation, for example, had difficulty in claiming appropriately activist credentials. By the end of the 1960s, environmental issues had become more securely fixed on political agendas, more broadly defined to encompass urban pollution questions, and more oriented towards national policies and the role of the Commonwealth authorities.

In addition the environmental movement became both larger and also more diversified. The variety of organizations with interests in environmental policy issues — in terms of memberships and constituencies, location on the spectrum of partisan politics, sources of funding, preferred strategies, the range of questions tackled, degree of interest in international matters, and other measures — is such that many generalizations about environmentalist opinion have doubtful validity. Davis has suggested five main categories of organizations: national umbrella organizations, such as the ACF or the Australian National Parks Council (ANPC); state coordinating committees, for example the Conservation Council of New

South Wales; specific issue bodies, such as the Tasmanian Wilderness Society (TWS) or the Fraser Island Defence Organization; environmental centres, with primarily an educational or consciousness-raising role; and international organizations such as Friends of the Earth (FOE) or Greenpeace, which exist as relatively autonomous branches of outside bodies. There are also a number of "quasi-environmental professional bodies" and voluntary research coalitions with links to global institutions such as IUCN or the World Wildlife Fund (WWF).[5]

Membership of such groups has expanded significantly since the mid-1960s. The first wave of recruitment by the new ACF led to a membership of more than 1,200 by 1967; the figure rose from 6,688 to 10,002 in the period 1978-81 alone.[6] The number of groups with "environmental" interests rose to an estimated 1,198 in 1978 and to around 1,350 in 1981; their total membership has been put at around 100,000 in the mid-1970s and at as much as 400,000 by the end of the decade.[7] Such figures have to be approached with some caution. Members of the same organization differ in their views on policy questions, and in their degree of interest in such issues; some individuals take up memberships in a number of like-minded bodies; some sympathizers may not take up membership at all. Group activities, moreover, do not necessarily translate into public interest or support. Increased memberships from 1976-80, for example, took place at the same time as evidence from public opinion poll data of a slight drop in attention to environmental issues.[8] However, there is here sufficient indication that the organized voice of conservation became more significant during the 1970s.

The ACF was in a sense a product of external pressures. In a visit to Australia in 1963, Prince Philip suggested some form of Australian contribution to the recently established WWF. It became clear during meetings of scientists and conservationists in subsequent months that no appropriate Australia-wide organization existed that could coordinate responses to international bodies of this kind. The ACF was founded late in 1964, following an initial meeting held in Canberra in August. A small secretariat, and an elected council, was put in place during 1966-67.[9] Its early character generated later controversies. In terms of issues, the Foundation was more interested in the nature conservation questions with which IUCN was identified internationally than with the emerging range of urban and industrial issues. The ACF also aspired to be an influential advocate at the elite rather than the grass-roots level. It was comfortable with the liberal assumption that through reasoned argument lay the route to influence and sound policies. Its choice of its leading figures (for example, Lord Casey, the Governor-General, as first Patron; Sir Garfield Barwick, Chief Justice of the High Court of Australia, as first President; Prince Philip as President later, in 1973-75) signalled its style and approach to environmental issues. The ACF membership has been predominantly middle-class. Of its members in 1984, approximately 64 per cent had professional, managerial, or other white-collar occupational backgrounds, and 77 per cent had completed some form of tertiary education studies.[10]

By that time, however, the ACF's orientation to policy issues had been affected by the changing character of environmental politics. Even in the early 1970s,

159

it bred growing frustration among its critics. Internal changes in 1973 ushered in a progressively more activist and open approach. It remained none the less the main body representative of a wide range of conservationist opinion, and also the one most generously funded by government. Other organizations implicitly challenged this role in the 1970s. The FOE organization, for example, was based on active branches in each state, and, unlike the ACF, it focused much more single-mindedly on a restricted circle of exploitable issues, such as whaling, uranium mining, or threats to Antarctica. Other bodies, such as Greenpeace, were candid about their readiness to make use of more direct and controversial tactics to bring about change. So were some trade unions, especially for a time those in the building and construction industry. In a number of "green bans," for example in relation to The Rocks, Sydney, and a proposed Newport power station in Melbourne, unions supported industrial action by members as a means of protecting the environment.[11]

The ACF, however, had the distinction, dubious at times, of retaining relatively good working relations with government and sympathetic parliamentarians. From the outset, too, it consistently fostered its role as a national body, and attempted to resist being drawn too deeply into environmental controversies of a purely local or regional character.[12] The Foundation's advocacy of stronger Commonwealth policies was a reflection in part of both an interest in international environmental policy developments, and also a conviction of the need for greater uniformity among the programmes of state governments. As its then President, Murray Wilcox, argued in 1980, Australia had a "mish-mash of eight systems of State or Territorial law upon which there has been recently imposed skeletal, and rather ineffective, federal law."[13]

The question of government funding of environmental groups was closely linked to the way they evolved. Both sides of the counter had a stake in this process. Benefits flowed to funding as well as to funded bodies. First, the absence of US-style tax deductibility for contributions was one of the first problems to beset the ACF. Its viability, and that of organizations like it, was recognized as calling for some input of public funds. The criteria and formulae for support, however, were far from self-evident. Secondly, environment officials in their dealings with other government departments, whether at the state or the federal level, also had an interest in cultivating a supportive non-governmental environmental constituency. The same consideration applied, particularly during ALP rule in 1972-75, to the Commonwealth as a whole in its relations with state governments.

This issue became a controversial one in the 1970s. The foundations of the funding policy, however, were laid before the Whitlam government took office — indeed before there was a serious possibility of it taking office. The first annual grants (of $20,000) were made in the ACF's first year of operations. In 1969, this was increased to $50,000, with a commitment to five years of funding; in September, 1972, the federal authorities raised this to $150,000.[14] This continued after Labor came to power. Though small as a proportion of government

160

expenditures, the figures were substantial from the recipients' point of view. The ALP government saw funding as a significant arm of its overall environmental policy. Awareness of conservationist criticism of the ACF led the government in 1973 to threaten a major cut in funds unless the Foundation brought about policy and constitutional changes to make it more responsive to the interests and aspirations of members.[15] The ACF, moreover, Cass said, had been "surpassed by other, more active conservation groups, and by the growth of bodies able to tender expert environmental advice."[16] This pressure for change was a central factor precipitating the internal crisis within ACF ranks in 1973, which led to a significant shift in its emphasis and priorities.[17] The government aimed, then, to spread funding support among competing groups and avoid placing all the Commonwealth's eggs in one basket. But it also wanted to stimulate coherence and efficacy. "Because we're handing out taxpayers' money," Cass said in 1974, "we don't want to subsidise incompetent organizations or fund trivial feuds."[18]

This policy made the government vulnerable to attack from a number of fronts. The conservative opposition, and the governments of New South Wales and other states,[19] portrayed it as a device to win support for the ALP. Mining, agricultural and industrial interests, increasingly restless about the general direction of government policies, particularly with regard to environmental impact provisions and heritage protection, saw in funding programmes the permanent entrenchment of officially subsidized opponents. Mining companies, recognizing the AFC as likely therefore to be an increasingly important element in the regulatory picture, made a number of attempts during the 1970s to influence its thinking.[20] The Fraser government's first funding cuts came quickly.[21] Yet it was more cautious in its approach than some of its supporters wished it to be. The aim was not to dismantle the programme, but rather to use it as a means of directing the course of the environmental movement along more "responsible" lines. The FOE, for example, was eliminated from the grants hand-out in 1977 because of what was regarded as its extremist political stance. The government argued that it should not subsidize "an organization that has been largely responsible for very violent demonstrations."[22] The action enhanced FOE's prestige in the eyes of many environmentalists, but this sacrificial offering to the anti-environment lobby also allowed the government to continue some level of funding, howbeit reduced in absolute as well as real terms, to other groups. However, the effective cases against funding mounted in parliamentary hearings in the late 1970s and early 1980s by bodies such as the New South Wales Livestock and Grain Producers Association and the Australian Chemical Industry Council clearly defined the limits of acceptability of such a policy.[23]

In many ways the issue was coming to a head at the same time that South-west Tasmania was providing environmental groups with additional evidence that conservationist views were more widely shared among the Australian public than the government realized. The Commonwealth's matching grants formula of the late 1970s was widely criticized on the grounds that it severely hampered the activities of the small organizations most in need of support. There was growing parliamentary acknowledgment at the turn of the decade of the contribution such groups made to public debate and environmental awareness.[24] Grievances were aired at a meeting of representatives of Conservation Councils and Environment Centres in Melbourne in July 1982.[25] The Tasmanian issue was thus useful not only because of the way it served to focus public attention on environment policy, and on the alleged shortcomings of the Fraser government, but also because the influx of members it attracted helped alleviate some short-term financial problems of organizations and supported the longer-term argument that the government's funding policies were misguided and counter-productive.

For the most part, such questions were significant primarily for domestic issues. Yet there were also some international implications. Government funding could be a decisive factor in the ability of groups to take part in debates on international developments, and more particularly in international meetings. The ACF could draw on resources to send representatives to some forums, such as the 1982 UNEP anniversary session in Nairobi; others, such as FOE or Greenpeace, maintained contact with NGO gatherings through their own transnational form of organization. Some had informal or formal links with government officials, for example through frameworks such as the Australian Committee for IUCN. Even so, groups increasingly in the early 1980s called for the government to provide funds for at least one NGO representative to attend international conferences as part of the Australian delegation.[26] Further, receipt of Commonwealth funds tended in many cases to be linked with groups' support of the federal government's role in making environment policy. The ACF's definition of its own role as a national body made it sympathetic to this line of argument, but some critics maintained that its dependence on federal funds pushed it into too great a readiness to support the Commonwealth line, or into interpretations of Australia's international obligations that implied significantly enhanced powers for the federal authorities. In part to counter this kind of trend, state governments had their own funding programmes for conservation groups. Like the Commonwealth, they were often selective in who they funded; the Tasmanian government stopped all funding to groups in 1982 because of the anti-dam campaign led by the TWS.[27] Organizations varied considerably, however, in the degree of attention they paid to the international developments affecting Australia. And, as we shall see shortly in connection with the Australian National Conservation Strategy, some groups argued strenuously in favour of the state, as opposed to the federal, level as the more appropriate basis of response to international issues.

Environmental groups and Australian public opinion

The ability of environmental NGOs to mould Australia's international policies, or its responses to international developments, has been shaped by their relations with Australian publics, international organizations, the federal government, Parliament and the state governments. We will first look at each of these relationships, and turn in the next section of this chapter to a more detailed study of specific instances of attempts to exercise influence.

The success of environmental groups in mobilizing large sections of Australian public opinion has been restricted to a handful of key issues, of which the best example is South-west Tasmania in the early 1980s. Public resistance to group messages is compounded by two factors: indifference to foreign affairs, and objections on broader ideological grounds. For conservative opinion, the regulatory spirit and the values represented by environmental groups were often indigestible. Environmental activists, Lang Hancock said in 1978, were "the Number One enemy of civilization, and hence Australia"; they were "dole-bludging dropouts", "subversives" working against the free enterprise system.[28] Even critics who could see some merit in conservationist arguments could easily be alienated by the way goals were defined and priorities ordered. The Tasmanian issue demonstrated for the *Australian Financial Review* "that emotional defence of the wilderness ranks well ahead of rational economic debate when it comes to party attention, media coverage, and even international interest..."[29]

Environmental bodies faced a different set of problems in attempting to muster support from the left. For many in the ALP, particularly at the state level, environmentalism implicitly rejected economic development, and hence the need to fight against unemployment. By the early 1980s, the federal ALP had been outflanked on this question by the younger Australian Democrats who, under Senator Chipp, made a determined bid for the conservation vote. Environmentalism was more in tune with Labor's thinking in the late 1960s and early 1970s. This often translated into impatience with existing bodies, identified by critics with the "good old-fashioned liberal means" of achieving goals such as endangered species protection or pollution abatement.[30] Although the ACF underwent changes in the mid-1970s, the changes were frequently found wanting. As a result, one critic argued later, it was "too radical for conservatives and too conservative for radicals. Too much effort is being put into securing that annual federal grant, and our aims are constantly being compromised for expediency."[31] In the longer term, conservation groups tended to suffer as the targets of radical politics shifted away from the environment and towards more promising topics such as employment, immigration, race relations and feminism.

Attempts to identify the main environmental issues facing the country have varied with the particular concerns of groups. They often provide a useful indication of the extent to which international questions fit into the thinking of environmental organizations. A characteristic list of the mid-1980s included the following: rainforests, woodchipping, softwood plantations, land degradation, weed infestation, mallee (a more specific focus on vegetation in arid areas), sandmining, the Great Barrier Reef — more specifically, threats from oil drillers, leases, giant clam and turtle poaching by Taiwanese fishermen, and tourism — uranium mining, pollution (including atmospheric carbon dioxide build-up), and endangered species.[32] There were significant international aspects of several of these, as there were to earlier questions such as oil pollution of the coastal zone, South-west Tasmania, and arid lands management. But there were limits to the appeal of globalist arguments, the view that action was required because it served a more universal good. Environmental groups that shared such perspectives on Antarctica, for example, or the ozone layer, had to present their case with considerable care if it was to stand much chance of being heard. On the other hand, exploitation of the international aspects of issues — for example, the international significance of the Huon pine in South-west Tasmania, the jarrah forests of Western Australia, or the rainforests of northern Queensland — could be a valuable tool once a conservation question already had a certain momentum in wider public debates.

Secondly, many environmental groups were, directly or indirectly, parts of larger international groupings. Membership of IUCN, for example, provided sources of environmental data, was an emblem of identification with global environmental values, afforded a potential means for levering external allies into place to fight domestic battles, and gave an opportunity to influence federal officials through participation in Australian delegations at international meetings. This meant that IUCN in particular had a centrality in Australian conservation debates it could not have secured alone. Links were strengthened with the establishment in 1979 of the Australian Committee for IUCN, consisting of the union's governmental and non-governmental members; one of its first steps was to draw up a report on the Darling Ranges in Western Australia for submission to the Director-General of IUCN.[33] The formation of WWF-Australia in 1978 was similarly a significant development, not least because of the symbiotic relationship between IUCN and WWF at the international level. Australians were able to use these links to secure IUCN intervention in domestic issues, for example in relation to Lake Pedder, the Tasmanian South-west, or crocodiles. Less directly, IUCN guidelines or pronouncements could be used as supports for advocacy inside Australia on such matters as the inadequacy of national park or protected area coverage, or state government land use planning in arid areas.[34] On questions of endangered species, a traditional concern of IUCN, activity by Australian groups designed to generate publicity and action served both external and domestic objectives.[35]

The obscurity of many of these questions made them unreliable as instruments for the persuasion of publics. They were, however, closely linked to the third set of relationships — that between NGOs and the Commonwealth. Not all groups enjoyed a productive rapport with politicians and bureaucrats. Many were instinctively suspicious of the politics of cosiness. Even the ACF, the most "official" of these groups, consistently baulked at the suggestion that it should move its headquarters from Melbourne to Canberra.[36] Yet, because of the way environmental issues were structured in Australia, many groups were also drawn towards the Commonwealth side of arguments about federalism: partly because of the funding relationship, but mainly because on many issues action seemed to be required by the federal authorities to bring reactionary state governments into line. Thus the South-west Tasmania issue became for the ACF in early 1982 "the test case for Commonwealth concern about the environment."[37] In addition, some Commonwealth bodies shared goals with the NGO constituency. In the late 1970s, both the AHC and the ANPWS suffered from the sensitivity of political leaders and central agencies to state government charges that these organizations were overstepping the limits defined by cooperative federalism in order to press environmental protection arguments. On the question of Daintree in 1985, for example, and the issue of rainforest conservation in northern Queensland, there was a widespread view in government that the AHC was "too independent."[38] A variety of formal and informal links strengthened the reciprocity between environmental groups and some segments of the federal bureaucracy, and some Commonwealth officials retained active connections with the domestic and international environmental movement.[39]

Fourthly, environmental groups had some ability, in the right circumstances, to mobilize opinion in Parliament. Apart from some issues in which a wider range of public interest was generated, however, such as kangaroo management, the trade in wild birds, or Tasmania, attention to environmental matters in the House of Representatives tended to be restricted to a handful of members. These members often faced an uphill battle. Dr. Jenkins, one of them, noted in 1981 in connection with the issue of Australia's position on the marine pollution conventions that "parliamentary consciousness of their existence is abysmally low and public awareness is practically nil."[40] Such endeavours met with more success where environmental issues seemed to provide a key to a larger political agenda, as was the case when the ALP pursued such issues from the opposition benches in 1970-72. The workings of the Australian electoral and parliamentary system often meant that this kind of minority interest was better represented in the Senate. The upper house, as one of its members said in 1971, had been "in the forefront of initiating parliamentary interest in the field of environmental pollution."[41] This began with the work of two key select committees, dealing respectively with air and water pollution, and continued, with some breaks, into the 1980s. The Senate's role was central, for example, to the wider debate on the international aspects of the South-west Tasmanian question, particularly since this was the chamber used by the Australian Democrats in 1982-83 to press for Commonwealth intervention. The party took a variety of initiatives on environmental issues in the 1980s, building in the process close consultative links with the ACF, TWS and other groups.[42] In both the 1983 and 1984 elections, many groups urged combinations of voter support for Labor and the Australian Democrats.

Finally, environmental groups frequently made much of the argument that the Commonwealth should exploit its constitutional powers to the full in the search for national action on the environment. They viewed the external relations power as an essential instrument in this regard, something that could and should be used in environmental areas where the Australian government had signed a related international convention; they successfully maintained pressure on the government to use its federal power to regulate Australia's sand exports from Fraser and Moreton Islands. Some groups, however, were also aware, even if reluctantly so, of the limits beyond which Canberra would not go in efforts to persuade state governments. For example, many strongly favoured tightening the implementation

165

provisions of the National Conservation Strategy in the early 1980s, which meant confronting directly the delicate question of state powers. The ACF took the matter up with federal officials in 1984; as a result "we didn't press this issue because of advice from [McMichael] that it would be tactically wiser not to do so, to leave this matter to be discussed by the Prime Minister with the Premiers, probably at a Premiers Conference."[43] Many groups were quick to voice support for beleaguered federal environmental officials in the late 1970s, and to protest the shift of significant environmental impact responsibilities from the Commonwealth to state governments.[44]

Even this short account indicates the very real constraints that affected the operations of environmental groups. More particularly, we can see that international considerations played various roles in their orientation to issues and to governmental and political actors. Such aspects were central, and an end in themselves, for some; but marginal for many. Organizations also varied a great deal in their respective capacities to exploit links with international bodies as a strategy in dealings with federal or state governments in Australia, and their willingness to appeal to international obligations as a rationale for domestic action. We now turn to a more detailed analysis of same of the cases in which sustained efforts were made to alter the course of government policy.

Influence strategies and environmental issues

In relation to two of the questions examined in earlier chapters — the protection of Australia's natural heritage, and the Australian response to IUCN's World Conservation Strategy — many groups seized the opportunity presented by international instruments to sharpen the focus of domestic environmental objectives.

The World Conservation Strategy came at useful juncture. By 1980, conservation groups had been seriously affected by funding cuts, and Commonwealth environmental legislation and institutions had been subjected to a major critical review inside government. Apparently more interested in soothing ruffled state feathers than in protecting Australia's environment, the Commonwealth authorities were facing increasing criticism on a growing number of issues. The launch of the IUCN *Strategy* by Prime Minister Fraser in 1980 was designed in part as a gesture of appeasement, and, since many of its provisions were sufficiently vague, one that would cost relatively little in terms of policy change. In pursuing the goal of translating the principles of the *Strategy* into concrete policies and programmes, environmental groups sought a number of objectives: the establishment of machinery to follow it through; assurance that the public and conservation groups would be well represented in this process; maintenance of the pace of debate and the design of specific policies; and resistance to attempts to deflect the *Strategy* into generalities devoid of policy content or compromises shorn of ecological soundness.

The idea of working towards a national version of the global document was already generally accepted within government. It took form with the Prime

Minister's announcement in September 1980 of plans for the phased development of a National Conservation Strategy. The ACF, like other groups, concentrated on efforts to secure wider public debate.[45] The two-year programme for development of the Strategy, endorsed by the steering committee at its June 1981 meeting, called for "participation by conservation and developer groups, individual citizens and professional experts." In December, a national seminar aired many of the issues. From then on, and particularly in light of the government's discussion paper that followed the meeting, the tone of commentary by environmental groups was increasingly negative. Representatives of conservation councils and environment centres, meeting in Melbourne in July 1982, urged preparation of an autonomous Strategy, rather than comment on a document "which contains no strategy, has no stated aims, and is not a true or appropriate synthesis" of the December 1981 deliberations.[46] The bases of discontent varied with individuals and organizations, but a common theme was the charge that the Commonwealth was failing to take a lead in defining environmental priorities and was proving to be too responsive to the concerns of industry and the jurisdictional fears of state governments. Dissatisfaction mounted when it became clearer that major change in the draft Strategy could not be accommodated. Groups called for a totally new draft, for a strengthening of its provisions (in terms of policy detail and implementation), and for more effective public consultations. The conference on the Strategy held in Canberra in June 1983 agreed on a text, and recommended its adoption by governments, but failed to meet these concerns.

The resulting Strategy, designed as an integrated package of development and conservation goals and programmes, defined a set of objectives and principles, and then attempted to define priority national actions in a number of areas: education and training, policy planning and coordination, legislation and regulation, research, international aspects, reserves and habitat protection, control of pollution, wastes and hazardous materials, use of living resources, and conservation of soils and water. The ACF and other groups attacked it as being heavily laced with generalities, and weak on substance; it did not point the way towards specific conservation measures, nor did it define the relative priorities among various conservation areas. The Strategy process was widely seen as the culprit. Conservation principles present in the original IUCN document had been watered down, it was argued, because the government had insisted that economic interests and state governments help shape the National Strategy. Thus "in the end the Strategy represents what industry and the more conservative government representatives were prepared to accept."[47] These interests, moreover, did not share the goal of open, public debate; on a number of issues, some industry and state representatives objected to the release of information regarded by environmental groups as essential for such discussions. In the final analysis, the Commonwealth authorities could not strengthen the implementation provisions of the Strategy because of reluctance to step into areas falling under state jurisdiction. Federal environmental officials resisted attempts by the ACF and others to secure a tighter definition of the implementation clauses with the argument that, in light of state sensitivities, this would be counter-productive.[48]

In the final stages of detailed committee work on the Strategy in 1984-85, environmental groups more or less abandoned hope in the enterprise. The enthusiasm of 1980 had evaporated. Some organizations, for example in Western Australia and Victoria, had increasingly ignored the federal level and concentrated attention on the development of state strategies. More radical green groups dismissed the exercise as one of futility and expediency.[49] There were calls from within the ranks of the ACF that the Foundation should withdraw its endorsement of the Strategy.[50] The economic realism of the new Labor government, moreover, as well as its caution in the aftermath of the Tasmanian crisis, made the IUCN *Strategy* unattractive as a framework for future environmental conservation programmes; and by the mid-1980s, there was little that even sympathetic organizations could do to stimulate media interest in the National Strategy.

By contrast, the existence of the World Heritage convention provided Australian environmental groups with an international instrument which played a significant role in the transformation of the Tasmanian issue. The general question of wilderness conservation in South-west Tasmania had been on their agendas at least since the mid-1960s, but it was not until the late 1970s that it took shape as a national political issue, of interest also to Australians outside the normal range of environmental groups. From the early days, environmentalists were forced to recognize federal realities. There was widespread ACF support in 1968 for Commonwealth intervention to secure the establishment of an adequate protected area in South-west Tasmania; but its President, Sir Garfield Barwick, pointed to "the many legal and political difficulties which prevented the Commonwealth government from moving into the National Parks field in the States."[51] This initial phase, centring on protests over the state government's plans to flood the Lake Pedder area, failed to bring about change in either Hobart or Canberra.

During the mid-1970s, several factors propelled these concerns into the centre of national debates. First, the environmental movement itself, and the audience for its various viewpoints, had grown substantially, as had parliamentary attention to conservation issues. Secondly, it was during the early and mid-1970s that the Commonwealth for the first time emerged as a significant environmental policy actor, as a result chiefly of the legislative and institutional developments associated with the Whitlam administration. More particularly, the establishment and growth of the national heritage protection programme afforded a continuous stream of opportunities for proposals, criticism and publicity. In 1976-77, for example, the apparently lower priority placed by the AHC on the inclusion of green sites, as opposed to cultural properties, in the list of heritage areas provoked complaints from conservation groups.[52] Inclusion of the South-west on the Register of the National Estate was urged as an essential feature of this programme.[53] Thirdly, it became clear during the 1970s that development activities and projects in the region constituted a mounting and seemingly irreversible set of threats to wilderness values. These included renewed interest in the potential of limestone quarrying and forestry resources, but centred on hydro-electric power generation. Though the specifics of HEC plans and Tasmanian government decisions in this field still had to be finalized, the fundamental strategy of moving towards dam construction in ecologically vulnerable areas of the South-west appeared to be inflexible.[54] Finally, the presence of the UNESCO World Heritage convention, and the Australian government's commitment in principle to support the convention's goals, threw into sharp relief the option of Commonwealth intervention. Given the climate of opinion in Tasmania itself, many environmental groups had concluded even before the fall of the Whitlam government in 1975 that action by Canberra would be the only way to resolve the impasse. Constitutional hurdles admittedly blocked this path, but, in view of the financial and other resources that a Commonwealth government with the political will to pursue federal options would possess, removal of the obstructions could, it was widely believed, be successfully negotiated. In this context, use by the federal authorities of powers under the World Heritage convention might be the crucial factor to guarantee success. By the late 1970s, the ACF had identified a total of 14 areas argued to be suitable for nomination to the World Heritage list, and was increasingly critical of the government's failure to submit proposals to the World Heritage Committee; the Tasmanian South-west was regarded as an obvious candidate, and the Franklin-Lower Gordon campaign generally became the Foundation's "prime focus" in 1978-79.[55]

The lead in this broader campaign was quickly taken in the late 1970s and early 1980s by the Tasmanian Wilderness Society. Founded in 1976, its membership by the early 1980s was around 5,000.[56] The success of the TWS in attracting support across Australia, and internationally, for its cause, can be attributed to several factors. One reason given by a commentator at the time was the character of the issues; the South-west as the focus of a campaign could attract more widespread support than could be mobilized by the long-running anti-nuclear campaign.[57] The Society's leadership undoubtedly possessed a flair for publicity. One small example was the superb colour photograph of Rock Island Bend on the Franklin River, included in newspapers at a crucial juncture in the March 1983 election campaign. The *Sydney Morning Herald* published an unprecedented 75 letters on the Tasmanian question.[58] The determination of Tasmanian government and HEC officials to pursue dam construction also presented the TWS with a continuing series of exploitable opportunities. In the crucial Tasmanian referendum held in December 1981, voters were not allowed to register disapproval of the dam option; at the urging of the TWS, many wrote in the "No dams" option on the ballot sheet, resulting in a high "informal" vote of almost 45 per cent and, additionally, in the defection of many Tasmanian ALP supporters to the TWS camp. Partly through its office in Canberra, the Society also engaged in lobbying federal politicians, particularly in the increasingly sympathetic Australian Democrats, and officials in the various environment and heritage institutions of the Commonwealth. The intensity of the confrontations of December 1982 and early 1983, marked by a prolonged civil disobedience campaign to block

169

dam construction activities following the Tasmanian legislation of November designed to prevent trespass on HEC land, took the events into a different phase of mounting disorder.[59]

The main groups active in the South-west campaign increasingly focussed on the potential electoral spin-off of the question from late 1982. A strategy of active campaigning in all key constituencies in the forthcoming general election was decided on at a meeting of 14 organizations in Melbourne in December.[60] Labor, with a record of earlier opposition to the flooding of Lake Pedder in 1973, stood to be the main beneficiary of any election fought around Tasmanian conservation; the ALP only needed eleven seats in the House of Representatives to form a government, and some key areas of Sydney and Melbourne were clearly vulnerable to anti-dam arguments.[61]

In what ways did international considerations enter this picture? We can identify three. First, the TWS, ACF and other organizations made good use of the proposition that Tasmanian energy development plans threatened not only state and national, but also global conservation values. The message was directed primarily towards mainland audiences, and pronouncements by outside figures, including Prince Philip, were regularly deployed as a means of strengthening this case. David Bellamy, the English botanist later arrested in the Tasmanian blockade, denounced dam plans in 1981 as an act of "international vandalism."[62] The receptivity of Australians to such opinions varied considerably, however; a barrage of external criticism could conceivably have resulted instead in a cohesive rallying of opinion around states' rights and the federal underpinnings of the Australian polity. That it helped to reinforce the opposite tendency — towards widespread condemnation of the development plans of a state government — is testimony to the shrewdness of TWS strategists in assessing, and exploiting, both the special features of Tasmania's place within Australian federal life and also the degree to which sustained exposure to fault-finding by outsiders could have a galvanizing effect on public opinion.

Secondly, the World Heritage convention, and the Australian nomination of the South-west for inclusion on the World Heritage list, provided groups with both political and constitutional ammunition. More specific demands followed. The Australian government could be urged simply to fulfil its putative obligations under the terms of the treaty. The extensive argumentation that grew up around the Commonwealth's external affairs power was significant politically for the way it put pressure on the federal authorities to address the issue of intervention in Tasmania. Increasingly, and certainly by December 1982, the Commonwealth refusal to use such means was made to appear not as a studied defence of federalist principles so much as an intransigent retreat from reality. Yet by such measures as withholding support for the Australian Democrats' bill to halt the project, which was passed by the Senate in December, the government was also counting on a widespread bedrock of opposition to Commonwealth activism of this sort. As Senator Carrick, government leader in the Senate, put it, the ALP "would use the bulldozer of very dubious federal powers to destroy the States."[63]

170

Thirdly, a small number of conservation organizations had some capability to manoeuvre international institutions closer to the battle lines. The TWS joined IUCN soon after its formation, and the longer-established ACF had its own productive contacts both with that body and also with federal environment officials linked to the Union's activities. In a 1980 letter to the Premier of Tasmania, for example, the IUCN secretariat maintained that there would probably be a "serious loss of wildlife and other unique wilderness values" if HEC plans were implemented. The South-west was considered by IUCN to be "one of the world's three largest temperate wilderness areas and hence of considerable scientific and conservation importance, and of world significance."[64] As an official advisory body to the World Heritage Committee, however, IUCN later faced constraints in terms of more active involvement in the issue. Other non-governmental organizations in Australia, such as FOE, were better placed, because of their transnational character, to publicize the Tasmanian issue abroad, particularly among conservation bodies in London. The Australian scientific community, which we will examine shortly, also had leverage with external opinion, particularly in areas of botany and archaeology central to the debates on Tasmanian conservation.

Following the 1983 general election and High Court ruling, public interest in the question visibly subsided. The post-crisis politics of the situation had a different character. Conservation groups maintained a close interest in management plans for the South-west, and especially in the question of the composition of the body designed to make decisions affecting areas within and adjacent to the World Heritage region. The management authority structure, which emerged in 1984-85 following prolonged negotiations between the federal and Tasmanian governments, was widely criticized for failing to build wilderness expertise firmly into decision-making processes, and for allowing HEC and other Tasmanian anti-conservationist viewpoints too great a role.[65] The Hawke government was also assailed for altering the world heritage nomination process generally in order to appease outraged state sensibilities.[66] But by this time the interests of publics, and governments, in Australia had largely moved on to other questions.

Some of the central lessons of the Tasmanian experience, however, were not lost on conservation groups. Even so, the world heritage option clearly had to be deployed with care. Over-indulgence could revive earlier complaints that so few world heritage nominations stood a chance of being successful that the whole enterprise should be ignored. The impact of the Tasmanian episode on conservation politics on this score can be seen by comparing cases in the 1970s with those of the 1980s. During the earlier period, for example, a number of national and Western Australian groups campaigned for protection of areas of jarrah forest threatened by bauxite mining and alumina refining. Activity included the initiation by the Conservation Council of Western Australia of legal action inside the US against the company concerned. Yet although the threatened area was widely portrayed as the only one of its kind in the world, pursuit of a world heritage strategy did not become central to the issue.[67]

In a later instance, by contrast, it did. This was the more successful, and more widely publicized, campaign of a large number of conservation groups against development plans in rainforest areas of northern Queensland. A variety of threats were posed by tin mining, logging, road construction, housing plans and tourism development. Politically, the campaign — which was already active in 1980-81 — benefited from the fact that the Queensland government was generally seen by potential sympathizers with the conservationist cause as the most obstructionist and reactionary in Australia. The issue developed in parallel with the Tasmanian question. In May 1982, the Australian Democrats introduced a rainforest protection bill in Parliament. The ACF, and local Queensland groups, took a cue from declared ALP policy to take action to conserve Australia's rainforests and urged creation of an effective Greater Daintree National Park, together with a world heritage nomination for the area. The Australian Heritage Commission was also, by 1984, known to be in favour of world heritage listing.[68] During 1984, Queensland groups focussed their energies on a particular road construction project and turned this effort into the centre of a large-scale public education and lobbying campaign that also included contingency plans for a Tasmanian-style blockade. The matter was discussed by the federal Cabinet in September 1984. A consensus was reached that the area fulfilled world heritage criteria, and that development plans, including logging and road construction, would destroy the ecological integrity of the region. In keeping with its post-Tasmania approach to these questions, however, the government decided against any unilateral Commonwealth action to nominate the area.[69]

Thus in the cases of both the IUCN *World Conservation Strategy*, and UNESCO's World Heritage convention, different kinds of international instruments significantly extended the repertoire of tools of influence available to environmental groups. In relation to Antarctic development, which we shall look at shortly, such groups faced substantial obstacles when trying to affect the course of government policy; and in the case of CITES, to which we now turn, the international document itself was so little known outside specialized conservation circles, and the questions it addressed so circumscribed in practice, that it afforded relatively few possibilities for campaign activism.

CITES did, however, make contact with some of the questions at the heart of Australian wildlife conservation debates, such as kangaroo management or the trade in wild birds. These were issues that pre-dated the convention. As the author of an ACF publication suggested in 1970, "To the great majority of Australians wildlife means kangaroos, first and foremost, and wildlife conservation means looking after kangaroos."[70] For environmental groups, the international aspects of the question were located in the context of the domestic argument that an annual cull, while necessary to protect the livelihoods of farmers and graziers, and also the basis of a profitable meat and hides industry, was applied in practice in ways that were destructive of the resource. In the case of wild birds, international trade, much of it illicit, was a central policy question. Evidence presented to a parliamentary committee in the mid-1970s indicated that the

172

overseas price of a smuggled pair of Crimson Rosellas was around $100; for a breeding pair of Golden-shouldered Parrots, an endangered species, the figure could be as high as $8-10,000. However, international smuggling centred on Sydney and Melbourne, was described as representing only a small percentage of a vast illegal trade in native fauna carried out across state borders within Australia.[71] For both kangaroos and wild birds, then, pursuit by conservation organizations of domestic goals was inextricably linked with the requirement for more effective international control measures.

Environmental groups did not, however, immediately seize the opportunity for domestic lobbying presented by CITES. Attention to the agreement grew during the late 1970s as organizations became more aware of international debates within the CITES framework of species of Australian fauna and flora. The government's pursuit of trade liberalization with regard to kangaroo products in the early 1980s was one factor which served to accelerate this process. The Nature Conservation Council of New South Wales, for example, recognized that there might be a need to cull certain kangaroo species, but maintained that an export ban was still needed.[72] Interest in CITES was also heightened by the Commonwealth's preparation of the bill that became the *Wildlife Protection (Regulation of Exports and Imports) Act* of 1982, designed to formalize Australia's implementation of the agreement. Leading conservation groups, including Greenpeace, Project Jonah, FOE and the ACF, announced their support for the measure.[73] In relation to the CITES framework itself, this generally welcoming tone grew louder and more insistent when it became apparent that external allies — various delegations of states attending the meetings of the parties — were making use of the convention as a means of directing international criticism at Australian policies. A particular case in point was the government's attempts in the early 1980s to secure changes in the listings of various crocodile species in order to lend international legitimacy to farming experiments in the Northern Territory, a move sharply criticized by environmental organizations.[74] On the other hand, the convention also raised some false expectations. The qualifications and understandings that governed CITES operations, as spelled out for example in the Berne criteria, meant that it fell short of the universal endangered species protection device some groups initially took it to be. The capacity of NGOs to engage in informed appraisals of CITES developments was enhanced by the establishment of an Australian section of TRAFFIC, the wildlife trade monitoring organization with headquarters in Cambridge.

At the same time, the complaints of farmers persisted. Representative associations, and sympathetic governments such as that of Queensland, were openly critical of the damage done to rural enterprises by insufficiently checked kangaroo populations. The resulting variation in state government kangaroo management programmes was increasingly criticized by the ACF in the mid-1980s, and this criticism spilled over into doubts about the principles and the application of the 1982 Act.[75] Early in 1985 farmers mounted a publicized campaign of dumping

173

the carcasses of galahs, little correllas, and cockatoos to underline the point that many wildlife species were simply pests.[76]

Compared to the Antarctica treaty system, the CITES framework was a more accessible instrument for conservation groups. The convention itself had a broader base of signatories, meetings of the parties were more open and publicized affairs, and treaty politics presented a number of opportunities for NGOs to influence delegation members and secretariat officials. By contrast, the restricted membership of the Antarctica framework, and the relative secrecy of the deliberations of members, constituted formidable obstacles for Australian environmentalists. The nature of Antarctic politics also posed dilemmas: would conservation values better be promoted by support for Australia's claims to sovereignty in the AAT, or by pursuit of internationalization options?

Interest in Antarctic conservation matters grew from the mid-1970s. The 1964 Agreed Measures failed to stimulate much debate in Australia. During the Whitlam years, however, several questions, including the disposal of radioactive wastes and concern about the environmental implications of oil exploration on the continent, led to the emergence of Antarctic environmental protection as an issue in Australian conservation politics. The ACF expanded its capacity to debate Antarctic policy in 1974.[77] The election of 1977 saw it, and several other organizations, making more determined efforts to situate Antarctica high on the agenda of Australian environmental issues. In part, these bodies were also responding to international developments, particularly the establishment by several institutions (the IUCN, the International Institute for Environment and Development, the Sierra Club, and the FOE) of a central Antarctica umbrella grouping earlier in 1977. During the late 1970s and 1980s, attention tended to be directed towards three interrelated objectives: the development and publicizing of conservationist policy positions on Antarctic issues, a call to restructure the policy process in Australia, and efforts to gain more secure access to the hidden pathways of that process.

In relation to the Antarctica regime as a whole, the ACF moved in the 1980s towards a compromise position that incorporated world heritage thinking while avoiding a frontal assault on Australia's sovereignty claims. The idea of international control in some form of world park was retained as a long-term goal; proposed intermediate steps included the nomination of the AAT for a place on the World Heritage list, pursuit by the Australian government of eventual nomination of all parts of the region, and, more generally, an invigorated re-emphasis on environmental conservation as the paramount objective of policy.[78] Similar attempts to entrench conservation goals more deeply in treaty processes were made in policy declarations by other groups, particularly FOE, Greenpeace, and also the TWS, and through efforts to stimulate media interest in Antarctic conservation issues.[79] Development of the AMLR convention during the 1970s, and Australia's leading role in this process, added pressure on groups to define policy positions. The ecosystem approach underlying these moves injected an additional incentive for groups to portray the convention as a test case of the

174

parties' seriousness with regard to conservation goals. As we saw in Chapter 5, nagging doubts came to outweigh optimism as evidence mounted that compromises were necessary to secure the support of the major fishing nations. One FOE critic, Michael Kennedy, referred in 1980 to "the extreme apprehension" of the world environmental community on this score. Taking all the convention's aspects into consideration — the restricted membership, the consensus system of decision-making, the provision for a lengthy (90-day) objection period against Commission decisions — there was a clear risk of overexploitation. The CAMLR was a compromise convention, "the primary beneficiary of which has been the fishing states."[80]

Secondly, criticism increasingly turned in the late 1970s and early 1980s to the character of the Antarctic policy process in Australia. This criticism was linked to a wider unease. Antarctic deliberations were not only restricted to a handful of states, they were also viewed as too sedate and protracted: "much too slow to cope with the accelerating events in Antarctic affairs," as one critic insisted. "This gentlemanly pace may have been quite appropriate for the first years of the Treaty; in the 1980s it is a liability."[81] Australian NGOs, however, had little if any capability to bring about change at this level. Tackling the Australian method of approach was more promising. Several groups participated actively in the wider Australian debates on government leadership, the adequacy of the commitment to research funding, and the structure of decision processes, that gathered momentum from the mid-1970s. The representation of mining interests on scientific advisory and policy bodies was singled out as an indication of the Commonwealth's vulnerability to powerful, anti-conservationist pressures.[82]

Thirdly, this genre of criticism reinforced, and partly reflected, continuing attempts by some groups to edge closer to the centre of Antarctic policy-making. The ACF and Greenpeace in particular, and also the IFAW, sought representation at various 1980s meetings within the CAMLR framework.[83] More contact of this kind had been achieved by the mid-1980s. As the convention's workings became more consolidated, so official Australian criticism of states with fishing interests to protect became less muted, with the result that a measure of consensus could be found between Commonwealth views on some topics and those of, for example, officials of the Greenpeace Antarctic campaign.[84]

The role of the scientific community

The scientific community has constituted a special case within the context of environmental politics in Australia. Scientific groups can be contrasted with the wider constituency of NGOs on such grounds as the professional expertise of members, the criteria for membership, and acceptance of common values and approaches. Scientific organizations have also been more likely to be fused with government bodies, the greater ease of access being a product of official perceptions of the dependence of some policy areas on outside advice. Organizationally, however, only a small minority of scientists, even of those working in related

175

disciplines, has demonstrated an active interest in environmental policy questions. Policy-oriented research, for some, is not good science; officially encouraged activity may lead to a soft-edged science marked by lack of rigour. Yet many individual scientists have also been associated with the world of environmental NGOs, or of international collaborative research efforts with a policy slant. Resistance to the dangers of contamination by "politics," nevertheless, has erected barriers to certain kinds of engagement in policy issues. The Australian Academy of Sciences (AAS), for example, took the view, when confronted by increased demands during the 1970s for its intervention in local conservation issues, that "it could not become involved in local disputation and still retain its stance of objectivity in enquiry and reporting."[85]

Scientific investigation, especially in botany,[86] was in a sense central to Australian nation-building in the nineteenth century: its natural vegetation was one of the most striking factors that distinguished Australia from Britain. Organized science was a post-federation development. It began with the establishment of a scientific advisory body, the forerunner of the CSIRO, as early as 1916. Debates on science policy have been a recurrent feature of Australian politics ever since.[87] As in other fields, interaction with developments overseas played its part in these events. The 1916 council, for example, was modelled on the experiment with organization for scientific research begun in Britain in 1915. The establishment of an Australian National Research Council in 1923 was, similarly, a response to an invitation to Australia in 1919 to participate in the work of the new International Research Council (later the ICSU).[88]

Scientific bodies began to play a growing role in environmental policy debates and processes from the 1950s (though "environmental" terminology tended to be a later development). Domestically, this activity tended to focus on national parks and protected areas, flora and fauna studies and conservation, and, later, environmental policy more generally. Much of the thinking lying behind it was important politically for the way it implicitly accepted the need for Australia-wide solutions to policy questions then falling almost exclusively within the preserve of state governments. This work thus prepared the ground for a Commonwealth role in the 1970s. On national parks in the 1950s and 1960s, for example, one prominent AAS viewpoint was that the process to create and maintain them suffered from a lack of consultation between states, and the absence of a nation-wide survey of areas and ecosystems upon which to base planning. National parks were "in reality State parks, except that the majority of them were of national significance." The criteria for choice and boundaries, moreover, were often not scientific, but rather based on "scenic grandeur and the special enthusiasm of influential individuals for particular areas."[89]

AAS lobbying had a more direct impact on the form taken by the Commonwealth's environmental policy role in the early 1970s. A long-running concern had been with fauna studies, with a particular focus on the requirement of a more organized and better funded national collection. Prime Minister Menzies was presented with specific proposals in this area in 1955, but the response to this and to subsequent pressure on officials in the Prime Minister's Department during the 1960s was that funds were not available.[90] More progress was made in the overlapping area of flora research and conservation. Plans for an Australia-wide biological survey were formulated in some detail by the late 1960s. Professor Frank Fenner, on behalf of the AAS, was instrumental in gaining wider parliamentary and party support for the idea in 1972 testimony to the House Select Committee on Wildlife Conservation. Both federal parties expressed a commitment to the idea in that year's elections. Consultations between the AAS and the Commonwealth environment minister and his staff were then instrumental in establishing the ABRS in 1973, and in its later emphasis on flora work.[91]

This early concentration on flora had a longer-term significance. It gathered momentum during the 1970s as a result of survey work carried out under ABRS auspices, botanical work by the CSIRO, the establishment of a Standing Committee on Flora in the AAS in 1972, and the continuing activity of the Committee on Systematic Botany of the Australia and New Zealand Association for the Advancement of Science (ANZAAS) from the 1950s. In 1973-74 this enterprise was taken a significant step further with the creation of the Australian Systematic Botany Society (ASBS).[92] Contacts among its members, numbering more than 300 by the end of the decade, and with botanists in other countries, played an important role in the early 1980s in focussing international scientific attention on conservation issues in South-west Tasmania.

Finally, the commencement of serious Commonwealth interest in environmental policy questions owed much to pressures from the scientific community. The development was more a product of wider political movements in Australia. Once recognized by the government as calling for some kind of organizational and policy response, however, the backlog of AAS thinking on the subject came into play. The Academy's proposal to the Prime Minister in 1970 for a Royal Commission on environmental questions was thus a key factor in the events leading to the creation of a Commonwealth Office of the Environment, the institutional forerunner of the environment department. The AAS also successfully put the case for an advisory body to the Australian government; when the AACE was established, it was appropriately enough chaired by the chairman of the AAS environment committee, Professor R.J. Walsh.[93]

Many of the participants in this policy-related scientific work were internationalist in their inclinations. The AAS had earlier become the central Australian point of contact for links with scientific bodies in the ICSU system, including organizations with environmentally related terms of reference, such as the SCOR and the SCAR. The thrust here has been primarily transnational rather than intergovernmental. As one of its histories has observed, AAS influence in the inter-governmental scientific area "has not been uniformly significant and certainly not of the same magnitude as its contribution to international non-governmental scientific matters...."[94] The International Biological Programme (IBP), from 1964, was the first significant cooperative venture in broadly environmental areas. Australian participation was constrained by financial difficulties, and also by the

177

criticisms some Australian scientists raised of the Programme on scholarly grounds. Of particular importance, nonetheless, was the conservation side (IBP/CT). Australian doubts about the classifications used by IBP in relation to plants prompted a new approach in the first Australia-wide survey of plant communities, the risks to them, and the conservation measures in place. This, the Specht report, both stimulated and had a major impact on Australian conservation debates after 1974-75.[95]

The Man and the Biosphere Programme (MAB) grew out of UNESCO rather than the ICSU. Australian association with it, and particularly with its main conservation activities, was approved by CONCOM in 1976. Although a number of prominent Australian scientists were active in the Programme, particularly Professor Slatyer as chairman of the International Coordinating Council, it faced some of the problems that beset the IBP. Ultimately, decisions to participate were those of individual scientists or research teams; government had limited capacity, even if it had the political will, to influence such choices. Many scientists were skeptical of the value of MAB engagement, critical of the methodologies underlying some projects and of their definitions and scope, and, on balance, inclined to suspect that such exercises were directed more towards consciousness-raising or the application of existing knowledge in developing countries than towards international collaboration likely to produce concrete benefits for Australian science. More important in environmental policy terms was the impetus MAB gave to the creation of an Australian network of biosphere reserves. The process which emerged in the 1970s was similar to that in other participating countries. Nominations — from governments, scientific bodies, or NGOs — were evaluated by the Australian MAB committee, which worked through the Australian National Commission for UNESCO, and forwarded for final decision to the International Coordinating Council in Paris. By 1983, a total of 226 such reserves had been designated in sixty-two countries, twelve of them in Australia.[96] Such designation had practical consequences not in itself, but because of the practice of nominating areas already accorded some kind of official protection; Danggali Conservation Park, for example, approved by the MAB Bureau in 1977, was protected as a conservation park by the South Australian authorities.[97]

Antarctica and the issue of South-west Tasmanian conservation are instructive examples of the role of the scientific community in broader political processes. In relation to the controversy over the Franklin dam, both the publicizing and the generation of scientific research were decisive steps in the unfolding of the issue. This was particularly because one of the chief defences of the various power-generation options by the HEC was that environmental impact would be minimal. There were no known archaeological sites or other evidence of Aboriginal occupancy, it was argued in the late 1970s; the Huon pine was held to be not rare, and also not significantly threatened by the proposed projects.[98] Establishing firm evidence to the contrary on each of these points proved to be crucial to the credibility of the case developed by the TWS and other groups. Archaeological findings dating back to investigations in 1974, and other sites explored later, were prominently featured in the anti-dam campaign. Threats to the flora of the area made a still larger political impact, especially in terms of external perceptions of the issue. Central to the TWS position was the estimate that as much as 35 per cent of the world's stock of Huon pine, many individual trees more than a thousand years old, would be destroyed if the Franklin-below-Gordon project went ahead. Australian botanists and other scientists played a pivotal role in attracting international scientific attention to these questions.[99]

The AAS, and leading individuals in the Australian Antarctic scientific community, also occupied key positions in the Antarctic policy debates of the 1970s and 1980s. The arguments here tended to revolve around the adequacy of research funding in general, the relative emphasis placed on different research priorities, and the role of scientific advice in the determination of policy, and only secondarily around questions of environmental protection. Links in the policy chain were forged early. In 1954, the AAS was invited by the Department of External Affairs to nominate a representative for the ANARE planning committee; it played a leading role in the mid-1950s in planning for the International Geophysical Year that later led to the construction of the Antarctica treaty; it carried out a major review of Antarctic scientific efforts at the request of External Affairs in 1966-67; and the AAS, and its committees and individual members, were active in the extensive debates of the 1970s and 1980s over the future direction of Australia's Antarctic research and policy.[100] On these kinds of matters, the relative smallness and compactness of the scientific community concerned, and the high-priority commitment of the Commonwealth to Antarctic research as a means of retaining and enhancing Australia's sovereignty claim and its role in the Antarctica treaty framework, together meant that the degree of fusion of scientific and official bodies was more complete than in other policy areas.

Domestic politics and the global environment

Environmental groups have varied considerably in their orientation towards international questions. For many, the local or state picture fills the horizon; others view Australian issues from the perspective of global ecological conditions. The specialized character of many international conventions can make them difficult for groups to exploit. The specific provisions and criteria built into CITES, for example, render it something quite different from the general wildlife conservation agreement that some environmentalists have misperceived it as. It none the less figured in pressure group strategies from the later 1970s once it became evident that regulation of the wildlife trade at the international level was a crucial aspect of the effective control of the illicit trade inside Australia. Organizations that have sought national leadership roles, such as the ACF, have usually been the most informed about the relevance of international developments to their overall goals; some, for example the TWS in connection with the anti-dam campaign, made careful and successful use of specific regime elements in their campaigns. Many groups have also enjoyed direct or indirect access to IUCN or to its

179

international partner, the WWF, and secured occasional interventions by international organizations in state or national policy debates on conservation issues.

Despite the oversimplifications of some critics, the environmental movement in Australia has in practice spanned a wide range of political opinion. Its membership and support have cut across traditional partisan divides, as the Australian Democrats began to appreciate in the early 1980s. Diversity, however, implies weaknesses as well as strengths. The attempts of the ACF, for example, to capture an environmental middle ground sometimes led to a loss of support from both radical activists and conservative naturalists. Other factors have affected the fortunes of groups. After 1983, the government lacked the political will to apply the precedent set by the Tasmanian issue to a broadly similar question, that of rainforest preservation in northern Queensland. Although its political calculations were different, the results, in terms of a wary respect for state sensitivities, were comparable to those under its predecessor. Party outlooks have also changed over time; Labor in office in the mid-1980s was in many respects a changed party, and much less susceptible than the ALP government of 1972-75 to appeals from environmentalists. Public responses to conservation arguments have likewise warmed and cooled at different times and in relation to different issues. The level and quality of interest in such questions in Parliament has also varied: the Senate took a leading role in public debate on air and water pollution in the early 1970s, on Tasmanian conservation in the late 1970s, and on rainforest issues in the early 1980s, but on many important international topics Parliament tended to be a bystander. The influence of conservation groups, moreover, has been in part a function of their capacity to withstand political pressures mounted from the opposite side of the argument. The National Conservation Strategy, and federal and state environmental impact assessment guidelines, were among a number of questions that were affected by the opposition of Australian industrial interests to a strengthening of environmental regulation.

Notes for Chapter 9

1 Cited by G.M. Bates, *Environmental Law in Australia* (Sydney: Butterworth, 1983), p. 9.
2 Sir Keith Hancock, *The Battle of Black Mountain* (Canberra: Society for Social Responsibility in Science, n.d.).
3 K. Tsokhas, *A Class Apart? Businessmen and Politics in Australia, 1960-80* (Melbourne: Oxford University Press, 1984), pp. 75-81.
4 Joseph Glascott, "Myles Dunphy, Conservationist," *Sydney Morning Herald*, 2 February 1985.
5 Bruce W. Davis, "Federalism and Environmental Politics: An Australian Overview," in R.L. Mathews, ed., *Federalism and the Environment* (Canberra: Centre for Research on Federal Financial Relations, 1985), p. 8.
6 *ACF Newsl.*, 2 (October 1967), p. 10; ACF, *The Green Pages* (Melbourne, 1978).
7 Alan Gilpin, *Environment Policy in Australia* (St. Lucia: University of Queensland Press, 1980), p. 81; Davis, "Federalism and Environmental Politics," p. 8.
8 Gallup Poll data, cited in *The National Estate in 1981. AHC Report, June 1981* (Canberra, 1982; PP 96), p. 9.

9 *ACF Newsl.*, 1 (April 1967); pp. 1-3 and 6 (January 1969), pp. 1-3.

10 Approximately 60 per cent of members were in the age groups 20-39; 57 per cent were male; only 2.9 per cent were tradesmen, 1.3 per cent blue-collar workers and 1.8 per cent unemployed (*ACF Newsl.*, 16(2), March 1984, p. 15).

11 Gilpin, *Environment Policy in Australia*, pp. 81-2.

12 *ACF Newsl.*, 1 (April 1967), pp. 2-3; "Main Policy Guidelines of the ACF," *ACF Newsl.*, 7 (April 1969), p. 3; and *ACF Newsl.*, 6(5), June 1974; pp. 2-3.

13 Murray Wilcox, "Conservation and the Law," *Habitat*, 8(3), June 1980, pp. 26-31. For a similar criticism of the sheer amount of legislation in one state, New South Wales, much of it conflicting and confusing, and of the institutional assumptions on which it was based, see G.C. Garbesi, "Main Features, Gaps and Recent Advances in Australian Environmental Law," *Habitat*, 4(4), September 1976, pp. 20-3.

14 *ACF Newsl.*, 6 (January 1969), pp. 1-2; and 4(4), September 1972, p. 1.

15 Cass, in *AFAR*, 44(9), September 1973, p. 607.

16 *AGD*, 1(3), 1973, p. 1003.

17 *Australia Environmental Report*, 21-73 (1973), p. 470.

18 *Australia and New Zealand Environmental Report*, 1-74 (1974), p. 15.

19 See for example Sir John Fuller, *New South Wales, Parliamentary Debates*, Vol. CXII (Session 1975-76), 18 March 1976, p. 4453.

20 Tsokhas, *A Class Apart?*, pp. 75-81.

21 *ACF Newsl.*, 8(2), March 1976, p. 1.

22 Newman, in a radio interview, cited at *ACF Newsl.*, 9(11), January 1978, p. 6.

23 Bill Ord, "Conservation — The Poor Relation," *National Times*, 492, 6-12 July 1980, p. 38.

24 DHAE, *Annual Report 1980-81* (Canberra, 1982; PP 35), p. 17. The possibility of a review was mentioned by the government (e.g. Webster, at *Commonwealth Record*, 4(46), 19-25 November 1979, p. 1807).

25 The last meeting had been held in 1978. Closure of the Environment Centre of the Northern Territory, and the difficulties faced by the Conservation Council of Western Australia, were among the main concerns at the meeting (*ACF Newsl.*, 14(8), September 1982, p. 4). The ACF grant in 1981 was set at $75,000 (*ACF Newsl.*, 13(1), February 1981, p. 1).

26 Jenkins, reporting on testimony given to the House subcommittee investigating international environmental organizations, at *House of Representatives*, 130, 28 October 1982, p. 2725.

27 Robert Milliken, "The Greenies Sharpen Their Political Teeth," *National Times*, 624, 16-23 January 1983, pp. 3-4.

28 Gilpin, *Environment Policy in Australia*, p. 83.

29 "The Economics of the Franklin," editorial, *Australian Financial Review*, 17 December 1982.

30 "Do's and don't's for doomwatchers," *Bulletin*, 15 July 1972, pp. 32-35.

31 Peter Springell, in *ACF Newsl.*, 10(3), May 1978, p. 7.

32 David Hickie, in *National Times*, 624, 16-22 January 1983, pp. 3-4, 7.

33 *The National Estate in 1981. AHC Report, June 1981* (Canberra, 1982; PP 96), p. 191. On the value of IUCN's mixed governmental-NGO character see John Sinclair (then ACF Vice-President), "IUCN: The world's conservation organization," *Habitat*, 10(4), August 1982, p. 12.

34 "Protecting Australia's arid lands," *ACF Newsl.*, 13(11), December 1981, p. 1.

35 Helene Marsh and George Heinsohn, "Conserving the dugong: Australia's responsibility," *Habitat*, 11(2), April 1983, pp. 29-30; Greg Roberts, "The saving of the Lord Howe woodhen," *National Times*, 679, 3-9 February 1984, p. 22. Both had IUCN priority as endangered species.

36 See the report on the 8th AGM, at *ACF Newsl.*, 6(10), November 1974, p. 4.

37 *ACF Newsl.*, 14(2): March 1982, p. 5.

38 J.G. Mosley, "Improvements needed in heritage policy," *ACF Newsl.*, 17(1): February 1985, pp. 1, 4.

39 Dr. McMichael, for example, later permanent head of the environment department, joined the ACF as Director in 1967, and left in 1968 to take up the position of Director of the new National Parks and Wildlife Service in New South Wales. He later also served in various roles in IUCN

and OECD, arising in the main from official responsibilities, and combined this with other tasks, such as chairmanship of the conservation programme of WWF-Australia.

[40] *House of Representatives*, 123, 2 June 1981, p. 2948.

[41] Byrne, *Senate*, 49, 12 May 1971, p. 1748.

[42] *ACF Newsl.*, 16(10), November 1984, p. 1.

[43] Murray Wilcox, "The problem of the National Conservation Strategy," *ACF Newsl.*, 12(4), 1984, pp. 6-7. The problem was "the familiar one called 'State sensitivities', which bedevils so much of good administration in this country."

[44] *ACF Newsl.*, 9(10), December 1977, p. 8 (report on the 11th AGM).

[45] *ACF Newsl.*, 12(4), May 1980, p. 2, and 12(10), November 1980.

[46] *ACF Newsl.*, 13(8), September 1982, p. 4, report by Peter Blackwell.

[47] J.G. Mosley, "The NCSA: A critique," *ACF Newsl.*, 15(9), October 1983, pp. 6-7; John Sinclair, "Difficulties for the Conservation Strategy," *ACF Newsl.*, 15(5), June 1983, p. 15.

[48] Murray Wilcox, "The Future of the NCS," *ACF Newsl.*, 12(4), 1984, p. 6. Vague implementation provisions were contained in paragraphs 10 and 36 of the document.

[49] Strider, "NCS: The Politics of Expediency," *Green Alliance Newsl.*, 10, November 1984, pp. 1-2.

[50] Peter Springell, in *ACF Newsl.*, 17(1), February 1985, p. 22.

[51] *ACF Newsl.*, No. 6 (January 1969), p. 4.

[52] *ACF Newsl.*, 9(4), June 1977, pp. 4-5.

[53] For example in testimony to the Advisory Committee on the South-west (ibid., p. 3).

[54] For a summary of HEC plans during this period see H. Bandler, "Gordon below Franklin Dam, Tasmania, Australia: Environmental Factors in a Decision of National Significance," *The Environmentalist*, 7(1), Spring 1987, pp. 43-54.

[55] *ACF Newsl.*, 9(3), May 1977, p. 3; April 1979, pp. 2, 4-5.

[56] Paul Malone, "The Courted Greenies — Can they give the extra percentage vote?" *Australian Financial Review*, 23 December 1982.

[57] *Ibid.*

[58] Bandler, "Gordon below Franklin Dam," p. 49, citing unpublished *Herald* sources.

[59] See further B. Burton, *Overpowering Tasmania* (Hobart: TWS, 1984); R. Connelly, *The Fight for the Franklin* (Sydney: Cassell, 1981); and K. Warner, "The Gordon-below-Franklin Dam: Obstructing the Police in the Execution of their duty," *Environmental and Planning Law Journal*, 1(3), September 1984, pp. 283-5.

[60] Robert Millikan, "The Greenies sharpen their political teeth," *National Times*, 624, January 16-22, 1983, pp. 3-4, 7.

[61] The government at the time had all five Tasmanian seats. Liberal strategists were clearly divided in their estimates of the likely electoral implications of the issue. See Paul Malone, "Federal Government in troubled waters over Tasmania dam issue," *Australian Financial Review*, 16 December 1982. Deputy Prime Minister Anthony later expressed the view that the no dams vote swung the March election (*ACF Newsl.*, 15(3), April 1983, pp. 1, 3). The national ALP had earlier developed a plan for compensation to Tasmania as part of its case against the Lake Pedder flooding (articles by Lance Norman, *Australian Financial Review*, 17 July 1973 and 1 August 1973).

[62] David Hickie, "In the wilderness of Tasmanian politics," *National Times*, 653, 15-23 November 1981, pp. 22, 24, 27.

[63] Malone, "Federal Government in troubled waters."

[64] *ACF Newsl.*, 12(4), May 1980, p. 6.

[65] Bruce Montgomery, "Conservation bodies 'black' Franklin Plan," *Weekend Australian*, 19-20 January 1985.

[66] J.G. Mosley, "Improvements needed in Heritage Policy," *ACF Newsl.*, 17(1), February 1985.

[67] *ACF Newsl.*, 10(6), August 1978; and 13(5), June 1981, p. 1.

[68] Though its report on the subject was released after the September 1984 Cabinet decision. See *ACF Newsl.*, 16(9), October 1984, p. 3.

[69] *ACF Newsl.*, 16(1), February 1984; 16(2), March 1984, p. 3; and 16(6), July 1984, p. 1. Parliamentary activity continued under Labour though the government was not satisfied with the 1982

Domestic Contexts: Environmental Constituencies in Australian Politics

bill (*Weekly Hansard*, Senate, No. 4, 1984, 5 April 1984: p. 1323, Sen. Evans). Senator Macklin, of Queensland, later introduced a north Queensland wet tropics protection bill (*Weekly Hansard*, Senate, No. 14, 1984, 10 October 1984, p. 1513; also *Daily Hansard*, Senate, 28 February 1985, p. 293).

70 Francis Ratcliffe, *The Commercial Hunting of Kangaroos* (Melbourne: ACF, 1970), p. 4.

71 *Trafficking in Fauna in Australia*, Second Report of the House of Representatives Standing Committee on Environment and Conservation, September 1976 (Canberra, 1977: PP 301), para. 10, 12, 22.

72 Cited at *ACF Newsl.*, 13(1), February 1981. The ACF's position was that the killing of kangaroos was acceptable "only in circumstances of proven conflict with agriculture where no other solution is possible" (*ACF Newsl.*, 13(5), June 1981, p. 3; and Geoff Mosley, "National Kangaroo Management. The Need for a Review," *ACF Newsl.*, 11(5), 1983, pp. 9-12).

73 *ACF News.*, 15(11), December 1983, p. 7.

74 *ACF Newsl.*, 15(3), April 1983, p. 6; and more generally Ross Burton and Michael Kennedy, "Endangered Species Treaty Gains Strength," *ACF Newsl.*, 11(5), 1983, pp. 12-13.

75 *ACF Newsl.*, 16(9), October 1984, p. 8. The Act came into force on 1 May 1984. See further ANPWS, *Kangaroo Management Programmes of the Australian States* (Canberra, 1984).

76 *Sydney Morning Herald*, 26 January 1985.

77 Primarily through the creation and work of an Antarctic Treaty subcommittee (*ACF Newsl.*, 6(8), September 1974, p. 2).

78 *ACF Newsl.*, 16(4), May 1984, pp. 6-7; and Geoff Mosley, "The natural option: the case for an Antarctic world park," in Stuart Harris (ed.), *Australia's Antarctic Policy Options* (Centre for Resource and Environmental Studies, ANU: CRES Monograph 11, 1984), pp. 307-26.

79 Keith Suter, *Antarctica: World Law and the Last Wilderness* (Sydney: FOE, 1980); Greenpeace's view on the world park option was put by Roger Wilson in the *Daily Telegraph* (Sydney), 11 July 1983; on the TWS entry to the campaign, see the *Melbourne Herald*, 14 February 1983; and in general "Greenies out to 'save' Antarctica," *Sydney Morning Herald*, 15 February 1983. There were regular newspaper reports of specific Antarctic developments during the 1980s, and threats posed by mining, waste, tourist development and so on. The IFAW campaign was directed primarily towards certain species, particularly penguins ("Save Antarctica before it's too late," *Woman's Day*, 28 September 1982). The news media also reported frequently on international debates on Antarctica (e.g., "UN may control Antarctic minerals," *Australian*, 18 January 1983).

80 Michael Kennedy, "AMLRs Conference — A compromise," *Habitat*, 8(5), 1980, pp. 8-9.

81 Barney Brewster, *Antarctica: Wilderness at Risk* (Sydney: A.H. and A.W. Reed, 1982), pp. 113-4.

82 *Ibid.*, p. 108. The reference is to one of the seven members of ARPAC, an official from Western Mining Corporation, Ltd. The issue was a central one in NGO campaigning since, according to Roger Wilson of Greenpeace, "mining will inevitably lead to the destruction of the very values which have made the Antarctic a paradise for scientific research and a model for international cooperation" (*Daily Telegraph*, 11 July 1983).

83 *Australian*, 14 July 1983. Several groups, including FOE, Greenpeace, Project Jonah and the ACF, also closely monitored the work of the 1980 conference.

84 See for example the criticisms by Wilson (of Greenpeace) and an Antarctic official in connection with the 4th meeting of the CCAMLR, *West Australian*, 16 September 1985.

85 Frank Fenner and A.L.G. Rees (eds.), *AAS: The First 25 Years* (Canberra: AAS, 1980), pp. 78, 126. There were some exceptions for historical and scientific reasons, such as concern for developments in Kosciusko national park, and the strom atolites in Hameline Pool, Western Australia.

86 See W.T Stearn, "Sir Joshua Banks (1743-1820) and Australian Botany," *Records of the AAS*, 2(4), May 1974, pp. 7024; and J.H. Willis, "The History of Botanical Investigations in Central Australia," in John Jessop (ed.), *Flora of Central Australia* (Sydney: A.H. and A.W. Reed, 1981), pp. xiii-xx.

87 On the early history see Sir George Currie and John Graham, *The Origins of CSIRO: Science and the Commonwealth Government, 1901-26* (Melbourne: CSIRO, 1966), Ch. 1. Some aspects of the debates on science policy from around 1974 were touched on in earlier chapters; occasionally these were focussed on by the media (e.g., Brian Hoad, "It's time Australians had a think about science," *Bulletin*, 12 August 1972, pp. 21-2).

183

[88] Australia was one of the sixteen countries invited to take part (*AAS: First 25 Years*, pp. 2, 62, 118-9).

[89] *Ibid.*, pp. 75, 79. For a similar complaint of selection for aesthetic and emotional reasons see R.L. Specht, "The Report and its Recommendations," in F. Fenner (ed.), *A National System of Ecological Reserves in Australia* (Canberra: AAS, 1975), pp. 11-12. AAS work on this topic was directed by its National Parks Committee, later the Standing Committee on National Parks and Conservation. See in particular its *National Parks and Reserves in Australia* (Canberra: AAS, 1968).

[90] *AAS: The First 25 Years*, pp. 62-65; and "The Australian Museum," *Australian Journal of Science*, 19 (1956), pp. 11-15.

[91] See Chapter 8 above. Until 1978 this worked through an Interim Council. On the background of AAS thinking see "Proposal to Establish a Biological Survey of Australia: Report by the Flora and Fauna Committee of the AAS," *Australian Journal of Science*, 31 (1969), pp. 377-82; and *AAS: The First Years*, p. 68.

[92] Jessop (ed.), *Flora of Central Australia*, Foreword by I.T Evans, and Introduction.

[93] *AAS: The First 25 Years*, pp. 84-87. The choice of Walsh in 1972 was made by the Prime Minister (*The Howson Diaries*, pp. 807, 832, 855, 867).

[94] *AAS: The First 25 Years*, p. 113. Also worth note, however, is Australia's contribution to UN arid lands work in the 1950s.

[95] *Ibid.*, pp. 147-51. For assessments of the importance of the Specht report, see Fenner (ed.), *A National System of Ecological Reserves in Australia; National Estate. Report of the Committee of Inquiry* (Canberra, 1975; PP 195), p. 77, para. 3.172; *AHC. 1st Annual Report 1976-77* (Canberra, 1978; PP 238), p. 3; and David Yencken, Introduction to *The Heritage of Australia: The Illustrated Register of the National Estate* (Macmillan of Australia, 1981), p. 45.

[96] On the criteria for selection see B.W. Davis and G.A. Drake, *Australia's Biosphere Reserves: Conserving Ecological Diversity* (Canberra: Australian National Commission for UNESCO, 1983), Ch. 1, 2: and R.O. Slayter, "Ecological Reserves: Size, Structure and Management," in Fenner (ed.), *A National System of Ecological Reserves in Australia*, pp. 23-25.

[97] *Australia's Biosphere Reserves*, p. 13.

[98] Quoted by Bandler, "Gordon below Franklin Dam," p. 50.

[99] See for example the sequence of communications published in *Nature*: V. Sarma, 300 (1982), p. 3; K. Kiernan, et al., 301 (1983), pp. 28-32; S.J. Paterson, 303 (1983), p. 354; R. Jones, 306 (1983), p. 726; and D.J. Mulvaney, *ibid.*, p. 636.

[100] For a review of the background see Department of Science, Antarctic Division, *Report for Year 1972-73* (Canberra, 1974; PP 251), pp. 5-13, para. 21-57.

III

THE POLITICS OF REGIMES

CHAPTER TEN

Australia and the Global Environment 1965-1985

By the mid-1980s, government environmental policy, in both its domestic and international aspects, had become firmly established in Australia. The setting up and evolution of state environment agencies, of federal government bodies and programmes, and of a federal-state cooperative machinery, represented a sharp contrast to the situation of the mid-1960s. A large and varied network of environmental organizations had also emerged, and governments and groups had confronted the dilemmas of cohabitation and the problems of mutual accommodation. In this period, too, the international milieu grew considerably more complex, as new organizations and activities developed and demanded policy responses from national governments. In this final chapter we examine the roots of change, the factors that have driven the policy process, and the significance of these events. The first two sections evaluate the making of policies and the impact they have had, in turn, on Australian politics and government. The third section sets Australia in the broader comparative perspective of other western countries, and focusses particularly on the ways in which Canadian policies in comparable areas have been formulated. Finally, we turn to some continuing problems of the international environmental regime highlighted by the study.

The making of Australia's international environment policy

The role played by the federal government provides the best clue to the nature of the policy process in Australia. This is despite the fact that state governments are constitutionally the main authors of official environmental action in Australia. Collectively they exercise the bulk of the responsibilities in areas such as pollution control, environmental impact assessment, protection of the natural and cultural heritage of the country, the creation and management of national parks, and wildlife conservation. On a minimalist reading of the constitution, the federal government is empowered to act only in relation to certain carefully defined areas: the Australian Capital Territory itself; the external territories, including the Australian Antarctic Territory; Commonwealth property located in states; and to some extent in the Northern Territory until such time as full statehood is achieved. If federal-state relations were to work along the lines of coordinate or classical federalism, the government in Canberra would be marginal. Its involvement in those areas of international relations which touch on the environmental and resource authority

187

of the states, moreover, would, according to some constitutional interpretations, be devoid of practical policy significance.

Yet this is clearly not what happened in the field of environmental policy, whether domestic or international, in the period 1965-85. The Commonwealth during this period acted in many ways as the engine of change. Its international activities did have important repercussions inside Australia. The critical role of the federal government is increasingly attributable to its occupation of the strategic points at which Australia's domestic and external policies converge. The rise of the administrative state in Australia and of the intervention of governments in the economy and society, together with the phenomenal growth, diversity and complexity of international arrangements in all policy areas touched by these governments, have combined to propel the federal government into a more pivotal role than that envisaged for it in 1900. The continuing constraints imposed by state powers, however, have deflected more ambitious federal governments from politically unacceptable degrees of central direction. Inter-governmentalism and more organic forms of federalism[1] have as a result become the hallmark of policy processes in many areas. Some distinctive features of the environmental policy area — its complexity, the fact that many issues cannot adequately be handled by state governments in isolation, the dependence of policy on reliable national data and scientific expertise, and the inherently international character of many of the questions addressed — reinforce these general trends and provide added impetus to effective cooperation among governments.

Thus a wide range of state interests is affected by, or has implications for, international environmental policy. While federal governments generally have maintained that their forte lies in the optimal blending of the national and international interests of Australia, their critics at the state level have been quick to anticipate and protest alleged violations of the federal compact. Questions of land use stemming from the parks, heritage protection or international conservation policies of the Commonwealth have been especially apt to spark tensions. As was documented in Part II of this study, the rise of cooperative federal-state structures, in particular the AEC and CONCOM, has served to douse many embers and to encourage a collaborative approach to political fire prevention. The institutions and practices of cooperative federalism in the environmental area, however, have proved incapable of containing all threats within a conflict-free, problem-solving milieu of technical cooperation and inter-governmental bargaining.

The factors that shape these relationships are many. Environmental legislation in the 1970s added significantly to federal funding powers. The ability of state governments to respond effectively to mounting, and shifting, pressures from publics and environmental groups became more dependent on financial support programmes controlled by Canberra. Federal funding of environmental groups themselves was a related development. State governments critical of this move in the early and middle 1970s claimed to see it as a Trojan horse designed to release waves of pro-federal activists inside state fortresses. This hyperbole required

188

of state governments in their public dealings with federal authorities rested on an element of truth. The availability of funds from Canberra was only one factor, and ultimately a marginal one at that, in the emergence and growth of an environmental constituency in Australian politics; but it served indirectly to foster a body of informed environmental policy opinion that was frequently inclined to advocate stronger federal authority in the area. Political appeals to the principle of states' rights — "probably the most important cultural expression in the lexicon of Australian federalism"[2] — have nonetheless retained their potency. The principle was translated during the 1970s into the greater recognition state governments received of their claim to be regarded as partners of the federal government in dealings with international institutions and conferences that affected their interests. In this arena, though, the states suffer from various weaknesses. It is the Commonwealth that possesses the main constitutional powers to act abroad. Where states have an interest in international environmental developments, they often lack the capabilities, including expertise in government and outside, to follow them through. Their access to international meetings, moreover, is dependent on representation formulae which assure that the Commonwealth retains the lead role. While membership of some organizations, such as IUCN, is open to state agencies, in general the workings of international regimes are not so flexible that sub-national actors in federal systems can be accommodated as participants with standing in their deliberations.

State governments have been able, however, to set limits to the federal authorities' exercise of constitutional powers in international relations. The principle that states should be consulted in early stages of treaty-making was recognized in agreements of the late 1970s. The fact that much of the substance, as well as the pace, of implementation may be dependent on the political will and resources of states looms inevitably over all phases of such processes.

Some international conservation conventions have progressed relatively smoothly through the Australian polity. The wetlands and migratory species agreements of the 1970s experienced some initial frictions, but after that the problem was more one of protracted federal-state exchanges. In some cases, as in the Ramsar wetlands convention, the federal government was able to by-pass states by exploiting its own land-use authority in the territories. Recognition of state powers in relation to offshore pollution similarly slowed down the progress of the various IMO conventions inside Australia. A related constraint, though, was self-imposed: the older federal government practice of waiting where possible until conventions were in force internationally before proceeding to formal ratification, even in cases where implementation was already being effected administratively or through legislation.

State authority acted as a powerful constraint in relation to the World Heritage convention. Nomination of sites, and their management as protected areas, was primarily a task for the states. The federal government clearly had to be a part of such decisions as the representative of Australia in international heritage forums, but it could not unilaterally initiate nominations or take responsibility for

189

management plans inside state territory. After 1984, indeed, procedures in such cases were revised in the light of the Tasmanian dam experience to ensure that the federal level, and its heritage body, could not manoeuvre free of state government influence. CITES affected state powers in relation to wildlife management and the protection of endangered species of flora and fauna. In many cases cooperation through the CONCOM group framework ensured consensus among federal and state officials on matters related to the convention's listings of species; and, particularly after 1975, the federal government was responsive to state requirements, for example in relation to kangaroo management.

Negotiation of a national version of the *World Conservation Strategy* would have been a complex matter even if Australia were a unitary state, since the international document touched on conservation needs in many sectors of national economies. The states added a significant dimension of their own. Any workable national strategy (like the evolving programmes of the 1980s for dealing with toxic chemicals or oil pollution of Australia's coastal seas) clearly had to be one that the states could live with. The negotiation by some of state strategies, as opposed to state components of a national strategy, indicates the degree of caution that such developments inspired. Endorsement of the *World Conservation Strategy* by the federal government signalled only the commencement of a process that was in large measure outside its control.

Bringing environmental questions on board the federal vessel was only one of a number of significant organizational changes instituted by the Whitlam government in the early 1970s.[3] The policy area was then subject to more general problems of policy coordination in Australian government. In interdepartmental committees, particularly those that have a direct policy role, Painter and Carey have observed that the defence of turf takes priority and that a variety of unsatisfactory compromises may be the only available products of such encounters.[4] Superimposed on this kind of conflictual interaction is the intrinsic tension of relations between line departments and central coordinating agencies.[5] This combination of horizontal and vertical constraints has been evident in the environmental area. Crucial aspects of the Tasmanian dam episode were handled inside government not by the environment department but by the Prime Minister's and Cabinet Department and others. Difficulties of administrative coordination have been the source of continuing problems in relation to the implementation of CITES.

On international questions, the voice of the environment bureaucracy of the federal government has sometimes been muted by the voice of others, particularly Foreign Affairs. In the early 1970s, Australia's international environment policy was relatively rich in foreign policy content. The issues were new, showed some promise of enhancing Australia's position in the UN system and OECD, embraced some critical concerns of the Australian government in areas such as marine pollution and dumping, and were being increasingly grasped by publics and the expanding network of conservation groups as a criterion for evaluating government records. The mixture has thinned in the period since. Many questions have been defined as specialized and discrete, and dealt with by technical bureaucracies. Yet there are still significant instances where environmental issues are considered part of broader Australian foreign policy objectives and subject, therefore, to influence from the Department of Foreign Affairs: the workings of the Antarctica system, for example, some of the UN environmental conferences, the linkages between the OECD's environmental and economic activities, or the role of environmental cooperation in the cultivation of relations with Japan. Both at this level and in relation to domestic policy questions, similar kinds of conceptual questions have formed the ingredients of political debates on government organization and policy processes: to what extent should environmental policy be viewed as a coherent area, and how much as being contingent on objectives in others such as trade policy, industrial development policy, or foreign policy?

Environmental groups have had a problematic relationship with federal policymakers. As we saw in Chapter 9, these groups are very diverse in their influence with government, aims, size and membership, and ideological definitions of environmentalism. It has sometimes been in Canberra's interest vis-à-vis state governments to cultivate a supportive national constituency. Within the federal government, environment departments and agencies have benefited in their dealings with others from the evidence such groups provide that environmental programmes have a broad base of public support. The public funding of groups, as an attempt to build an informed body of environmental policy opinion outside government, has been one upshot. As in the later years of the Fraser period, however, a relationship of mutual dependence between government and groups can be a vulnerable one. Cutbacks in funding and other programmes, revisions to federal environmental legislation, administrative and programme changes designed to appeal to state governments, and growing restlessness on the part of some groups with the political implications of dependence on federal funds, especially in a situation of mounting dissatisfaction with government policies, were among the factors which soured relations in the late 1970s and early 1980s. Many groups were able to regain lost ground as a result of the political dynamism, largely unexpected, of the Tasmanian dam issue. Partly because of changes in the political climate in the mid-1980s, however, and the declining fortunes of environmentalism on left-wing agendas, this did not usher in a new empowering phase of pressure group activities.

There have nonetheless been significant continuities in the approaches of groups to international questions. A relative ease of access to some international bodies, such as IUCN, combined with the international scientific advisory work of some government officials and scientists, has at times made the pursuit of external intervention in Australia's affairs seem attractive. The more closed framework of the Antarctica treaty system rules out such options. Some groups have been able, however, to profit from the frustration of federal officials at their own inability to effect change on such matters as the working of the AMLR convention, and establish working alliances with the Canberra environmental agencies. Collaborative links between officials and group representatives have

191

also been noticeable in forums such as the meetings of the CITES parties. Federal officials have been brought by such relationships into intermediary roles between groups and government structures, as when they informally advised groups to refrain from pressing for speedier federal action on the national Strategy in deference to state sensitivities. In these developments, the smallness of the environmental policy community in Canberra — officials, group representatives, the attentive media, occasional parliamentary committees — has facilitated the growth of informal contacts as well as more formal working relations through such forums as the Australian Committee for IUCN.

Environmental policy appears to have been conditioned by the more general tendency for Parliament in Australia and Canada to occupy a comparatively marginal role in the determination of federal government policy and in the resolution and negotiation of federal-state differences.[6] The weakness has been reinforced by the inexpertise, and low levels of interest, of members of both Houses on environmental policy questions, especially questions with significant international dimensions. The influence of Parliament has been indirect. Some parliamentary committees — for example, the Senate air and water pollution committees and the House wildlife conservation committee of the early 1970s — played a role in focussing attention on the need for more effective government organization in these areas. Others, such as the Senate committee on the South-west in the late 1970s, were important in educating the public and in clarifying issues and interests. A more active role has followed when political parties have used Parliament as a forum for attacking government policies, as the ALP did on international environment policy prior to the 1972 election, or as the Australian Democrats did in relation to Tasmania and rainforest conservation issues in the early 1980s. Committees have also explored relatively little known questions and tried to inject the results into wider debates, as on Australia's policies in international environmental organizations;[7] but on many questions, such as law of the sea or Antarctica policy, Parliament's handicaps, in terms of resources for research, lack of knowledge and political will to sustain systematic investigations, have been all too evident.

Impact of the external milieu

What, in turn, have been the consequences for Australia of this steadily growing involvement with international environmental matters? We can identify five main sets of effects. First, the range of actors with some capacity to influence Australian policies has expanded to include inter-governmental organizations, transnational non-governmental organizations, and governments of other states represented in international conferences and other settings. Attempts at direct influence originating in international bodies are relatively rare, but more general policy recommendations directed towards member-states of IGOs have left their mark on Australia. Often this process has been assisted by various intermediaries, as when environmental groups or parliamentarians took up and magnified calls for the signing and ratification of international marine pollution conventions. Similarly, direct approaches by IUCN tended to have more impact when re-transmitted by Australian bodies, such as the AHC within government or the ACF outside. Thus during the 1970s and 1980s, in policy areas as diverse as endangered species protection, conservation of the Great Barrier Reef, or the registration of toxic chemicals, a variety of international environmental institutions could be considered as legitimate participants in the framing of Australian policies. These also provided a means by which the diffuse external interest in the Australian natural environment, evident at least since the 1920s, could be organized and targeted on Australian policy-makers. The resulting difficulties for Australian officials in CITES meetings over crocodile farming and other questions are a case in point.

Secondly, the form taken by the federal government's organization for environmental policy-making and programme administration, and also the pace of institutional change, were at times significantly influenced by international regime developments. The Stockholm conference of 1972 was an important turning-point in this regard. Being able to demonstrate at the UNCHE sessions that Australia's own administrative house was in order, both at the federal level and in terms of federal-state consultations, accelerated and directed the organizational steps initiated in 1970. Comparable organizational capabilities were called for in connection with Australia's participation around the same time in the early stages of OECD approaches to environmental problems faced by the western industrialized nations.

More specialized institutional requirements for meeting Australia's obligations under CITES and other conventions were later grafted onto this basic machinery. Arrangements for managing Australia's Antarctic policies were in place before the environmental policy changes that began in the late 1960s; but here too institutional responses, and extensive debate within official and scientific communities about the adequacy of existing policies, were a visible by-product of Australia's deepening engagement in the Antarctica treaty system from the mid-1970s.

There have been related consequences, thirdly, for federal-state relations. Although international conventions generally treat federal countries as equivalent for their purposes to unitary states, in practice Australian official and informal dealings within convention frameworks were hampered in situations where federal and state interests were in conflict — and, perhaps more importantly, where this conflict was well known outside the country. Canberra, that is, has needed a significant measure of state government support, or at least tacit acquiescence, in order to be effective as an actor in international environmental regime developments. This dependency, however, is not incapacitating. The states, for their part, have not made as much use as they might of the potential bargaining strength this relationship affords them; and the rules of the international system, on such matters as formal participation in inter-governmental organizations and attendance at treaty-making conferences, work in favour of leadership from the federal side. The states have nonetheless attempted to set limits to federal policies, as in New South Wales' attempts to check Australia-US kangaroo conservation moves in the early 1970s, Tasmania's unsuccessful interventions in the world heritage process a decade or so later, and Queensland's protracted resistance to federal (and international) thinking on protection of the Great Barrier Reef and the northern rainforests. For some, the decision of the courts in the case of the Tasmanian dam issue in 1983 appeared to stamp with approval a stance of Commonwealth interventionism. The political realities of federalism, however, and the accumulated residues of past encounters, suggested that future federal governments would be unlikely to cross more and more state boundaries by exploiting the device of flourishing an international convention as a passport.

Fourthly, a number of particular policies and programmes owe their origins to developments in international regimes. One prominent example was the evolution of federal policies on toxic chemicals. These took their cue in the early 1980s directly from recommended approaches negotiated among OECD member-states. In other cases, the impact of international developments has been to reinforce moves already under way in Australia, or to shift emphases in more globalist directions. Much official Australian work on endangered species protection or heritage conservation, whether at the federal or state level, was either autogenous or else influenced by external stimuli more by way of comparative lesson-learning than as a result of direct pressures from other countries or international organizations. The existence of the World Heritage convention, and Australia's active role in its institutional arrangements, lent to federal heritage programmes a more distinctively international character than they would otherwise have had; not least, the AHC, as the federal government's agency on heritage matters, became as a consequence one of the strongest advocates of the need for Australia to take a global view of its heritage responsibilities. The form taken by Australia's international wildlife trade legislation in the early 1980s, and the administrative practices put in place before that, similarly reflected in large measure the extensive background of Australian involvement in CITES developments since 1973.

Finally, the activities of domestic groups in Australia have been moulded in part by their appreciation of international events. Some are transnational in character, almost instinctively tuned to viewing Australian problems through global lenses. The art of mobilizing external allies in domestic battles was skilfully demonstrated by the TWS and others in the Tasmanian dam controversy. As in the initially enthusiastic response to the *World Conservation Strategy* and to planning for a national version, international regime developments can at times exert a significant impact on domestic conservation politics. However, there is no guarantee that outside events can be manipulated or exploited to further the cause of domestic goals, or that the objectives of international bodies will be consonant with those of Australian groups. State governments resistant to federal entreaties on environmental conservation are unlikely to be more responsive to approaches by international bodies. Such organizations have frequently been used by groups more as a means of bolstering arguments being put to domestic publics by showing that their views correspond to international opinion. There are clear

194

limits to the efficacy of such tactics. They depend for their success on the dubious proposition that Australians know of the existence of these organizations or, if they do, that they are likely to be impressed by statements issuing from them. There has been a longer-term trend, nonetheless, of international bodies strengthening domestic group attention to developments at that level through conferences, publications, joint activities and other contacts.

Australia in comparative perspective

Western industrialized nations began to face comparable sets of environmental policy problems during the 1960s and early 1970s. Many questions were not new in themselves. Legislation on various aspects of air pollution, the protection of special areas or wildlife species, the use of hazardous chemicals, sanitation and water quality, and other matters that later entered the environmental policy mix, had been in existence in some countries from the middle and late nineteenth century. What was novel, rather, was the integration of these policy areas with newer ones into qualitatively different, coherent frameworks. The rise of the environmental movement in western countries during this period reflected, as well as pushed forward, government programmes. Political conflicts emerged as the demands of environmentalists created stresses in the traditional approaches of governments to agricultural, industrial and resource policies and the activities of the private sector.

These developments provide a helpful perspective for viewing the Australian record. While a systematic comparison of policies and processes in western countries is beyond the scope of this study, a brief overview lends some useful insights. More particularly, a look at Canadian international environmental policies is illuminating because of broader constitutional, political and economic similarities between the two countries.

The OECD countries produced a variety of answers to the problem of incorporating environment policy into government. In some countries, parts of existing government departments dealing with pollution and other problems were welded together into new agencies. The Canadian approach in the early 1970s is a good example. In others, notably the United States and Japan, regulatory agencies with broad powers were specifically created to deal with environmental issues. The definition of environmental policy was stretched in some countries, and contracted in others. In Britain, for example, the new environment department of the 1970s was a super-ministry embracing housing and other major policy areas as well as those that were rapidly becoming identified with environmentalism.

There was considerable variation, too, in approaches to fundamental questions of environmental regulation and administration. Regulatory approaches in the US and Britain, for example, were in sharp contrast. As David Vogel has noted, the US approach is rule-oriented and rigid, more so than in any industrial society, while that in Britain falls at the opposite extreme of flexibility and informality.[8] Use of environmental impact statements, for example, is optional in Britain, but

195

required in the US; self-regulation by industry is the norm in Britain, but is almost entirely absent in the US; use of the courts to ensure company compliance with regulations is frequent in the US, but extremely rare in Britain. Countries varied also according to the level of government at which different aspects of environmental policies and regulations could be formulated. In the Federal Republic of Germany, for example, air pollution, control of hazardous substances, and other matters fall under the concurrent jurisdiction of the federal and state governments, the Länder being empowered to legislate in such areas only if Bonn has not; the federal government has constitutional authority to pass only broad framework laws in areas such as nature protection and land use, with the state governments being responsible for passing detailed implementing laws.[9] The case of the transformation of the environmental movement in West Germany into a network of groups with an organized, if unconventional, political party at its centre is well known.[10] This is by no means the norm, however, and there has been wide diversity in the patterns of environmental politics and group activities among western countries.

Attention to international and transboundary questions, and to the links between these and domestic environmental policies, has likewise varied across political systems. Structures of government are one factor. In the United States, Congress became during the 1970s a significant governmental actor in relation to international environmental policy, for example by building provisions into laws requiring the executive to pursue international cooperation on environmental matters; or by regulating aspects of US international trade policies in such areas as hazardous chemicals exports to bring these into greater conformity with domestic regulatory norms.[11] In countries with parliamentary forms of government, or where environmental issues have had less prominence, or where the external reach of government and companies is significantly less, the profile of the legislative body has tended to be comparatively lower. The geographical and ecological situations of different countries help shape the kinds of issues that characterize their environmental politics, and also to some extent the range of policy options pursued by governments. Cooperation among the Nordic countries on migratory bird and other environmental matters is a product both of traditional regionalism, but also of the nature of the environmental policy problems each confronts. International policy, moreover, has to fit within the broader context of foreign policy and approaches to the making and domestic implementation of international law. Switzerland, for example, while eschewing membership of many organizations, has none the less actively pursued the gradual institutionalization of international cooperation on environmental conservation.

Comparative studies of Australian government and politics have tended increasingly, however, to turn to Canada. We can usefully touch on aspects of Canadian international environmental policies and policy processes that have the most direct bearing on the specific questions examined in earlier chapters in relation to Australia.

Despite clear parallels between Canadian and Australian environmental conditions — both countries occupy large geographical areas, and both have long coastlines and resource-rich economies — significant differences have also shaped their respective political agendas. Canada, to take some obvious examples, has no offshore barrier reef; its interest in polar politics is restricted to the Arctic, and is not therefore situated within a complex regime like that of Antarctica; and its climatic and ecological zones are less diverse than Australia's. Most importantly, and unlike Australia, Canada shares a continent with the world's leading economic power. Bilateral cooperation in the environmental field, the Joint Committee on Canada's International Relations observed in 1986, is "literally forced upon Canada and the US by the cross-border transport of the airborne pollutants that cause acid rain, the flow of water across the boundary, and the need to regulate industrial developments in one country that will affect the other."[12] Cooperation has a long history, beginning with the North American Conservation Conference and the Boundary Waters Treaty of 1909 and the 1916 Migratory Birds Convention. As the more recent record of acid rain politics amply demonstrates, however, functional cooperation of this kind has a limited capacity to generate binding resolutions of major policy differences between Washington and Ottawa.

This bilateral context has implications for the way in which Canada has approached international environmental institutions and conventions. At the Stockholm conference in 1972, for example, Canada sought firmer international recognition of the fact that pollutants do not respect international boundaries and of the principle that states had an obligation to minimize environmental damage to others resulting from their own activities. The delegation drafted two of the Declaration principles related to this point. High on the Canadian agenda at UNCHE was the goal of strengthening international controls over ocean dumping, restricting large tankers to routes that avoided ecologically sensitive areas, and promoting international cooperation in marine science. Like Australia, Canada viewed UNCHE partly from the perspective of related oceans developments, particularly the forthcoming IMCO conference on marine pollution and the start of the UNCLOS III negotiations The minister, Jack Davis, considered that the greatest contribution of the delegation at Stockholm was "on the marine side. Freedom of the high seas must not include the freedom to pollute."[13] Canada had "a big stake in international arrangements of this kind. As a nation with a vast territory, with the largest continental shelf and one of the largest coastlines in the world, we have much to gain from the enunciation of a universal good neighbour policy — a global environmental ethic — by the UN."[14] This interest, and the more general foreign policy goal of supporting UN economic and social activities, led to collaboration in subsequent UNEP programmes such as GEMS, INFOTERRA and the IRPTC.

Both countries have been active within many of the same institutions, though Australia is excluded from two taken seriously by Canada: the UN Economic Commission for Europe (ECE), and, to a lesser extent, the NATO Committee

197

on Challenges of Modern Society. Both have also tended, on balance, to view the OECD's environmental work as more germane to their interests than UNEP, particularly, in the 1980s, its activities related to toxic chemicals management.[15] Similarly, scientists and officials from both Canada and Australia have been among the leading figures in the IUCN and in the events preceding its formation. Shortly after World War I, Canadian scientists began to explore the possibility of reviving or replacing the defunct Consultative Commission of 1913, and there was a significant Canadian presence at the 1949 Lake Success conference on world conservation.[16] Canadian experts have been active in IUCN Commissions, particularly those on National Parks and Protected Areas, Ecology, and Species Survival (especially the wolf and polar bear groups). Partly through normal consultative processes, and partly because of the role of officials appointed or seconded to the IUCN Secretariat in Switzerland (including its Director-General, David Munro, during a key period), Canadians also played a significant role in shaping the *World Conservation Strategy*. Related activities across the full range of UN bodies have been supported. Thus Canada has been a strong proponent of cooperation on chemicals, for example through the pesticides residues work of the WHO- and FAO-sponsored Codex Alimentarius Commission.[17] ECE negotiations, which led to the 1979 Convention on Long-Range Transboundary Air Pollution, and the 1985 Protocol on Reduction of Sulphur Emissions or Their Transboundary Fluxes, took on special importance for Canada because of widespread European member-state support for transboundary pollution controls and the potential this particular forum had for bringing multilateral pressure to bear on US policies.

Canada, like Australia, has been interested in most international environmental conventions. It signed the World Heritage convention in 1976 and commenced a term of membership on the World Heritage Committee in 1985, by which time nine Canadian sites were included on the world list. Canadian contributions to the UNEP Coordinating Committee on the Ozone Layer from 1977 were an important part of the preparatory work for the international ozone layer agreements of 1985 and 1987, the meeting for the latter being hosted by Canada. The international polar bear convention of 1973 reflected more distinctively Canadian interests. Scientific support for such an instrument began in the early 1950s, and Canadian representatives were active both in keeping Arctic questions central to IUCN agendas during the following decade and in drafting the agreement itself in the early 1970s.[18]

Even this brief summary indicates something of the depth of Canadian engagement in international environmental regime developments. A study of the policy process in Canada also reveals some illuminating parallels with Australia. The creation of a federal environment department in 1970-71 is a case in point. Anticipation of UNCHE put a premium on the consolidation of a clear federal presence in the formulation of environment policy in Canada, particularly in light of the Trudeau government's interest in crafting a special role for Canada in the new world order issues of the decade. Growing tensions in Canadian-American relations were also a factor; setting up such a department was designed in part to give a signal to Washington that environmental issues were regarded as important by Canada.[19] As in Australia, public awareness of environmental questions helped create an atmosphere of receptiveness towards an expanded federal role. In Canada in 1970, moreover — as in Australia after the 1972 election — the federal government was led by a Prime Minister with strong views of the requirement for an enhanced degree of central direction in the affairs of the nation, and a predisposition to see environmental issues as one means to secure this goal.

The place of the Department of the Environment (DOE) in government has been influenced by two factors: the problem of giving operational force to a politically acceptable definition of the term "environment," and the fact that several federal departments and agencies have shared responsibilities in the area. The department has tried to resist attempts by others to pigeon-hole it. Ministers and officials have argued, within government and outside, that any adequate definition of environmental problems must embrace a wide span of policy areas and, by implication, rest on a larger role for the DOE. Changing environmental philosophies articulated by the department have put increasing emphasis on linkages with broader questions of the economy and social justice.[20] In 1984 the department maintained that "the interdependency between society, the economy and the environment is much more fundamental and pervasive than generally thought. . . . The focus is no longer on single issues, such as water or air quality, but rather is fundamentally concerned with the worldwide husbandry of global resources over the long term."[21]

In practice, the DOE has been constrained by the same kind of limitations as its Australian counterpart. The department is only one of several environmental voices in the federal government. Indeed it was formed out of pieces from five departments grafted on to the former Department of Fisheries and Forestry.[22] Health and Welfare, for example, as the department managing relations with WHO, is the major player in dealings with the IRPTC and the International Program of Chemical Safety. The main northern policy actor has been Indian Affairs and Northern Development, with roles played also by Fisheries and Oceans; Transport; Energy, Mines and Resources; and National Defence as well as the DOE, together with ten other departments and agencies of the federal government.[23] The Health Protection Branch of Health and Welfare, and the Plant Health and Plant Products Directorate of Agriculture Canada, coordinate Canada's role in FAO and WHO work on pesticide chemicals.[24] Questions of marine pollution have traditionally been based more in Transport than in the DOE.[25] All of this naturally creates coordination problems. One recent study has highlighted several weaknesses in Canada's administrative arrangements for CITES. The DOE acts as the Canadian Management Authority and Scientific Authority under the terms of the convention, with the primary duties falling to a special unit of the Canadian Wildlife Service (CWS) . Closely related tasks, however, are carried out by Fisheries and Oceans, Agriculture, National Revenue, Customs and Excise, and the Royal Canadian

199

Mounted Police, and these various agencies "appear to operate automonously, with little harmonization of their activities."[26]

On international questions of any kind the Department of External Affairs has to be taken into account. Here the DOE has achieved a certain autonomy. Indeed as one official has put it, "In many instances DOE plays a more leading and active role in both representational and technical functions than does External Affairs which nevertheless retains nominal responsibility for relations with other countries and inter-governmental organizations."[27] The two departments share responsibilities for Canadian (and joint Canadian-American) submissions to the World Heritage Committee and in connection with Canadian representation on the UNEP Governing Council. As in Australia, the environment department is the main federal actor in the OECD Environment Committee, but this has to be seen in the context of External Affairs' role in relation to the organization as a whole. External Affairs also takes the lead in convening inter-departmental consultations on Canadian policies in UN bodies. The DOE handles Canada's relations with the IUCN and the main international conventions in the conservation area; the department represents Canada, for example, on the executive body of the Convention on Long-Range Transboundary Air Pollution. Acid rain, on the other hand, has been an issue high on the Canadian foreign policy agenda. Bodies such as External Affairs' Bureau of USA Affairs and the Division of Transboundary Relations have thus taken the key role rather than the external relations components of the DOE. External Affairs (like Foreign Affairs in Australia) was similarly the major player in the UNCLOS III negotiations.

Complexity at the federal level, however, is only a part of the picture. The provinces, like the Australian states, are in many ways the foundation of environment policy. At the same time, the constitutional framework provides for a significant role by the federal government, so that in practice there is considerable jurisdictional overlap in resource and environment areas.[28] Ottawa has jurisdiction in the Territories and Indian lands, and also for national and historic parks and migratory bird sanctuaries. Significant environmental dimensions are involved in the federal government's powers in relation to coastal and inland fisheries, oceans, navigation and shipping, and transboundary and international questions. The Canadian Council of Resource and Environment Ministers (CCREM), the main federal-state forum, has suffered from some of the tensions that have affected the AEC in Australia. Indeed provincial annoyance at federal trespassing led in 1973 to the temporary disbanding of the CCREM. The DOE is itself decentralized, to facilitate provincial and regional participation in environmental policy. Its capabilities on this criterion have been criticized; Paul Brown has argued that both the complexity of the environmental mission, and the weight of centralist thinking in the department, are factors that seriously hamper the prospects for effective administrative decentralization.[29] Yet federal-provincial cooperation also nourishes an infrastructure of diverse programmes. In 1986-87, the DOE was administering a total of 56 agreements, or sets of agreements, with provincial governments on a wide variety of questions, such as the Canadian Heritage Rivers system and bilateral frameworks such as the Canada-Ontario Wildlife Conservation Agreement.[30]

Canada's efficacy as an international actor in these matters is thus dependent in part on effective cooperation with the provinces. In the late 1960s, seven governments had regulatory competence for polar bears and there was wide diversity on questions such as hunting seasons; domestic coordination was an essential prerequisite for active Canadian participation in the international convention-making process that culminated in the 1973 agreement.[31] Similarly, Canada's negotiating position with the US on acid rain has been weakened by regulatory gaps at the provincial level; parallel sulphur dioxide emission agreements negotiated with the governments of Ontario and Quebec in the mid-1980s were thus an essential accompaniment of this process. The *World Conservation Strategy* was endorsed by Ottawa in 1981. Following a provisional implementation plan produced in 1982 by the DOE for areas within federal jurisdiction, events then slowed down. As in Australia, problems arose particularly in exchanges with provincial governments, many of which considered the document insufficiently development-oriented and also a possible vehicle for enhanced federal powers. In consultations prior to Canadian ratification of CITES, some provinces perceived the envisaged administrative machinery as a threat to their existing wildlife management programmes. Cooperation has since assured provincial participation in several ways: through the issue of provincial CITES export permits for wildlife and wildlife products originating within their jurisdictions; through the nomination of provincial representatives on Canadian delegations to CITES meetings; and through biennial federal-provincial meetings convened to address common CITES concerns.[32] Ottawa has also acted as an international defender of provincial interests, as in the joint Canada-Newfoundland delegation which visited IUCN and WWF headquarters in 1979 to voice concern over these organizations' position on the harp seal question.[33]

Public attention to environmental questions in Canada has in general not reached the peak of intensity that marked the final stages of the Tasmanian dam confrontation, but acid rain has been a more protracted issue, with higher levels of public interest over a significant length of time than any in Australia. There is also a regional dimension. Public awareness of acid rain questions in the 1970s was high in Ontario, for example, but relatively low in Quebec.[34] For the most part, though, a sustained interest in environmental questions, whether domestic or international, has tended in both Canada and Australia to be a minority concern. Yet in both, the pattern of group politics has a remarkable diversity, in terms of the degree of specialization of groups, their strategies and tactics, targets and definitions of the environmental arena. On the other hand, a shared body of underlying goals can also produce implicit or direct collaboration between groups such as Greenpeace, Pollution Probe, the Canadian Coalition on Acid Rain, or the Federation of Ontario Naturalists. Somewhat apart from this often turbulent world has been the steady volume of unpublicized scientific activity in relation to international cooperative exercises such as the MAB Programme.[35] As in

Australia, groups' relations with government vary. The Canadian Nature Federation has occasionally influenced official policy on matters such as access to national parks and the extension of the northern parks system.[36] From the outset, the DOE has attempted to nurture this constituency, but its ability to do so has been constrained by the unwieldy diversity of environmental networks, and its own vulnerability to broader political, and budgetary, forces within the federal government.

These kinds of similarities suggest some distinctive features of the Australian case. The contrasting environmental situations of the two countries are a central consideration. In Australia, environmental questions have been much more divisive internally than they have in Canada. Part of the reason is that the major targets of group and public pressures have been domestic ones: the governments of Queensland over the Great Barrier Reef or northern rainforests, for example, of Tasmania over the South-west, or of Western Australia over mining threats to jarrah forests or the resource exploitation activities of Australian companies. Comparable issues are not, of course, absent from Canada. The priority attached to acid rain issues, however, has focussed attention rather on external targets — the policies of the US Administration or of various state governments — largely missing in the Australian setting.

More general factors are also relevant. Australian politics, Don Aitkin has argued, is "partisan, ideological and tough to a greater degree, I think, than is true of the politics of any other Anglo-American democracy."[37] Australian political culture appears to elevate the values of political combativeness and to disparage mere consensus-seeking of the Canadian variety. The rise of the environmental movement, and its mobilization on key issues, may also reflect the distinctive character of Australian political parties. James Jupp has characterized Australian democracy as "the interplay of small bureaucratized elites insulated from popular pressure by institutions, including the parties. Rather than links with the masses, the small hierarchical parties may be barriers to mass involvement."[38] The Australian Democrats in the early 1980s were able to exploit environmentalist criticism of a cautious Labor traditionalism unsure of the wisdom of putting ecological issues on a par with jobs as a party priority. Labor, earlier the natural home of environmentalist opinion, suffered too from the more general retreat from Keynesianism of the late 1970s and 1980s[39] and its consequences for the political acceptability of the regulatory intervention implied by environmentalism. Conservation groups thus both benefited and lost from a perception of their identification with the left; the former in that groups could tap support from a broad ALP-oriented constituency, the latter because resort to partisan slogans provided critics with ammunition lacking in the more pragmatic Canadian context.

Theory and practice in regime construction

Regime change is a continuing process. The international environmental regime that faced Australian policy-makers in the early 1970s is not that of the early

1990s. Indeed in some respects the international questions that began to emerge in the middle and late 1960s, and which continued during the first decade of the life of UNEP, may in retrospect eventually appear as minimal or highly circumscribed approaches to global ecological issues.

During the 1980s more emphasis was placed on linkages between environmental conservation, on the one hand, and broader questions of the management of economies on the other. There are strong elements of continuity. Concern for the protection of wild flora and fauna, for example, is still high on environmental agendas, though the rationales and the motivations of actors have increasingly focussed on the economic, scientific, medical and other tangible benefits of conservation. Complex special-purpose regimes for the oceans, Antarctica, the ozone layer and other areas continue to evolve in light of the interests of states. Other developments impinge more directly on economic and resource policies, as in the spread of environmental impact assessments in international development assistance agencies,[40] evolution of environmental components of codes of conduct for multinational corporations, or the tightening of environmental criteria in the determination of export rules. These kinds of trends will likely push environmental and related issues still higher on international political agendas in the future.

Australia's experience is not unique. As in other countries, environmental policies have been a complex and changing function of external events and pressures and domestic requirements. At important stages in the formulation of policies and programmes, the structuring of the international regime had an important effect on the organization of government in Australia, the pace of institutional and policy change, relations between governments at different levels, and the strategies of pressure groups. Australia's definition of its own interests, however, and constraints set by a variety of domestic actors, set limits to the federal government's readiness to take part enthusiastically in regime developments. Nor should we assume that environmental groups are automatically oriented towards internationalist solutions. Some are; but others remain localized in their concerns, or if not, antipathetic towards an international level of organization perceived as remote, bureaucratic and conservative.

Environmental issues contain the potential for both cooperation and conflict between national governments in their approaches to these decisions. States do cooperate for tangible, common ends; only a few want to stand alone. Yet such cooperation is not an inevitable product of ecological interdependence. Issues vary considerably in the degree to which they determine the ease and the likelihood of effective international cooperation. Transboundary pollution, particularly where major industrial sectors are involved, is intrinsically more difficult to control than are questions of the conservation of sites for migratory birds. The problems raised for Australia by the latter issue, however, were more internal than external, since in many cases relevant land use powers were not at the disposal of the federal government. This suggests internal complexity is the most striking feature of nations in the contemporary international system, and the most relevant for determining the nature of the international arrangements they enter. As the range of issues regularly or routinely handled in international forums expands, so attention is directed more towards such matters as the internal structures of government, the diverse world of public groups, and the multiple connections between these and international regimes.

Political conflict within and between countries also marks the environmental area, as the respective examples of South-west Tasmania and acid rain in Canada-US relations indicate. Assessing the balance between the gains and costs of cooperative ventures requires political decisions. No set rules or procedures suggested an easy solution of the Tasmanian dam question; those that did exist pointed towards respect for the authority of the state government, while the eventual resolution of the issue took a quite different course. Internal processes seem far more conflict-prone than the more courtly exchanges between national governments across national boundaries.

These considerations have a bearing on the more general question of the significance of international arrangements. Answers have in the past depended in part on the orientations of different traditions of scholarship. Students of public policy in western industrialized nations, for example, have often tended to view selected countries in isolation, or else to group two or more together for comparative analysis; either way, the question of the role of international arrangements such as deliberations within OECD forums in forming national policies and programs can easily be overlooked, and the assumption that domestic policy frameworks can in practice be viewed as autonomous or insulated may remain untested. Students of the workings of international institutions or regimes, similarly, have tended to focus more on the international negotiations that lie behind such arrangements, or to assess these arrangements mainly in the light of the contribution they might indirectly make to peace, or to look at domestic political settings primarily as sources of possible influence on the external actions of governments. The parallel assumption, that matters of domestic implementation and response can be taken for granted as a low research priority, can go unrecognized. The wider domestic ramifications of the international activities of states may as a result be neglected. Study of public policy, and of particular topics such as the effects of and consequences for government organization, the structures and processes of federalism, or the forms of international regimes, is increasingly an area in which no individual disciplinary, or sub-disciplinary, tradition can direct us towards the most fertile questions.

The evolution of national and international arrangements to tackle environmental problems has already produced some novel organizational forms. The convention on Antarctic marine living resources, for example, while flawed in the eyes of some conservationist critics, none the less creatively adapted ecosystem thinking as a basis for regime formation. In the future, research on global linkages between atmosphere and climate, ecosystems, non-living resources and economic activities, may lead to arrangements based on as yet unanticipated conceptual underpinnings. While the decisions of nation-states will remain central to these political processes, it is also evident that the phenomena of governance cannot be neatly contained within their borders.

Notes for Chapter 10

1 Kenneth Wiltshire, *Planning and Federalism: Australian and Canadian Experience* (St. Lucia: University of Queensland Press, 1986), p. 128.

2 Kenneth Wiltshire, "Working with inter-governmental agreements: the Canadian and Australian experience," *Canadian Public Administration*, 23(3), Fall 1980, pp. 356-57.

3 Four departments were disbanded and nine new ones created. See Elaine Thompson, "The Public Service," in A. Patience and B. Head (eds.), *From Whitlam to Fraser: Reform and Reaction in Australian Politics* (Melbourne: Oxford University Press, 1979), pp. 70-87.

4 Martin Painter and Bernard Carey, *Politics between Departments: The Fragmentation of Executive Control in Australian Government* (St. Lucia: University of Queensland Press, 1979), p. 62.

5 Geoffrey Hawker, R.F.I. Smith, and Patrick Weller, *Politics and Policy in Australia* (St. Lucia: University of Queensland Press, 1979), p. 107.

6 Richard Simeon has argued that in both Canada and Australia, a combination of parliamentary government, strict party discipline, and centralization within both levels of government, has acted to inhibit the effectiveness of national legislatures as arenas for adjustment. See his *Federal-Provincial Diplomacy: The Making of Recent Policy in Canada* (Toronto: University of Toronto Press, 1973), pp. 302-3.

7 House of Representatives, Standing Committee on Environment and Conservation, *Australia's Participation in International Environmental Organisations* (Canberra, October 1982).

8 David Vogel, *National Styles of Regulation: Environmental Policy in Great Britain and the United States* (Ithaca: Cornell University Press, 1986), p. 21.

9 Richard D. Brown, Robert P. Ouellette, and Paul N. Cheremisinoff, *National Environmental Policies and Research Programs* (Lancaster: Technomic, 1983), p. 34.

10 Elim Papadakis, *The Green Movement in West Germany* (London: Croom Helm, 1984).

11 Maria H. Grimes, "Congress and international environmental policy: an overview," *Journal of Public and International Affairs*, 5(1), Winter 1985, pp. 84-93.

12 *Independence and Internationalism. Report of the Special Joint Committee of the Senate and of the House of Commons on Canada's International Relations* (Ottawa, June 1986), pp. 35-6. Often forgotten is Canada's "other" border, the maritime one with Greenland. There have been modest levels of effective bilateral cooperation with Denmark on such matters as marine pollution control and the impact of offshore development in the eastern Arctic. See Frances Abele and E.J. Dosman, "Inter-departmental coordination and northern development," *Canadian Public Administration*, 24(3), Fall 1981, p. 438.

13 *House of Commons*, 28th Parliament, 4th Session, vol . IV, June 21, 1972, pp. 3333-34.

14 *House of Commons*, 28th Parliament, 4th Session, vol . III, June 2, 1972, p. 2791.

15 For an evaluation of Canadian approaches, see Peter N. Nemetz, et al., "Toxic chemical regulation in Canada: preliminary estimates of costs and benefits," *Canadian Public Administration*, 25(3), Fall 1982, pp. 405-19.

16 UNESCO, *International Technical Conference on the Protection of Nature*, Doc. Cont. 2/15 (1949), pp. 499ff.

17 See further R. Boardman, *Pesticides in World Agriculture: The Politics of International Regulation* (London: Macmillan, 1986), pp. 65, 67, 71, 128.

18 "The Banff General Assembly," *IUCN Bull.*, 3(10), October 1972, p. 43.

19 See further Don Munton, "Dependence and interdependence in transboundary environmental relations," *International Journal*, 36 (1980-81), p. 155; Michael S. Whittington, "Department of the Environment," in G. Bruce Doern (ed.), *How Ottawa Spends* (Toronto: Lorimer, 1981), pp. 99-100.

[20] J. Blair Seaborn, "Attitudes Change," *Contact*, 4(7), no. 80, p. 3; L.J. D'Amore, "New slant on environmental thinking," *Environment Update*, 5(1), March 1984, p. 9.

[21] Environment Canada, *Sustainable Development: A Submission to the Royal Commission on the Economic Union and Development Prospects for Canada* (Ottawa, February 1984), p. 5.

[22] *Environment Canada: Its Evolving Mission* (Ottawa: September 1982), p. 13. In 1979, the Department of Fisheries and Oceans was formed out of Environment's fisheries and marine component; and Parks Canada joined from Indian and Northern Affairs.

[23] Abele and Dosman, "Inter-departmental coordination," p. 434.

[24] Bengt v Hofsten and George Ekström (eds.), *Control of Pesticide Applications and Residues in Food* (Uppsala: Swedish Science Press, 1986), pp. 98-99.

[25] R.M. M'Gonigle and Mark W. Zacher, "Canadian foreign policy and the control of marine pollution," in Barbara Johnson and Mark W. Zacher (eds.), *Canadian Foreign Policy and the Law of the Sea* (Vancouver: University of British Columbia Press, 1977), pp. 147-48.

[26] On problems of post-entry enforcement, see Douglas Hykle, "Canadian Administration of the Convention on International Trade in Endangered Species," unpublished MES thesis, Dalhousie University, (1988), p. 226.

[27] Robert Lederman, "The Canadian Government and international environmental cooperation: The UN experience", paper presented at the Symposium on Global Issues and the Future, Trent University, 8 February 1985, p. 1.

[28] Marsha Chandler and William M. Chandler, *Public Policy and Provincial Politics* (Toronto: McGraw-Hill Ryerson, 1919), p. 263.

[29] M. Paul Brown, "Environment Canada and the pursuit of administrative decentralization," *Canadian Public Administration*, 29(2), Summer 1986, pp. 218-36.

[30] Federal-Provincial Relations Office, *Federal-Provincial Programs and Activities: A Descriptive Inventory, 1986-87* (Ottawa, May 1987), pp. 64-101. Wiltshire has estimated that overall Canadian and Australian figures are comparable ("Working with inter-governmental agreements," p. 358).

[31] C. Jonkel, "Some comments on polar bear management," *Biological Conservation*, 2(2), 1970, pp. 115-19.

[32] Hykle, "Canadian Administration of CITES," Chapter 3.

[33] *IUCN Bull.*, 10(2), February 1979, p. 11.

[34] *Still Waters. Report of the Sub-committee on Acid Rain of the Standing Committee on Fisheries and Forestry* (Ottawa, 1981), p. 99. One reason put forward was the publicity given to the issue by the Government of Ontario.

[35] Contributions to MAB projects have covered a wide span, with emphasis on vegetation and flora studies. See for example Gerald B. Straley, et al., *The Rare Vascular Plants of British Columbia*, *Syllogeus*, No. 59, 1985.

[36] *Nature Canada*, July/September 1979, p. 21; *Nature Canada*, January-March 1984, p. 42. For a useful perspective on phases in the growth of the Canadian environmental movement, see Maxwell Cohen, "Building on the Canada-US experience," in John Holmes and John Kirton (eds.), *Canada and the New Internationalism* (Centre for International Studies, University of Toronto and the CIIA, 1988), pp. 112-3.

[37] Don Aitkin, "Australian politics in a federal context," in R.L. Mathews, ed., *Public Policies in Two Federal Countries: Canada and Australia* (Canberra: Centre for Research on Federal Financial Relations, Australian National University, 1982), p. 49. He suggests as reasons the professionalism of politicians, the age of the party system, and its flavour as an amalgam of late nineteenth-century ethnic, religious and class antagonisms.

[38] James Jupp, *Party Politics: Australia, 1966-1981* (Sydney: Allen and Unwin, 1982), p. 187. For a development of the argument of rigidities in Australian politics, see David Kemp, *Authority and Politics in Australia: Some Key Dynamics of Australian Politics* (Melbourne: Oxford University Press, 1987).

[39] See Marian Simms, *A Liberal Nation: The Liberal Party and Australian Politics* (Sydney: Hale and Iremonger, 1982), Ch. 8.

[40] V.J. Hartje, "Environmental Impact Assessment for development projects: institutional constraints in international development cooperation," *Journal of Public and International Affairs*, 5(1), Winter 1985, pp. 49-57.

Bibliography

Aitkin, Don (ed.) *The Howson Diaries: The Life of Politics.* (Ringwood: Viking Press, 1984).

Albinski, Henry S. "Australian External Policy, Federalism and the States," *Political Science* 28(1), July 1976, pp. 1-12.

_____, *Australian External Policy under Labor: Content, Process and the National Debate.* (St. Lucia: University of Queensland Press, 1977).

Auburn, F.M. *Antarctic Law and Politics.* (Canberra: Croom Helm, 1982).

Bailey, K.H. "The Constitutional and Legal Framework," in J.A. Sinden (ed.), *The Natural Resources of Australia.* (Sydney: Angus and Robertson, 1972).

Bandler, H. "Gordon below Franklin Dam, Tasmania, Australia: Environmental Factors in a Decision of National Significance," *The Environmentalist*, 7(1), Spring 1987, pp. 43-54.

Barwick, Sir Garfield. *Economic Growth and the Environment* (Melbourne: ACF, Occasional Publication No. 7, 1971).

Bates, G.M. *Environmental Law in Australia.* (Sydney: Butterworths, 1983).

Birrell, Robert, et al. (eds.) *Quarry Australia? Social and Environmental Perspectives on Managing the Nation's Resources.* (Melbourne: Oxford University Press, 1982).

Boer, B.W., and Donna Craig. "Federalism and Environmental Law in Australia and Canada," in Bruce W. Hodgins, et al. (eds.), *Federalism in Canada and Australia: Historical Perspectives, 1920-1988.* (Peterborough: Broadview Press for the Frost Centre, Trent University, 1989), pp. 301-16.

Burmester, Henry. "The Australian States and Participation in the Foreign Policy Process," *Federal Law Review.* 9 (1978).

_____, "Australia and the Law of the Sea: The Protection and Preservation of the Marine Environment," in K.W. Ryan (ed.) *International Law in Australia.* 2nd ed. (Sydney: Law Book Co., 1984).

Burton, B. *Overpowering Tasmania.* (Hobart: Wilderness Society, 1984).

Caldwell, L.K. *International Environmental Policy.* (Durham, N.C.: Duke University Press, 1984).

Castles, A.C. "International Status of the Australian Antarctic Territory," in D.P. O'Connell (ed.), *International Law in Australia.* (Sydney: Law Book Co., 1965), pp. 341-67.

Cole, J. "Environmental Law and Politics," *University of New South Wales Law Journal* 4, (1981).

Connell, D.W. *Water Pollution.* (St. Lucia: University of Queensland Press, 1974).

Connelly, R. *The Fight for the Franklin: The Story of Tasmania's Last Wild River.* (Sydney: Cassell, 1981).

Coombs, H.C. *The Fragile Pattern: Institutions and Man* (The Boyer Lectures). (Sydney: ABC, 1970).

Cooper, M. *The Franklin Dam Case* (Sydney: Butterworths, 1983).

Costin, A.B. and H.J. Frith (eds.) *Conservation*. (Melbourne: Penguin, 1971).

Davis, Bruce W. "The Struggle for South-west Tasmania," in Roger Scott (eds.) *Interest Groups and Public Policy*. (Melbourne: Macmillan, 1980), pp. 152-69.

_____, "Federalism and Environmental Politics: An Australian Overview," in R.L. Mathews (ed.), *Federalism and the Environment*. (Canberra: Centre for Research on Federal Financial Relations, 1985).

Dempsey, Rob (ed.) *The Politics of Finding Out: Environmental Problems in Australia*. (Melbourne: Cheshire, 1974).

Dragun, Andrew K. "Hydroelectric Development and Wilderness Conflicts in South-West Tasmania," *Environmental Conservation*. 10(3), Autumn 1983, pp. 197-204.

Early, G.P. "Character of Commonwealth/State Environmental Policy-making in Australia," Paper for Environmental Studies Section, ANZAAS Congress, Adelaide, 12-16 May 1980.

Edwards, P.G. *Prime Ministers and Diplomats: The Making of Foreign Policy, 1901-1949*. (Melbourne: Oxford University Press, 1983).

Fenner, F. (ed.) *A National System of Ecological Reserves in Australia*. (Canberra: AAS, 1975).

Fisher, D.E. "An Overview of Environmental Law in Australia," *Earth Law Journal* 3 (1977), pp. 47-67.

_____, *Environmental Law in Australia: An Introduction*. (St. Lucia: University of Queensland Press, 1980).

Fogg, Alan S. "The Environment, Property, and Community Participation in Australia," *Earth Law Journal* 3(1), 1977, pp. 69-88.

Fox, A.M. "The Australian National Parks and Wildlife Service," *Parks and Wildlife* 2(3-4), 1979, pp. 154-60.

Frith, H.J. *Wildlife Conservation* rev. ed. (Sydney: Angus and Robertson, 1979).

Galligan, Brian. "Federalism and Resource Development in Australia and Canada," *Australian Quarterly*, 54 (1982).

_____, "Writing on Australian Federalism: The Current State of the Art," *Australian Journal of Public Administration*, XLIII (2), 1984, pp. 177-86.

Garbesi, G.C. "Main Features, Gaps, and Recent Advances in Australian Environmental Law," *Habitat*, 4(4), 1976, pp. 20-23.

Gee, H. (ed.) *The Franklin: Tasmania's Last Wild River*. (Hobart: TWS, 1978).

Gilpin, Alan. *Air Pollution*, 2nd ed. (St. Lucia: University of Queensland Press, 1978).

_____, *Environment Policy in Australia*. (St. Lucia: University of Queensland Press, 1980).

_____, *The Australian Environment: Twelve Controversial Issues*. (Melbourne: Sun, 1980).

Gunson, Neil. "Australian Antarctic Territory," in G. Greenwood and N. Harper (eds.), *Australia in World Affairs, 1956-60*. (Melbourne: Cheshire, 1963), pp. 384-418.

Harper, N., and D. Sissons. *Australia and the United Nations*. (New York: Manhattan, 1959).

Harris, Stuart (ed.) *Australia's Antarctic Policy Options*. (Canberra: Centre for Resource and Environmental Studies, Monograph No. 11, 1984).

Harris, Stuart and Geoff Taylor (eds.) *Resource Development and the Future of Australian Society*. (Canberra: Centre for Resource and Environmental Studies, Monograph No. 7, 1982).

Harry, Ralph L. "Australia's Role in the Evolving UN," *Australian Outlook*, 34(1), April 1980, pp. 13-19.

Hastings, Peter and Andrew Farran (eds.) *Australia's Resources Future: Threats, Myths and Realities in the 1980s*. (Melbourne: Nelson, 1978).

Herr, R.A. and B.W. Davis, "The Impact of UNCLOS III on Australian Federalism," *International Journal*, XLI (3), Summer 1986, pp. 674-93.

Hocking, B. "Pluralism and Foreign Policy: The States and the Management of Australia's External Relations," *Yearbook of World Affairs*, 38 (1983).

Howson, Peter. "Australia in the World Environment" (23rd Roy Milne Memorial Lecture) (Sydney: AIIA, 1972).

Hudson, W.J. *Australia and the League of Nations*. (Sydney University Press, 1980).

Hughes, Owen. "Bauxite Mining and Jarrah Forests in Western Australia," in Roger Scott (ed.), *Interest Groups and Public Policy*. (Melbourne: Macmillan, 1980), pp. 170-93.

Johnstone, G.W. "A Review of Biological Research by Australian National Antarctic Research Expeditions," *Polar Record*, 16 (1972), pp. 519-32.

Jones, Richard (ed.) *Damania: The HEC, Environment and Government in Tasmania*. (Hobart: Fullers Bookshop, 1982).

Kellow, A. "Public Project Evaluation in an Australian State: Tasmania's Dam Controversy," *Australian Quarterly*, 55(3), Spring 1983, pp. 263-77.

Kelly, G. "Commonwealth Legislation relating to Environmental Impact Statements," *Australian Law Journal*, 50 (1976), pp. 498-512.

Lloyd, C. *The National Estate: Australia's Heritage*. (Melbourne: Cassell, 1978).

Lumb, R.D. "Australia and the Law of the Sea: Recent Developments," *International and Comparative Law Quarterly*, 29(1), January 1980, pp. 151-65.

Lyster, S. *International Wildlife Law*. (Cambridge: Grotius Publications, 1985).

Mackie, J.A.C. (ed.) *Australia in the New World Order*. (Sydney: Nelson and the AIIA, 1976).

Marshall, A.J. *The Great Extermination*. (Melbourne: Heinemann, 1966).

Martin, Angus. *Pollution and Conservation in Australia*. (Melbourne: Lansdowne Press, 1971).

McKinney, Judith W. "The Loss of the National Estate," *Australian Quarterly*, 4 (December 1976), pp. 7-14.

McMichael, D.F. "Australian Government Action to Conserve the Great Barrier Reef," *Environmental Conservation*, 3(1), Spring 1976, p. 58.

Millar, T.B. *Australia in Peace and War: External Relations, 1788-1977*. (Canberra: Australian National University Press, 1978).

Miller, Alan S. "Conservation, Politics and the Law," *Habitat*, 6(1), April 1978, pp. 19-23.

Mosley, J.G. *National Parks and Equivalent Reserves in Australia: Guide to Legislation, Administration and Areas.* (Melbourne: ACF, Special Publication No. 2, n.d.).

_____, "Australia's Heritage Areas," *Habitat*, 11(1), February 1983, pp. 16-26.

Ovington, J.D. *Australian Endangered Species: Mammals, Birds and Reptiles.* (Melbourne: Cassell, 1978).

Peacock, Andrew. "The Politics of Pollution," *Australian Quarterly*, September 1970.

Pearman, G.I. (ed.) *Carbon Dioxide and Climate: Australian Research.* (Canberra: AAS, 1980).

Porter, Colin F. *Environmental Impact Assessment: A Practical Guide.* (St. Lucia: University of Queensland Press, 1985).

Powell, J.M. *Environmental Management in Australia, 1788-1914: Guardians, Improvers and Profit. An Introductory Survey.* (Melbourne: Oxford University Press, 1976).

Recher, H. "Failure of our National Parks System," *Australian Natural History*, 18(11), 1976, pp. 398-403.

Renouf, Alan. *Malcolm Fraser and Australian Foreign Policy.* (Mosman, N.S.W.: Australian Professional Publications, 1987).

Ride, W.D.L. "Towards a National Biological Survey," *Search*, 9 (1978), pp. 73-82.

Roddewig, R.J. *Green Bans: The Birth of Australian Environmental Politics.* (Hale and Iremonger, 1978).

Routley, R. and V. *The Fight for the Forests.* (Canberra: Research School of Social Sciences, 1973).

Ryan, K.W. (ed.) *International Law in Australia.* 2nd ed. (Sydney: Law Book Co., 1984).

Saddler, H. et al. *Public Choice in Tasmania: Aspects of the Lower Gordon River Hydroelectric Development Proposal.* (Canberra: Centre for Resource and Environmental Studies, 1980).

Schneider, J. *World Public Order of the Environment.* (University of Toronto Press, 1979).

Serventy, Vincent. *A Continent in Danger* (London: Deutsch, 1966).

_____, *Australia's Wildlife Conservation.* (Sydney: Angus and Robertson, 1968).

_____, *Australia's National Parks.* (Sydney: Angus and Robertson, 1969).

Sharman, G. Campbell. "Australian States and External Affairs," *Australian Outlook*, 27(3), December 1973.

Sinclair, John. "IUCN: The World's Conservation Organization," *Habitat*, 10(4), 1982.

Slatyer, Ralph. "The Natural Legacy," *The Courier.* (UNESCO), December 1988, pp. 16-22.

Smith, Graham. "The Tasmanian House of Assembly Elections, 1982." *Politics*, 17(2), November 1982, pp. 121-7.

Smith, R.F.I. "Australian Cabinet Structure and Procedures: The Labour Government, 1972-5," *Politics* XII (1), May 1977, pp. 23-37.

Specht, R.L. et al. (eds.) *Conservation of Major Plant Communities in Australia and Papua New Guinea.* (Melbourne: CSIRO, 1974).

Suter, K.D. *World Law and the Last Wilderness*, 2nd ed. (Sydney: Friends of the Earth, 1980).

Swan, R.A. *Australia in the Antarctic: Interest, Activity and Endeavour.* (Melbourne University Press, 1961).

Tarrant, Valerie. *Conserving Australia.* (Melbourne: Cambridge University Press, 1974).

Thomson, J.A. "A Torrent of Words: A Bibliography and Chronology on the Franklin Dam Case," *Federal Law Review*, 15 (1985).

Tisdell, Clement A. "An Economist's Critique of the World Conservation Strategy, with examples from the Australian Experience," *Environmental Conservation*, 10(1), Spring 1983, pp. 43-52.

Tran, K.P., and D. MacRae. "Promoting INFOTERRA in Australia and Internationally," Paper to the 2nd INFOTERRA Network Management Meeting, Moscow, 1-6 October, 1979.

Triggs, Gillian. "Australia's Ratification of the International Covenant on Civil and Political Rights: Endorsement or Repudiation?" *International and Comparative Law Quarterly*, 31(2), April 1982, pp. 278-301.

Warner, Kate. "The Gordon-below-Franklin Dam: Obstructing the Police in the Execution of Their Duty," *Environmental and Planning Law Journal*, 1(3), September 1984, pp. 283-5.

Watt, Alan. *The Evolution of Australian Foreign Policy, 1937-65.* (Cambridge University Press, 1967).

Webb, L., et al. (eds.) *The Last of Lands.* (Milton, Qd.: Jacaranda Press, 1969).

Whalan, D.J. "The Structure and Nature of Australian Environmental Law," *Federal Law Review*, 8, 1977, pp. 294-318.

White, D.C. and C.S. Elliot (eds.) *Man, the Earth and Tomorrow. An Introduction to the Conservation and Use of Australia's Natural Resources.* (Melbourne: Cassell, 1969).

Wilcox, Murray. "Conservation and the Law," *Habitat*, 8(3), June 1980, pp. 26-31.

Wiltshire, Kenneth. "Heritage," in R.L. Mathews (ed.), *Federalism and the Environment.* (Canberra: Centre for Research on Federal Financial Relations, 1985).

Wright, J. *Conservation as an Emerging Concept* (Melbourne: ACF, Occasional Publication No. 2, 1970).

——————, *The Coral Battleground: An Account of the Fight to Prevent Oil Drilling on the Great Barrier Reef.* (Nelson, 1977).

Zines, Leslie, "The Environment and the Constitution," in R.L. Mathews (ed.), *Federalism and the Environment.* (Canberra: Centre for Research on Federal Financial Relations, 1985).

Index